Live
by the Sword

Live

by the ## Sword

Israel's Struggle for Existence
in the Holy Land

JAMES ROTHROCK

Lt. Colonel U.S. Air Force (Ret)

WESTBOW
PRESS
A DIVISION OF THOMAS NELSON

WestBow Press books may be ordered through booksellers or by contacting:

WestBow Press
A Division of Thomas Nelson
1663 Liberty Drive
Bloomington, IN 47403
www.westbowpress.com
1-(866) 928-1240

Because of the dynamic nature of the Internet, any web addresses or links contained in this book may have changed since publication and may no longer be valid. The views expressed in this work are solely those of the author and do not necessarily reflect the views of the publisher, and the publisher hereby disclaims any responsibility for them.

Any people depicted in stock imagery provided by Thinkstock are models, and such images are being used for illustrative purposes only.

Certain stock imagery © Thinkstock.

ISBN: 978-1-4497-2520-4 (sc)
ISBN: 978-1-4497-2521-1 (hc)
ISBN: 978-1-4497-2519-8 (ebk)

Library of Congress Control Number: 2011915277

Printed in the United States of America

WestBow Press rev. date:10/10/2011

Dedicated to

Staff Sergeant Gilad Shalit, an Israeli soldier held hostage by terrorists since June 2006; six Israeli soldiers missing in action; and all the brave and courageous men and women of Israel's Defense Forces.

Also by James Rothrock

Divided We Fall: How Disunity Leads to Defeat.

Contents

List of Maps and Charts

Preface

As a career military officer in the United States Air Force, I have followed with professional interest Israel's major military engagements and its day-to-day struggle to protect its people from indiscriminant terrorist attacks. My admiration of Israel's military forces and the people of Israel has grown as I watched them rise to meet the challenges to their survival. They have shown incredible courage and iron will in fighting against invading Arab armies, which usually outnumbered them many times over, and in combating terrorist attacks that ranged from suicide bombings to indiscriminate rocket and mortar fire on their homes and schools. I have also marveled at how the Israeli people have gone about their daily lives, never knowing when they send their children off to school or family members off to work if they will ever see them alive again.

In the first several decades of its existence, the new State of Israel was faced with attacks by the combined armies of scores of Arab nations, including Egypt, Jordan, Syria, Lebanon, Iraq, Saudi Arabia, Yemen, and others. The first four of these countries have common borders with Israel. Considering the small geographical area of Israel, the presence of unfriendly countries bordering on the North, South, East, and Northeast has made defense in-depth almost impossible. The common borders also make it difficult to prevent infiltration by terrorists. Consequently, from a military and national security standpoint, Israel has had to overcome almost insurmountable obstacles in developing tactics and strategy to defend its people and nation.

As the title of the book suggests, the people of Israel have been compelled to live by the sword since their first day of statehood. They have fought and survived six major wars and numerous confrontations with terrorist organizations. Although the probability of a conventional war with Arab armies is less than it was in the past, Israel still faces grave dangers to its existence. Terrorist organizations like Hamas and Hezbollah have grown stronger, and their primary objective is the annihilation of Israel. These organizations are essentially surrogates of Iran and Syria and have been supplied with enormous quantities of modern weapons along with millions of dollars to support their terrorist operations. These four entities—Iran, Syria, Hamas, and Hezbollah—form what I have identified as the **Alliance of Terror**, which threatens Israel's very existence. Iran's quest for nuclear weapons makes this threat even more foreboding.

Israel is the only country in the world that has lived under the threat of annihilation since the first day of its existence. It is in recognition of this and Israel's relentless fight for survival that I have chosen to write this book. More to the point, my reasons are threefold:

1.   To inform of the dangers and sacrifices the people of Israel have endured since the birth of the Jewish State of Israel—major wars at regular intervals and indiscriminate terrorist attacks.

2.   To inform of the extraordinary performance of the Israeli Defense Forces (IDF)—how they met and defeated multiple Arab armies against overwhelming odds; how the army, navy and air forces performed as one; and how they maintained the highest level of fighting spirit and morale.

3.   To inform of the looming dangers that Israel faces today—the Alliance of Terror, Iran's nuclear threat, and the repeated threats by Iran's Ayatollah Khamenei and President Ahmadinejad to wipe Israel off the map.

As I conducted research for this book, I found that many of the sources included the names of towns and villages that would probably be unfamiliar to people outside of Israel and neighboring Arab states. Accordingly, to promote the ease of reading, I have attempted to avoid the use of such names where possible and substituted general references, such as "a settlement near the border in northern Israel."

My hope is that this book will promote an awareness of the many sacrifices the Israeli people have made in their fight to preserve the existence of a Jewish state in the Holy Land and the grave dangers they face today. Most importantly, it is meant to awaken the United States and the Western nations of the disastrous consequences for them and Israel if they fail to stand with Israel against Islamic extremists and a nuclear Iran.

Acknowledgements

My profound gratitude goes out to the following sources that provided a wealth of timely, clear, and accurate information for this book:

The Meir Amit Intelligence and Terrorism Information Center, part of the Israel Intelligence Heritage & Commemoration Center (IICC).

The Israel Project, Washington, D.C. and Jerusalem.

The Jewish Virtual Library of the American-Israeli Cooperative Enterprise (AICE).

Israel

Map 1. Israel Today
Source: CIA World Fact Book

Relative Size of Israel

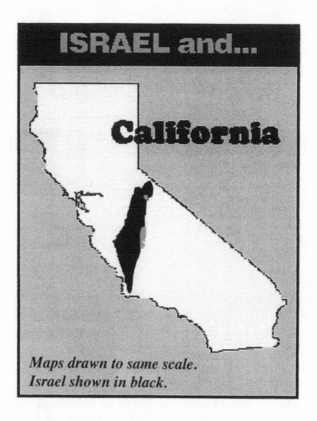

Map 2. Israel's Size Relative to California
Source: Jewish Virtual Library.
A Division of the American-Israeli Cooperative Enterprise

Relative Size of Israel

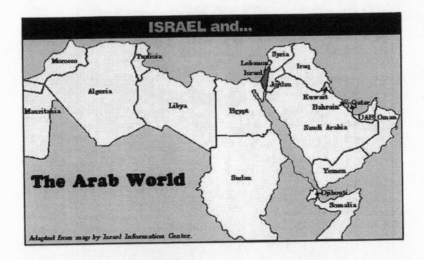

Map 3. Israel's Size Relative to Middle East
Source: Jewish Virtual Library.
A Division of the American-Israeli Cooperative Enterprise.

Chapter 1

If the Arabs put down their weapons today, there would be no violence. If the Jews put down their weapons today, there would be no more Israel.

—Benjamin Netanyahu

Dawn of a Jewish State

Moshe Dayan, former Israeli Minister of Defense, once remarked that his generation had been condemned to *live by the sword* for the foreseeable future.[1] The history of Israel since its founding in 1948 has been marked by one armed conflict after another with the Arabs. This has made living by the sword the way of life for the Israeli people. The late Prime Minister of Israel, Yitzhak Rabin, once commented, "Even when it was not engaged in outright combat with the Arab enemies, Israel remained in…a 'dormant war' that, 'like a volcano,' could erupt with little warning into a major conflagration."[2]

Quest for a Homeland

The course of the Jewish people's quest for a home in the Holy Land in modern history was influenced by two significant events that foreshadowed the genesis of a sovereign Jewish state in Palestine. The first was the Belfour Declaration of November 1917, in which the British Government endorsed, and the Allied Powers approved, the establishment of a national home for the Jewish people in Palestine. The British government pledged to use its best endeavors to achieve this objective.[3] Soon thereafter, at the San Remo conference of 1920, the world powers in attendance voted to give Britain the mandate to oversee establishment of a Jewish national home in Palestine. On July 22, 1922, the League of Nations ratified the San Remo recommendations and assigned Britain a mandate to set up a national home for the Jewish people in Palestine. The British accepted what became known as the Mandate of Palestine with the objective of putting into effect the League's dictate, which in essence, mirrored the Belfour Declaration.[4]

Soon after the Mandate became effective, the British established the civil administration for control of Palestine. Encouraged by the prospects of a homeland in Palestine, Jewish immigration and land purchases increased sharply. This gave rise to growing discontent among the Arabs, who soon resorted to violence against the Jews throughout Palestine. Casualties on both sides were heavy. The British High Commissioner of Palestine regarded Jewish immigration as the source of the problem. In an effort to allay Arab fears over the growing Jewish immigration and construction projects, which signaled that the Jews were building a national home in Palestine, the British government abandoned its commitment to the Belfour Declaration. Strict limitations tied to the economic capacity of the country were placed on Jewish immigration.[5]

British restrictions notwithstanding, 63,000 Jewish immigrants arrived in Palestine between 1924 and 1926, having left Poland amidst growing anti-Semitism. The Jewish economy in Palestine progressed quickly, and more immigrants arrived in 1928 and 1929. In the latter year, the actions by the Zionist Congress in Zurich to set up the Jewish Agency headquarters in Jerusalem angered the Palestinian Arabs, who saw it as another step toward establishing a Jewish state in Palestine. Another wave of violence broke out and spread from Jerusalem to Jewish settlements in other parts of Palestine. In the first week, 133 Jews were killed and 339 were injured. Six Arabs died at the hands of the Jews, and British police killed 110 Arabs and wounded 232.[6]

Between 1932 and 1939 another wave of Jewish immigrants from Poland and Germany arrived in Palestine. Arab fears of being swamped by the rising tide of Jewish immigrants led to open rebellion by the Palestinian Arabs in 1936. Driven by growing nationalist sentiments in neighboring Arab states, a ten-member Arab Higher Committee (AHC) was established to serve as the national leadership. The leader of the AHC, Haji Amin, the chief Arab dignitary of Jerusalem, declared a general strike that quickly turned into a full-scale uprising throughout Palestine. Attacks were directed at the Jews as well as the British Mandate officials, who were confronted with an Arab demand for an end to the Jewish immigration into Palestine.[7]

The British attempted to quell the uprising by force, even resorting to executing some of the Arab guerrillas. The British pacified the Arabs by backtracking on the idea of the two-state partition and issued a White Paper severely restricting Jewish immigration. Thus, on the eve of World War II, when the Jews were seeking refuge from Nazi Germany, immigration was restricted to no more than fifteen thousand per year over the next five years. At the end of that period, Jewish immigration was to be allowed only with Arab consent. In the event of a future independent state, Jews were to be limited to no more than one-third of the total population of Palestine. The stark revelations in the White Paper dealt a severe blow to world Jews, who saw it as the end of all hope for a Jewish state and abandonment of European Jews to a fate of persecution at the hands of the Nazis. The Arabs were also dissatisfied with the measures in the White Paper; they demanded immediate creation of an Arab state in Palestine and the complete end of Jewish immigration.[8]

World War II

With the outbreak of World War II, the conflict over Palestine was put on hold for most of the war. The Jews in Palestine chose to join the British in the war, but they did not give up the fight against the White Paper. About 85,000 Jewish men and 54,000 Jewish women registered for war service with the British forces. During the war, an all-Jewish brigade was established and fought against the Germans in Italy. As many as 30,000 served in all the branches of the British forces. This experience was to prove valuable in the creation of the Israel Defense Forces (IDF) in the conflicts that lay ahead. The Arab sympathies were mostly with the Axis during World War II. A poll in 1941 found that 88 percent of the Palestinian Arabs favored Germany, and only 9 percent were for Britain.[9]

During the war, the Jews in Palestine fought against the British restriction on immigration. The Jews did everything within their means to help refugees enter Palestine. Over 50,000 illegal immigrants found their way into Palestine during the war years, despite actions by the British to intercept and turn away ships carrying refugees. In one tragic incident, the British refused to allow the ship, *Struma*, to land in Palestine. The ship was turned away and later sank in the Black Sea with 768 Jewish refugees aboard.[10]

The British government's refusal to allow admission into Palestine of displaced Jews from war-torn Europe gave rise to armed opposition against the British forces in Palestine. The fledgling Israeli Army, the Haganah, led the fight that focused mainly on tearing down the British barrier on "illegal" immigration. Two dissident Jewish underground organizations also engaged the British. The group known as the Irgun (National Military Organization) was led by Menachem Begin, who, in an unusual twist of fate, became the Prime Minister of Israel in 1977 and held that office until 1983. The other more militant group was known as Lehi or the Stern Gang, named after its leader, Avraham Stern. The Lehi went underground and launched attacks against British installations and servicemen.[11]

The White Paper

Soon after the end of World War II, Ernest Bevin, Britain's Foreign Secretary, announced that the White Paper of 1939, which favored the Arabs and severely limited Jewish immigration, would remain in effect. This further outraged the Jews and led to the merger of the Jewish defense force, the Haganah, with the two dissident groups, Irgun and Lehi. The three organizations formed a united resistance movement and launched an armed campaign against the British. The British brought in an additional 80,000 troops to Palestine in an effort to put down the Jewish rebellion. However, the Jewish attacks continued with casualties on both sides. In retaliation for a bombing of a hotel in Jerusalem that housed the British government offices and military headquarters, the

British undertook a massive military offensive, arresting hundreds of Jews, killing fifteen, and confiscating arms caches.[12]

Undeterred by British policies to restrict the flow of immigrants into Palestine, Jewish allies in Europe purchased ships for transporting survivors of the Holocaust to Palestine. The British were just as determined to stop the flow of Jewish refugees into Palestine and used naval action on the high seas and police action to prevent landings in Palestine.[13]

In 1945 the British government rejected a plea by President Truman to permit 100,000 refugees from Europe to be admitted to Palestine. In 1946 the British government turned down a recommendation by a joint commission of United States and British officials to permit 100,000 refugees to be admitted to Palestine. These actions enraged the Jews and led to renewed retaliation against the British. One of the operations by the Jews involved destruction of all bridges and roads leading to nearby Arab countries. As a result of the rapidly escalating conflict with the Jews, Britain found it necessary to increase its troop strength in Palestine to 100,000. The British soon realized they were involved in a major armed conflict that was costing lives and depleting resources that were needed at home for reconstruction following World War II. The decision was made to turn the administration of Palestine over to the world community. On February 18, 1947, the British Government announced it had decided to refer the Mandate of Palestine to the United Nations.[14]

The UN Resolution

On May 15, 1947, the United Nations appointed an eleven-member committee, the UN Special Committee on Palestine (UNSCOP), to propose a settlement of the Jewish and Arab struggle over the Promised Land (Palestine). While the UN committee investigation was underway in Palestine, an incident took place that raised the level of concern around the world for the plight of Jewish refugees in Europe. The riverboat, *Exodus,* crammed with 4,539 Jewish displaced persons, attempted to break though the British blockade that was guarding the entry into Palestine. The British refused to allow the refugees, survivors of the Holocaust, to land in Palestine. The ship was turned back to its port of origin in Europe. This caused outrage among the Jews and received attention around the world. It also made a strong impression on the UN delegation and was influential in their decision on the future of Palestine.[15]

After months of deliberations, a majority of ten nations represented on the UNSCOP committee recommended partitioning the land in Palestine into separate Jewish and Arab states, with Jerusalem, Bethlehem, and surrounding suburbs to be an international zone under UN control. On November 29, 1947, the United Nations General Assembly voted to accept the committee's recommendation to partition Palestine. UN Resolution 181 implemented this decision and called for partitioning Palestine into two sovereign states, one Jewish and the other Arab. The Holy City of Jerusalem, sacred to Muslims, Christians, and Jews, was to be governed under a UN Trusteeship Council. Soon, thereafter, the British government announced that its forces would be withdrawn from Palestine on May 15, 1948.[16]

When the UN voted to divide Palestine into two states, the territory of Palestine consisted of approximately ten thousand square miles, about the size of the State of Maryland. The Arabs, with 1,364,330 inhabitants, retained 4,300 square miles. The Jews, numbering 608,230, were allotted 5,700 square miles.[17] The land for the Jewish state included major parts of the arid Negev Desert. It also comprised three separate segments connected by small, difficult to defend passageways (See Map 4 at end of this chapter). This configuration was to have significant consequences as the inexperienced Jewish state attempted to structure its government and defend against its enemies. Nonetheless, in Tel-Aviv the Jews rejoiced over finally being granted a homeland.[18]

The Arabs rejected UN Resolution 181, and in Arab capitals there were violent demonstrations. "We are solidly and permanently determined to fight to the last man against the existence in our country of any Jewish state, and no matter how small it is, Jamal al-Husseini, Vice-President of the Arab Higher Committee (AHC), the effective government of the Palestinian Arabs, told the General Assembly as it was about to cast its vote [on Resolution 181], that if such a state is to be established, it can only be established over our dead bodies."[19] An AHC circular was even more threatening: "The Arabs have taken into their own hands the final solution of the Jewish problem. The problem will be solved only in blood and fire. The Jews will soon be driven out."[20]

When the final vote was cast at the UN General Assembly, signifying that a Jewish state would be formed in Palestine, the General Secretary of the Arab League, Assam Pasha, led the Arab delegates out of the Assembly. His last words were, "The partition line will be nothing but a line of fire and blood."[21] (Note: The Arab League was formed in 1945 and consisted of Egypt, Saudi Arabia, Syria, Lebanon, Iraq, Yemen, and Transjordan, now Jordan.).

The Rising Threat

The stage was set for over 60 years of endless struggle for existence by the people of Israel. The conflict with the Arabs over the Jewish state in Palestine began within minutes after the UN voted to establish a Jewish state in Palestine. The first of these was the War of Independence, which was followed by a half dozen other major armed conflicts with the Arabs and day-to-day terrorist attacks from all directions against every settlement and city of Israel. In forthcoming chapters, the struggle of the Jewish people to survive and overcome these conflicts will be covered. The main emphasis will be on the more recent struggles with terrorist organizations, such as Hamas, Hezbollah, the Palestinian Islamic Jihad, and others. The support for these terrorist groups by Iran and Syria will be given special attention, along with Iran's threat to annihilate Israel and its drive to obtain nuclear weapons.

Before moving on, it is important to lay the groundwork for the reason that the Arabs have used major armed conflict, unconventional warfare, and suicide attacks to prevent the Israelis from making a home in Palestine. Most importantly, it must be understood that it is not a fight over land or resources, as in many other major conflicts, such as Japan's imperialist designs on Asia and the Pacific or Hitler's quest to take over all of Europe. In Palestine it is an ideological collision driven by the religious fervor of the Muslims who will not tolerate having Jews in their midst. If the UN had voted to settle a group of

Muslim refugees in Palestine, would there have been a campaign of all the surrounding Arab nations to expel them or drive them into the sea? In all probability they would have welcomed them with open arms! As further evidence, consider the following Islamic Hadiths (sayings of the Prophet Muhammad):

> Sahih Bukhari, Book 52, Number 177, narrated by Abu Huraira: Allah's Apostle said, "The Hour (of the Last Judgment) will not be established until you fight with the Jews, and the stone behind which a Jew will be hiding will say, 'O Muslim! There is a Jew hiding behind me, so kill him.'"[22]

> Sahih Bukhari, Book 52, Number 176, narrated by 'Abdullah bin 'Umar: Allah's Apostle said, "You (Muslims) will fight with the Jews till some of them hide behind stones. The stones will (betray them) saying, 'O 'Abdullah (slave of Allah) there is a Jew hiding behind me; so kill him.'"[23]

> Sahih Muslim, Book 004, Number 1080, compiled by Sahih Muslim. Abu Huraira reported: The Messenger of Allah (may peace be upon him) said, "Let Allah destroy the Jews for they have taken the graves of the apostles as places of worship."[24]

> Sahih Muslim, 002.191 Shakir: "And kill them wherever you find them, and drive them out from whence they drove you out, and persecution is severer than slaughter, and do not fight with them at the Sacred Mosque until they fight with you in it, but if they do fight you, then slay them: such is the recompense of the unbelievers."[25]

No other nation in modern history has been under such continuous threats of annihilation as Israel, and no other has been subjected to over 60 years of endless struggle for survival. For a small nation the size of New Jersey, surrounded by 22 Arab nations, most of which have tried to drive Israel into the sea at one time or another, it is nothing short of miraculous that Israel has been able to survive. The ability of the Israelis to hold out in the face of overwhelming odds is a testament to the courage, strength, and iron will of the Jewish people. Many Israelis have lived most of their lives in a constant state of war or periods of limited peace punctuated by terrorist attacks, suicide bombers, and an endless shower of rockets indiscriminately fired into civilian populations.

It brings to mind, how would the American people manage to live year-after-year under these conditions, with daily threats of suicide attacks on buses, malls, theaters, schools, markets, discos, restaurants, etc., not knowing if their children would come home safely or if their home would be destroyed by rockets?

In Israel, men and women 18 years of age have compulsory military service obligations (Christians, Muslims, and Circassians serve voluntarily). Enlisted men serve 36 months, women serve 21 months, and officers serve 48 months. Men have a reserve obligation until age 51. Women are required to serve in the reserve to age 24. Graduates of officer or pilot's schools or special military technical schools are required to sign on for career service.[26] Many Jewish men and women have been called several times to serve in the six major wars that Israel has faced in the past 60 years. Over 22,123 have given their lives between 1948 and 2006 in the fight for their homeland.[27]

In recent years, new threats have come from non-state organizations, such as Hamas in Gaza and Hezbollah in Lebanon. In the forthcoming chapters, you will learn about these terrorist groups, their charters to destroy Israel, and their backing from Iran and Syria. It is revealing to see how the leaders of these current threats view their mission and reason for existence. The sermons of the Imams broadcast from the mosques over Hamas, Hezbollah, and Palestinian Authority television leave little doubt of their intensions:

> Allah warned his beloved Prophet Muhammad about
> the Jews, who had killed the prophets, forged their
> Torah, and sowed corruption throughout their history.

With the establishment of the State of Israel, the entire Islamic nation was lost, because Israel is a cancer spreading through the body of the Islamic nation, and because the Jews are a virus resembling AIDS, from which the entire world suffers.

You will find that the Jews were behind all the civil strife in this world. The Jews are behind the suffering of the nations.

They are committing worse deeds than those done to them in the Nazi war.

Listen to the Prophet Muhammad, who tells you about the evil end that awaits Jews. The stones and trees will want the Muslims to finish off every Jew.[28]

Anti-Semitism and calls to kill Jews are common themes in the sermons broadcast from mosques in Gaza under Hamas control. Dr. Ahmad Abu Halablya, a member of the Hamas Parliament, recently made the following broadcast live from the Zayed bin Sultan Aal Nahyan mosque in Gaza:

Have no mercy on the Jews, no matter where they are, in any country. Fight them, Wherever you are, kill those Jews, and those Americans who are like them—and those who stand by them—they are all in the same trench, against the Arabs and the Muslims—because they establish Israel here, in the beating heart of the Arab world, in Palestine. They created it to be the outpost of their civilization—and the vanguard of their army, and to be the sword of the West and the Crusaders . . . they wanted the Jews to be their spearhead.

Let us put our trust in Allah, close ranks, and unite our words, and the slogan of us all should be, "Jihad! Jihad! For the sake of Palestine and for the sake of Jerusalem and Al-Aqsa!"

We will not give up a single grain of soil of Palestine, from Haifa, and Jaffa . . . and all the land, and Gaza, and West Bank. Allah, deal with the Jews your enemies and the enemies of Islam. Deal with the crusaders, and America, and Europe behind them. O Lord of the worlds.[29]

Sheikh Ibrahim Madhi spoke at the Sheik 'Ijlin Mosque in Gaza which was broadcast on Palestinian Authority television:

The Jews have exposed their fangs. Nothing will deter them, except the color of their filthy people's blood; nothing will deter them except for us voluntarily detonating ourselves in their midst. They have nuclear power, but we have the power of the belief in Allah. We blow them up in Hadera; we blow them up in Tel Aviv and Netanya.[30]

Similarly, Sheikh Ibrahim Madhi stated this in a sermon at the Sheikh 'Ijlin Mosque in the Gaza that was broadcast on Palestinian Authority television:

Our belief is that this war, between us and the Jews, will continue to escalate until we vanquish the Jews and enter Jerusalem as conquerors, [and] enter Jaffa as conquerors. We are not merely expecting a Palestine state with Jerusalem as its capital; we are heralding an Islamic caliphate with Jerusalem as its capital.[31]

For centuries the Jewish people have dreamt of a home in the Holy Land. From the first day the United Nations approved a home for the Jewish people in Palestine, they have had to fight every day to hold onto that dream. The sermons given at mosques reveal the ideological and religious hatred that the Jewish people have had to endure for many years. In the forthcoming chapters, you will see how the Jewish people have had to use every ounce of their strength, courage, ingenuity, and self-sacrifice in the struggle for their very existence. It will become clear why the Israelis have had to *live by the sword* since the day in 1947 when the United Nations approved their homeland in Palestine. On that day, the first major conflict with the Arabs began—the War of Independence.

The Partition Plan Map

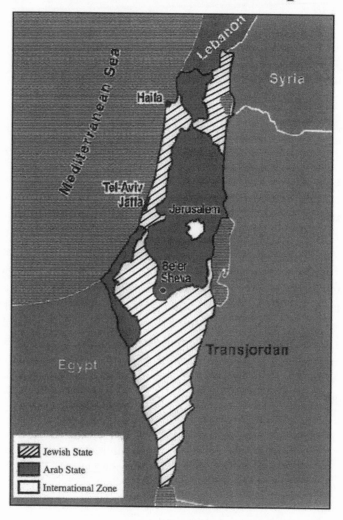

**Map 4. The United Nation's Partition Plan for Palestine
Source: Jewish Virtual Library.
A Division of the American-Israeli Cooperative Enterprise.
By Israeli Ministry Foreign Affairs.**

Chapter 2

War of Independence

The people of Israel were thrust into living by the sword on that day in November 1947 when the United Nations approved the plan to partition Palestine into two sovereign states, one Arab and one Jewish. The League of Arab States immediately announced its intention to "take whatever measures were required to prevent implementation of the [UN] resolution."[1] At the same time, several Arab countries proclaimed that "they would attack and destroy the Jewish state the moment the British pulled out of the area."[2] Arab mobs began rioting and attacking Jews before sunset on the first day of the UN resolution. Rioters killed seven Jews and injured many more. Violence against Jews broke out throughout Palestine and spread to many countries in the Middle East, North Africa, and parts of Europe. By the end of December 1947, 205 Jews and 120 Palestinian Arabs had died in the fighting. At a refugee camp in British-ruled Aden, 75 Jews were killed and 78 were wounded. There was widespread rioting in Yemen, Syria, and Egypt. Untold numbers of Jews were injured or killed when their homes, shops, schools, and synagogues were attacked.[3] Thus, the War of Independence, or the First Palestine War as the Arabs called it, was underway.

The Civil War

The first phase of the War of Independence was essentially a civil war between the Palestinian Arabs and the Jews, although volunteers from other Arab countries entered Palestine to fight beside the Palestinians. To some extent, this was a conflict between Arab and Jewish communities in Palestine, which at first was characterized by small units and volunteers engaged in guerrilla warfare. David Ben-Gurion, the leader of the Jewish population in Palestine, envisioned the inevitable conflict that lay ahead. In mid-1947 he began preparing the Haganah (forerunner of Israel Defense Forces) for war. He organized the military forces and deployed them to strategic locations in preparation for the expected invasion by Arab armies. He also led the drive to acquire arms and establish military training programs. His efforts to obtain arms and volunteers from outside Palestine were severely handicapped by British naval and air blockades. These efforts were further hampered by a British law that made the possession of weapons by Israelis punishable by death. Oddly enough, the Arabs were not bound by this rule and were allowed to move about freely with weapons.[4]

Israel began the civil war with militia and paramilitary forces, many of whom had no military training. Some had just arrived from refugee camps and received only a few hours training on how to load and shoot a weapon before going into battle. From this collection of essentially civilian soldiers, the Jews could muster a fighting force of approximately 45,000. Of this number, 30,000 were needed for local defense of Jewish villages throughout Palestine. It left a regular force of around 15,000 men and women. These forces were augmented by the two dissident groups, Irgun and Lehi, which could raise several thousand more fighters. The Israelis also suffered from a dire shortage of weapons and ammunition. They had only one weapon for every three fighters and had to share small rifles and light machine guns. There were no heavy machine guns, artillery, anti-aircraft weapons, or armored vehicles in their inventory. Ammunition was also in short supply. Early in the fighting, the Israeli air arm consisted of about a dozen light, civilian Piper Cub aircraft, which were vastly inferior to the fighters, bombers, and reconnaissance aircraft available to the Arab countries.[5]

The Palestinian Arabs outnumbered the Jews two to one; however, for the most part, they lacked the national identity needed for development of a cohesive fighting force. Their military value consisted primarily of armed bands and village militia. Historian Benny Morris, a recognized scholar of the Arab-Israeli wars, contends that the weakness of the Palestinian Arabs was overcome by direct support from neighboring

Arab states. According to Morris, "The largest and best organized Arab formation fighting in Palestine until the pan-Arab invasion of May 1948 was the ALA [Arab Liberation Army], consisting mainly of volunteers from Syria, Iraq, and Palestine who were recruited by the Arab League in Syria. The volunteers were trained at Syrian Army camps...."[6] They were told "they were going off to jihad to help the persecuted Arabs of Palestine...."[7] The ALA had 4,000 to 5,000 troops, augmented by hundreds of local volunteers. The extent of Arab involvement in the "civil war" becomes evident when we look at the nationality of the officers leading the ALA. They included mostly army officers from Syria and Iraq, with a smattering of Jordanian, Lebanese, Egyptian, and Bosnian officers.[8]

In the beginning of the civil war, Israel was on the defensive. The shortage of weapons forced the Israelis into a defensive strategy while they waited for the arrival of arms shipments from outside of Palestine—mainly Czechoslovakia. They were also faced with the dilemma of defending their centers of population, as well as the many Israeli villages spread throughout Palestine. The Arabs took advantage of this situation and concentrated on cutting the supply lines between Israel's urban centers and the outlying settlements. Their main objective was to cut the link between Jerusalem and Tel Aviv. The Arabs held the high ground along this road, which made it nearly impossible for the Israeli forces to protect convoys of food and other supplies destined for the besieged Jews in Jerusalem. Israeli casualties mounted as they fought to keep the road to Jerusalem open. In one convoy, 17 Israelis were killed on their way to Jerusalem. The Arabs also attempted to cut off Israeli efforts to deliver supplies and reinforcements to other villages under attack. As the village defenders fought off Arab attacks and Israeli convoys fought their way through ambushes, they took heavy casualties. In one engagement, Israel Defense Forces in Jerusalem dispatched a Special Forces platoon of 35 men to rush aid to nearby villages. En-route they were ambushed by Arab forces. The Israelis fought valiantly to the last man.[9]

While the civil war progressed to the end of 1947, over 600 foreign volunteers entered Palestine to reinforce the Arab militia. In early January 1948, units of the ALA began crossing into Palestine from

Syria and Lebanon. One battalion was commanded by a Syrian officer and was composed mostly of Syrian troops. Another was commanded by an Iraqi officer and consisted mostly of Iraqis. By mid-April the ALA had infiltrated 7,000 to 8,000 fighters into Palestine. The civil war was rapidly taking on the complexion of an international conflict. In one of the first actions by the ALA, a battalion supported by irregulars attacked a Jewish kibbutz in western Galilee. The defenders, greatly outnumbered, fought off several assaults. After suffering 30 killed and 60 wounded, the ALA withdrew. In a similar action, about 600 ALA troops attacked a kibbutz defended by 115 Israelis. The defenders drove off the Arabs, who retreated leaving behind 40 to 60 dead. While some Arab units concentrated on attacking Jewish villages and halting Jewish traffic on major roads, others turned to the now familiar terrorist practice of exploding bombs in populated areas. In one such bombing, three stolen British trucks loaded with explosives were set off outside of two hotels in Jewish Jerusalem, killing and wounding scores of people.[10]

A discussion of Israel's fighting spirit would not be complete without mentioning the accomplishment of the air service. The light, civilian Piper Cubs, piloted by a handful of British, American, and Israelis, performed unbelievable feats with aircraft that were not meant to be used in combat. They flew missions ahead of convoys to spot Arab ambushes; they dropped ammunition and supplies to troops and villages under siege; they threw bombs on enemy positions; they strafed the enemy with handheld machine guns; they operated out of makeshift landing fields; and they provided the communications link to units and villages that were cut off. They carried out these missions in the face of heavy ground fire in aircraft with no more armament than the fabric that covered their wings and fuselage.[11]

By the end of March, Israel had made significant increases in the size of its armed forces, and arms from Czechoslovakia had begun to arrive. In April three shipments arrived bringing thousands of rifles and machine guns with an abundance of ammunition. Israel was now in a position to begin offensive operations. In switching to the offensive, the Haganah launched large-scale, well-organized operations, taking advantage of the Arabs small-scale, dispersed militia. The Arab militia was quickly overcome when the Israelis embarked on an operation to secure the areas specified by the UN for Jewish statehood and the Jewish settlements located outside the Jewish designated areas. At the same time, the Israelis secured roads and borders where the Arab invasion was expected to cross into Palestine. They did not have long to wait, for in the first week of May 1948, the Arab League decided to invade Palestine as soon as the British mandate ended, which was scheduled for May 15. Immediately following that decision, the Chiefs of Staff of the Arab armies met and approved the invasion plan.[12]

As the Jews prepared for the invasion, they feared they would face annihilation if they failed, and rightly so, for the Secretary General of the Arab League proclaimed that the invasion would be a war of extermination and a momentous massacre. Israelis was facing the awesome task of fighting enemies on multiple fronts advancing from all directions. On the north border was Syria and Lebanon, to the east was Transjordan (now Jordan), to the south they faced the armies of Egypt, and to the west their back was up against the Mediterranean Sea. These border states were joined by army units from Iraq, Saudi Arabia, and Yemen. Each of the Arab countries had trained, standing armies, fully equipped with modern weapons. Egypt, Syria, and Lebanon had an air force with fighter and bomber aircraft. All had heavy artillery and some had tanks and armored vehicles. Against this juggernaut, there was the fledgling Israel Defense Forces (IDF), about half of which was made up of civilians who recently arrived in Palestine. They had very little military training and only limited weapons and equipment. They also lacked artillery and armored vehicles, and their air force was still made up of light Piper Cub aircraft.[13]

The Proclamation of Independence

May 14, 1948, marked a major turning point in the future of Israel. On that day, David Ben-Gurion, the Jewish leader of Palestine, made the official proclamation of Israel's independence. He stated, "By virtue of the natural and historical right of the Jewish people, and of the resolution of the General Assembly of the United Nations, we hereby proclaim the establishment of the Jewish state in Palestine, to be called Israel."[14] Several provisions of this historic Declaration of Independence are quoted here:

> THE STATE OF ISRAEL will be open for Jewish immigration and for the ingathering of the Exiles; it will foster the development of the country for the benefit of all its inhabitants; it will be based on freedom, justice and peace as envisaged by the prophets of Israel; it will ensure complete equality of social and political rights to all its inhabitants irrespective of religion, race or sex; it will guarantee freedom of religion, conscience, language, education and culture; it will safeguard the Holy Places of all religions; and it will be faithful to the principles of the Charter of the United Nations....

> WE APPEAL—in the very midst of the onslaught launched against us now for months—to the Arab inhabitants of the State of Israel to preserve peace and participate in the upbuilding of the State on the basis of full and equal citizenship and due representation in all its provisional and permanent institutions....[15]

It is noteworthy that the two sections of the Declaration just presented go to extraordinary lengths to assure the Palestinian Arabs who reside in the areas designated for the Jewish state that they would have full and equal citizenship, the same as Jewish citizens. It is unfortunate that the Arabs chose not to avail themselves of this chance to live side-by-side with the Jews but instead chose to use force to deny the Jewish people a home in Palestine. They also chose to ignore Israel's offer to preserve peace and together build a new nation.

The Arab Invasion

In addition to the Declaration of Independence on May 14, the same day in May was also significant in that it marked the end of the British Mandate over Palestine and an end to British control or influence over events within Palestine. However, it also opened the gates for the Arab invasion. Publicly, the Arab states described the purpose of their invasion as saving Palestinian Arabs. They also spoke of other less noble goals, such as eliminating the Jewish state, eradicating Zionism, and sweeping the Jews into the sea.[16] Four Egyptian Spitfires attacked Tel Aviv on the morning of May 15, signaling the beginning of the Arab invasion. The Egyptians were the first to cross into Palestine. A force of fifteen thousand marched out of the Sinai Peninsula in two columns. One moved along the western coast toward Gaza Strip, with the objective of driving northward to Tel Aviv, while the other force took the central route into the Negev Desert with the objective of striking north toward Jerusalem. The Egyptian invasion force was backed by tanks, artillery, and an air force of three squadrons of fighters, one squadron of bombers, and a few reconnaissance aircraft.[17]

Next, troops from Transjordan attacked from the east. A force of nine thousand of the Arab Legion, commanded by former British officers and noncommissioned officers, crossed the River Jordan into the part of Palestine that was allotted to Palestinian Arabs in the UN partitioning plan. The Arab Legion, known to be a highly professional army, was later renamed the Jordan Arab Army. In consonance with a 1947 agreement between King Abdullah of Transjordan and the Jews, the area of Palestine west of the River Jordan was to be divided between these two parties. Consequently, the Israelis did not engage this force at first; however, when the Arab Legion drove west toward Jerusalem, fierce fighting broke out as the Israeli's and Legion fought for control of the city. By the end of May, the Legion had gained control of the Jewish Quarter of the Old City and the Wailing Wall. The loss of the spiritual center of the Jewish community dealt a major psychological blow to the Jews.[18]

Syria and Iraq attacked Israel from across the northern border on May 15. A Syrian infantry brigade, supported by artillery and a company of tanks, crossed into Palestine with the aim of capturing several Israeli kibbutzes around the Sea of Galilee. However, the kibbutz defenders held out, and the Syrians were only able to capture one kibbutz, which they abandoned after failing to accomplish other objectives. They then withdrew to the hills in the east. Their only significant accomplishment was taking and occupying a single kibbutz one day before the first truce went into effect on June 11.[19] Their poor showing was no surprise to the

Israelis, as one of them observed, "The Syrians would generally fight in the morning. During the afternoon they would take a light siesta...."[20]

An Iraqi force of two infantry and one armored brigade entered Palestine from northern Transjordan. Finding two bridges across the River Jordan destroyed, they forded the Jordan and set out to attack a nearby kibbutz and a police fort. After five days of fighting and Israeli counterattacks, the Iraqis, cut off without bridges for re-supply, withdrew back across the Jordan. Joined by two other brigades, the Iraqi forces drove southward along the eastern bank of the Jordan and later crossed over a bridge to the west bank. During the first truce, two additional brigades joined the Iraqis on the west bank, together making up an Iraqi force of eighteen thousand troops.[21] The Iraqis advanced westward and took up positions around several villages about halfway to the Mediterranean coast. As the Iraqis launched an attack toward the coastal village of Netanya, Israeli forces drove them back, preventing them from reaching the coast, which could have cut the Jewish state in half. At that point, Israeli and Iraqi forces reached a stalemate that held until the first truce on June 11.[22]

The Arab invasion plan included the Lebanese Army advancing from the north and down the coast toward Haifa; however, at the last minute, the President of Lebanon and the army chief of staff decided against taking part in the invasion. To keep favor with the Arabs, they assisted an invasion force of the Arab Liberation Army (ALA) with logistical support and covering artillery fire as they advanced into Palestine. The ALA battalion, augmented by Lebanese, Iraqi, Syrian, and Yugoslav volunteers, pushed across the border into Palestine to an abandoned Arab village. There they clashed with a battalion of Israeli commandos. Outgunned by the enemy artillery and mortars, the Israelis were driven back, taking with them as many as 150 dead and wounded. Several days later the Israelis were able to attack the enemy from the rear and retake the village. As the first truce drew near, the Lebanese Army crossed into Palestine and assisted the ALA in recapturing the village.[23]

While the war progressed on multiple fronts, Israel shifted forces between fronts to meet the invading Arab armies. The Israeli forces held their own and even consolidated their hold on some mixed

Arab-Israeli towns. However, several weeks into the war, they were still unable to break Transjordan's control on the passage into Jerusalem. The imbalance between Arab and Israel's forces reached a significant turning point in late May and early June with the arrival of a contingent of aircraft for Israel's fledgling air service. World War II vintage Messerschmitt, Spitfire, and Mosquito aircraft arrived in Israel, flown by volunteers from Britain, Canada, America, and South Africa. By June 11, eleven Messerschmitt were operational. The Israelis immediately began attacking Egyptian and Iraqi troops. Just days before the first truce, the Israeli high command ordered the air service to bomb several Arab capitals in the belief that it would hasten an end to the war. In one of these raids, a twin engine Dakota transport aircraft was used to bomb the Syrian capital of Damascus. In a display of "modern" airmanship, the Dakota made several passes while crew members threw bombs out of the rear cargo door. The raid was a big success, causing the Syrians to divert more of their air force to home defense, away from the battles in Palestine.[24]

The First Truce

The UN Security Council adopted a resolution on June 7, 1948, calling for a truce to begin on June 11 for the duration of four weeks. The resolution followed several weeks of negotiations by Count Bernadotte, a special mediator appointed by the Security Council. Once the truce was in effect, Count Bernadotte exerted pressure on the Arabs to accept a political settlement. However, the Arabs continued to reject the existence of a Jewish state. Both sides ignored the provisions of the truce that disallowed any actions to improve their military position. The Arabs reinforced their lines with fresh units and occasionally opened fire on the Israelis. The Israelis circumvented the embargo. They brought in more troops and weapons, regrouped, and consolidated their positions. With the Arab Legion still in control of the main roads to Jerusalem, food and supplies for the Jewish people in Jerusalem remained critical. During the truce, the Israelis worked to improve the Burma Road that was to be used as a bypass to deliver supplies to Jerusalem.[25]

Count Bernadotte's efforts to extend the truce were rejected by the Arab League. On July 8, the day before the truce was scheduled to end, Egypt launched an offensive with the intent of catching the Israelis off guard. The next day Israel seized the initiative and attacked on all fronts. The respite in fighting had given Israel a chance to organize and prepare to take the offensive. Fighting raged for ten days, with the outcome mainly in Israel's favor. As Israel's air service expanded, the air war picked up, with Israeli fighters flying ground support missions and maintaining air superiority over enemy air forces. Soon after the resumption of fighting, the Israeli air service received three B-17 bombers, purchased from America before the invasion began. During the ten days between the first and second truce, the Israelis used the B-17s to strike targets in Cairo and Damascus. The Egyptians retaliated, bombing Tel Aviv several days in a row. The UN Security Council reacted to the increase in fighting and brokered a second truce which became effective on July 18, 1948. No end date was set. The truce was to continue until lasting peace agreements were reached. Some Arabs opposed the truce, mainly the Iraqis who argued for continuing the war. However, several Arab forces suffered from a critical shortage of ammunition and supplies and were not eager to continue the fight. The superiority demonstrated by Israel's military forces during the ten days of fighting had given Arab leaders reason to want an end to the fighting.[26]

In the early days of the truce, both sides maneuvered to improve their position. In violation of the terms of the truce, the Egyptians denied the Israelis passage to re-supply some of their settlements in the Negev Desert region, and firefights erupted as the Israelis attempted to send convoys to these enclaves. The Egyptians also held a large part of Palestine, mainly the Negev region and its northern approaches, which had been allocated for the Jewish state. Without this territory, Israel would have been marginalized in space and access. Fearing a decision by the UN to settle the conflict based on existing occupancy of territory, the Israelis saw it in their interest of survival to breach the truce and extend their control over the Negev Desert. This move would give them access to the Red Sea and the Gulf of Aqaba, which was an important avenue for commerce. The Israelis were successful in driving a wedge between the Egyptian forces and cutting the supply lines to parts of the Egyptian Army. They also captured the city of Beersheba, the capital of the Negev region, which was deep into the territory held by the Egyptians. During the renewed fighting, the Israelis took the opportunity to improve their access to Jerusalem. They drove the Lebanese Army out of Palestine and occupied several villages in southern Lebanon.[27]

A New Truce

On November 16, 1948, the Security Council imposed a new truce and called on all parties to negotiate and work toward an armistice. A few weeks later, the UN General Assembly passed a resolution that established a commission, consisting of representatives of the United States, France, and Turkey, to function as the UN mediator to negotiate a peace settlement and initiate measures to resettle the Palestinian refugees. Before the mediation had a chance to begin, Israel again breached the truce, this time with the intention of driving the Egyptian Army from Israeli soil. The attack sent the Egyptians retreating into the Sinai Peninsula, with the Israelis on their heels. International pressure and another call from the UN Security Council convinced Israel to resume the truce and withdraw from the Sinai. The new truce went into effect on January 7, 1949. This essentially ended the fighting and set the stage for negotiations to begin between Israel and the Arab states.[28]

Armistice Negotiations

The lead negotiator for the UN was Dr. Ralph Bunche, an American diplomat. Soon after the final truce, he began armistice negotiations with Egypt and Israel. Following several weeks of negotiations, the armistice between Egypt and Israel was signed on February 24, 1949 (see Map 5 at end of chapter). The agreement set the borders between the two states where the front lines existed when the fighting ended. Israel was left in control of the Negev region, and Egypt held onto the Gaza Strip along the western coastline. The Egyptian brigade at Faluja, which had been surrounded by the Israelis for weeks, was allowed to return to Egypt. The armistice agreement between Lebanon and Israel was concluded on March 23, 1949, with both sides retuning to their previous international lines. In response to Israel's demand, the agreement included the withdrawal of Syrian forces from Lebanon.[29]

The agreement with Transjordan was drawn out while both sides maneuvered for certain territory. Israel insisted on free passage to various places in and around Jerusalem, including the Wailing Wall. Israel also pushed for the Jordanians to give up some of the land they occupied on the West Bank. In the end, the Jordanians yielded a narrow strip along the western edge of the West Bank to Israel, and the armistice was signed on April 3, 1949. Negotiations with Syria were drawn out for several months, with the Syrians insisting on keeping several strips of Israeli territory on the northeast border with Syria. Finally, on July 20, 1949, the two sides agreed to limit military forces along each side of the border, and the Syrians withdrew to the international line. The contested area along the border became a demilitarized zone (DMZ). The Iraqi forces withdrew from the small areas they held in Palestine but refused to negotiate for an armistice. They did not share a common border with Israel, and they did not want to commit to recognition of Israel.[30]

The next step in the peace process was envisioned to be formal peace treaties between Israel and the neighboring Arab states. Many years were to pass before this was to become a reality. The reason the Arabs rejected the permanent peace settlement was their refusal to recognize the existence of a Jewish state in Palestine. This was to be at the heart of the conflicts between the Arabs and Israel for many years to come. Israel paid a heavy price from the beginning of the declaration of a Jewish state in Palestine. In the War of Independence, six thousand Israelis were killed, which at that time was one percent of Israel's population. As a career military officer, this author is awe struck by how this fledgling nation defended itself and was victorious against overwhelming odds, while fighting on multiple fronts against trained armies equipped with tanks, armored vehicles, artillery, and air forces.[31]

Chaim Herzog, who served in the War of Independence as a teen and later became the President of Israel, has written: "Israel's victory was the result of self-sacrifice and determination of a people to fight for its existence."[32] It was that and a lot more. It was the courage, daring, heroism, boldness, and undaunted spirit of the Israeli people. It was their willingness to die for a homeland they had longed for over the centuries. Many of the new arrivals from Europe had gone through the

Holocaust and were steeled to fight for their freedom. They had strong leaders with courage and vision who led their fight for independence, very much like those who led America's struggle for independence. As you will see in forthcoming chapters, they have had to meet the challenge to their very existence on many other occasions.

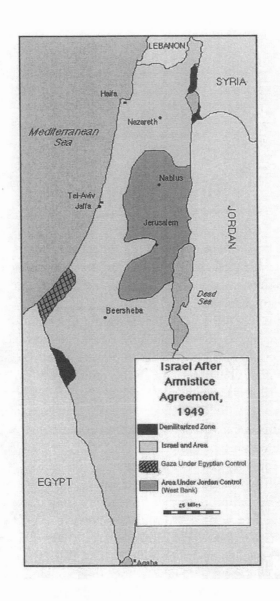

Map 5. Israel after the War of Independence 1949
Source: Jewish Virtual Library.
A Division of the American-Israeli Cooperative Enterprise.

Chapter 3

Sinai-Suez War

The War of Independence, and the subsequent armistices with its Arab neighbors, did not lead to true peace for Israel. Since Israel became a state in 1948, its cargo shipments attempting to pass through the Suez Canal were intercepted by the Egyptians and destroyed. This continued in spite of the UN Security Council's call for an end to all interference with shipping. In overt contempt of the UN, the interference actually increased with Nasser's ascension to power following the overthrow of the Egyptian monarchy.[1] To further complicate the international scene, in 1950 Jordan annexed the land west of the Jordan River, which became known as the West Bank. This was mostly territory that was granted by the UN as part of a Palestinian state. The Israelis saw this as less a threat than it would have been under the Palestinian Arabs and did not oppose the move by Jordan. At the same time, Israel had its hands full with thousands of Palestinian Arabs in refugee camps and a massive influx of Jewish immigrants from Europe and North Africa. By the end of 1951, 690,000 Jewish immigrants arrived, doubling Israel's population in about three years. These events put almost insurmountable hurdles in the path of the Israelis in building a new nation, with the task of developing a functioning government and economy. However, the most critical challenge remained the absence of peace, for the Arab neighbors periodically renewed the threat of jihad war against the Jewish state. The Israeli people were once again under constant fear of terrorism and renewed war as cross-border attacks by the Arabs became commonplace.[2]

A Terrorist Organization is Born

The conflict between the Israelis and Palestinians increased when thousands of previous inhabitants, who had fled during the war, attempted to cross back into Israel to resettle in their homes. Israel would not allow them to return. This resulted in an escalation of fighting between the Israelis and infiltrators. The Israelis resorted to severe reprisals, including cross-border attacks against Jordan and Egypt in an effort to persuade them to stop infiltration into Israel. One of these attacks took place in February 1955, when an element of the Israel Defense Forces attacked an Egyptian Army base in the Gaza Strip.[3] President Nasser of Egypt responded by organizing Arab volunteers into a terrorist group known as the Fedayeen. The Fedayeen were trained and equipped by Egypt's Intelligence Service to infiltrate into Israel and commit sabotage and murder. It was a new tactic by Nasser to carry out a low-level war with Israel while he built up his arsenal with massive supplies of modern weapons from the Soviet Union. On August 31, 1955, Nasser announced:

> Egypt has decided to dispatch her heroes, the disciples of Pharaoh and the sons of Islam and they will cleanse the land of Palestine.... There will be no peace on Israel's border because we demand vengeance, and vengeance is Israel's death.[4]

The Fedayeen began regular attacks against Israel's civilian population. They operated from bases in Egypt (the Gaza Strip), Lebanon, and Jordan. Between 1949 and 1956 Arab terrorists killed and wounded 1,300 Israelis. The terrorist attacks across the borders violated the armistice agreements, but it was Israel that was condemned by the UN for retaliatory attacks.[5] The terrorist attacks were not the only danger facing Israel. Nasser had just completed a deal with the Soviet Union for a major buildup of Egypt's military arsenal. This gave Israel every reason to be concerned about the threat from Egypt. Israel's leaders began weighing the prospect of taking out Egypt's new military arsenal before it could become operational and shift the balance of power in Egypt's favor. Coupled with this alternative, the Israelis were confronted with Egypt's blockade of access to the southern tip of the

Sinai Peninsula, which prevented Israel's sea passage through the Straits of Tiran and entrance to the Red Sea. This effectively closed Israel's access to commerce in East Africa and the Far East.[6]

Stranglehold

From the economic and security standpoint, Egypt had put a stranglehold on Israel's existence. Shipments via the Suez Canal were blocked; access to commerce by way of the Straits of Tiran was cut off; Egypt was sponsoring Fedayeen terrorist attacks on Israel; Nasser had embarked on a major buildup of military forces that overshadowed Israel's defense forces; and together, these factors greatly hindered Israel's efforts to strengthen its over-burdened economy. Israeli leaders reached the conclusion that Egypt intended to launch an all-out war against them as soon as it completed its arms buildup. As a further indicator of Egypt's intentions, Israel's leaders learned of a joint military command established between Egypt and Syria in late 1955. Jordan joined the command in 1956. These events led Israel to conclude that a preemptive strike against Egypt was necessary for its national survival. Egypt's massive arms deal with the Soviet Union was also of concern in Washington, so much so that the administration decided to withdraw its offer to help Egypt build a dam on the upper Nile River. This enraged Egypt's President Nasser, who retaliated by nationalizing the Suez Canal on July 27, 1956.[7]

The Suez Canal was within Egyptian sovereignty; however, it was regulated by an international agreement and under the administration of an international company owned mainly by British and French shareholders. The canal was the only land bridge between Africa and Asia and provided the shortest link between the Mediterranean Sea and the Indian Ocean. It was an important avenue of commerce and strategically important since two-thirds of Europe's oil passed through it.[8] Diplomatic efforts by Britain and France failed to alter Nasser's decision to take over the canal. Britain and France quickly reached the decision to jointly use military action to regain control of the Canal. There are conflicting stories on how Israel became a part of the British-French plan to attack Egypt. One report has it that Israel's Minister of Defense, Shimon Peres, approached the French to inquire about Israel joining in an attack on Egypt.[9] Another account has it that Israel was invited by France to take part in the operation.[10] In either event, Israel made it known that it was ready to take part.

In mid-October 1956, a secret meeting of top French, British, and Israeli officials took place in Sevres, France, to finalize plans for the operation. The plan called for Israel to begin the attack with a paratroop drop near the Canal and an assault on Egyptian forces in the Gaza Strip and Sinai Peninsula. In pretense, the British and French would issue an ultimatum for the Israelis and Egyptians to withdraw from the Canal area. It was assumed that Nasser would reject this demand, which would give the British and French the justification to seize control of the Canal. Before the end of the Sevres meeting, the French agreed to provide Israel extensive military reinforcements. This was critical for Israel's participation, considering the massive buildup of Egypt's arsenal.[11] As a further concession to Israel's participation in the attack on Egypt, France agreed to build a nuclear reactor in southern Israel and provide the uranium to fuel it.[12]

The Campaign

The Israelis initiated the campaign on October 29, 1956, with a bold parachute drop of 395 troops deep inside the Sinai just east of the Suez Canal. At the same time, another Israeli force crossed into the Sinai from the northeast with the objective of linking up with the paratroops. Egypt was slow to react to the Israeli assault, not knowing if it were a cross-border retaliation or a full-scale attack. In an effort to further confuse the Egyptians about their real intent, Israel sent troops to the Jordanian border feigning an attack in that direction. As prearranged, the day after Israel launched its attack, Britain and France called upon Israel and Egypt to withdraw their forces from the Canal area. As expected, the Egyptians rejected the ultimatum. This gave Britain and France the pretext to begin their assault. They immediately began bombing Egyptian airfields in preparation of their attack. Meanwhile, the Israelis seized the opportunity and set out to accomplish their objectives. They attacked the Egyptian Army and within days had destroyed or captured much of the war material Egypt had received from the Soviet Union and captured six thousand Egyptian soldiers. Israel occupied the entire

Sinai Peninsula and ended the Egyptian blockade of the Straits of Tiran. During the same time period, the Israelis took over the Gaza Strip and destroyed the Fedayeen bases that were harbored there. In the first 48 hours of the war, nine Egyptian fighter aircraft were shot down by the Israelis. Israel lost two jet fighters and nine propeller-driven aircraft, most of which were brought down by heavy ground fire.[13]

On the morning of November 6, the first British troops landed at Port Said, at the north end of the Canal. French troops landed at Port Fouad, a short distance from the British landing. Pressure from the international community was strong and swift. The Soviets threatened military action, including an attack on Israel. President Eisenhower was angered over attempts to use force to gain control of the Canal and threatened to terminate all aid to Israel. He was concerned that the attack on Egypt and the Suez Canal would lead to a much larger war. The United Nations General Assembly demanded an immediate ceasefire. The British government was the first to give in to the international pressure and agreed to a ceasefire. France and Israel were left with no other choice but to follow Britain's lead. Thus, the war ended not long after it began, with a ceasefire on November 8, 1956.[14]

Israel came under intense pressure from the UN and the United States to withdraw from the areas it had just occupied. It held out for assurances that the blockade of the Straits of Tiran would end and attacks by the Fedayeen from Egyptian territory would cease. Pressures from the United States eventually forced Israel to withdraw from the lands it had captured, but only in return for guarantees of passage through the Straits of Tiran and the UN's participation in the administration of the Gaza Strip. A UN Emergency Force was established, which replaced Israeli forces in the Sinai and Gaza. Unfortunately, the UN forces lost control of the Fedayeen in the Gaza Strip and gave in to Egyptian demands to move out of Gaza. The UN forces withdrew from the Gaza Strip and took up positions along the borders between Israel and Egypt but retained a post at Sharm el-Sheikh to assure Israeli passage through the Straits of Tiran. The removal of UN forces from the Gaza Strip weakened the UN's effectiveness and did little to stop the cross-border raids into Israel by the Egyptian-sponsored Fedayeen.[15]

The Aftermath

Even though he Egyptians were driven out of the Sinai and Gaza by the Israelis, Nasser was elevated to the leader of the Arab world for retaining control of the Suez Canal and fighting against Israel and the allied forces. He gained favor in the Arab world for vowing to renew the struggle with the Jewish state at the appropriate time. To further amplify the gravity of the threat, the Soviet Union and Eastern European bloc countries began accelerating delivery of weapons to Egypt and Syria. Israel heeded the warning and continued a buildup of its own defense forces.[16] While that was in progress, they still had to deal with continued cross-border raids by the Fedayeen. In another affront to peaceful existence, the Syrians began to launch attacks against Israel across the border. They shelled Israeli settlements from positions they occupied in the Golan Heights, laid land mines in Israeli territory, and instigated a war of attrition along the north western frontier with Israel. Israel Defense Forces (IDF) responded with a raid on Syrian posts near the Sea of Galilee. However, the Syrians continued their attacks, targeting Israeli fishing boats, shelling villages, and shooting at Israeli workers in the demilitarized zone near the frontier.[17]

Another Terrorist Organization is Born

At an Arab summit in Cairo in 1964, the heads of state in attendance decided to establish a joint Arab command to confront Israel. This organization came to be known as the Palestinian Liberation Organization (PLO). It was made up of Palestinian refugees led by Yasser Arafat who was head of al-Fatah, the largest armed group. The Arab states sponsored their own PLO subgroups. Egypt set up the Marxist Popular Front for the Liberation of Palestine, Syria sponsored the Palestine Liberation Front, and Iraq backed the Popular Democratic Front for the Liberation of Palestine. Israel considered the PLO and the subgroups as another move to drive them out of Palestine, and rightly so, for the founding charter of the Palestinian movement called for Israel's total destruction.[18] The complete PLO Charter is included in Appendix A. Several key articles of the Charter are quoted below.

Article 9. Armed struggle is the only way to liberate Palestine and is therefore a strategy, and not tactics. The Palestinian Arab people affirm its absolute resolution and abiding determination to pursue the armed struggle and to march forward toward the armed popular revolution, to liberate its homeland and return to it.

Article 10. Fedayeen action [paramilitary and terrorist attacks by armed Palestinians] forms the nucleus of the popular Palestinian war of liberation....

Article 19. The partitioning of Palestine in 1947 and the establishment of Israel is fundamentally null and void, whatever time has elapsed.... [19]

This is the threat environment that Israel faced as it sought to build a new nation and defend its very existence. Relations between Israel and Syria grew more contentious when in May 1967 the Soviets fed a false report to Syria and Egypt that Israel was massing troops along its border with Syria in preparation for an invasion. Although the report was a complete fabrication, it nevertheless served to increase tensions between Israel and the Arab nations and stoke the fires for the next major conflict that was just over the horizon—the Six-Day War.

Chapter 4

1967

Six-Day War

Nineteen years after Israel declared its independence, Israel was still faced with many of the same threats to its existence. The Arab states and the Palestinian Arabs still rejected the two-state solution mandated by the UN and refused to recognize Israel's right to exist as a Jewish state in their midst. Calls for destroying and liquidating Israel echoed from Voice of the Arabs broadcasts.[1] Still smarting from his defeat at the hands of Israel during the Sinai-Suez conflict, Egyptian President Gamal Abdel Nasser was unrelenting in his bellicose promises to one day restore the honor of the Arabs. As early as 1960, he began rallying the Egyptian people and neighboring Arab states to prepare for the liberation of Palestine.[2] In 1962 he proclaimed, "We will launch total war [against Israel] at the right moment."[3] Later that year he said, "There is no avoiding war in Palestine. As long as Israel exists, war is bound to break out."[4] In 1965 he declared, "When we enter Palestine, the soil will not only be covered with sand; it will be drenched with blood!"[5]

In a speech to Arab Trade Unionists on May 26, 1967, President Nasser proclaimed that they, the Arab states, had been waiting for the time when they would be prepared to liberate Palestine, and they were at last strong enough to enter into battle with Israel. "When we enter war," he said, "The battle will be a general one and our basic objective will be to destroy Israel."[6] Israel was not unaware of the rising tide of another war with the Arabs. The Palestinian refugee problem had been a thorn in the side of the Arab states since the War of Independence, when thousands of Palestinian Arabs fled their homes and settled in refugee camps in Jordan, Syria, and Lebanon. The plight of the refugees was exploited by some Arab leaders to achieve their political aims and rally the Arab world to drive the Israelis out of Palestine.

Plight of Refugees

Unfortunately for Israel, it received all the blame for the plight of the refugees. Israel was accused of forcing the Palestinian Arabs to leave Palestine and preventing them from returning to their homes after the war. In truth, the primary source of the refugee problem was the war. It should be remembered that it was the Arabs of Palestine who launched a civil war against the Jews on the same day in 1947 when the UN declared petitioning, and it was the surrounding Arab states that launched a full-scale war against the Jews of Palestine on the very same day in 1948 that Israel became an independent state. A convincing case can be made that if there had been no war, the Arabs of Palestine would not have been driven from their villages. Moreover, had the Arabs accepted the UN resolution for a two-state solution and agreed to live side-by-side with the Israelis, there would have been no reason for war and thus no refugees.[7]

Almost two decades after the War of Independence, thousands of Palestinian Arabs still languished in miserable refugee camps in Palestine and the surrounding Arab states. The camps became breeding grounds for Palestinian nationalism and terrorist organizations.[8] Although the Arab states had done little to improve the lot of the refugees, the hate that festered in the camps was directed at the Jews. Young and old Palestinians longed for the day when Palestine would be liberated, but they were essentially without leadership until the PLO was formed. The PLO provided direction for the Palestinian movement and gave a voice to those in the refugee camps. The original covenant of the PLO called for the destruction of Israel. The plan was to draw the Arab states into a war against Israel.[10] The PLO pulled together the various factions that sought the liberation of Palestine, the most notable of which was the Movement for the National Liberation of Palestine, al-Fatah. The ultimate goal of Fatah was to capture Jerusalem and set it up as the capital and holy city of a Palestinian nation. The strategy of Fatah was to devote itself solely to attacks on Israel, with the hope of stirring Arab unity and provoking war between Israel and the Arab states.[11]

Cross-Border Raids

In 1965, Fatah guerillas began crossing into Israel from the Jordanian border. Squads of armed men raided Israeli villages where they demolished houses, water installations, grain silos, and other civilian targets. As the raids on the civilian population became bolder and more numerous, Israel responded with retaliatory commando raids against suspected guerrilla camps in Jordan and Lebanon. Israel met with representatives of the UN Armistice Commission and demanded an end to the cross-border raids from Jordan. Although Jordan did not support the guerrilla activity from its territory, the armistice line with Israel stretched for 392 miles over rough terrain and was impossible for Jordan to secure in its entirety.[12]

The radical regime that came to power in Syria in 1966 supported Fatah and allowed the guerrillas to operate freely from its territory. As incursions and acts of sabotage from Syria increased, Israel warned Syria there would be consequences if it continued to allow cross-border attacks by Fatah. Nonetheless, the raids continued, taking the lives of several Israeli farmers. Israel retaliated with air strikes inside Syrian territory against heavy equipment that was being used to divert river water away from Israel. A month later, hostilities again erupted between Israel and Syria in a battle that involved fighter aircraft and artillery. Israeli pilots shot down two Syrian, Soviet-made MIG aircraft. Angry over the UN's failure to condemn Israel, Syria announced its intensions in future clashes to attack targets and bases inside Israel. The Syrians also left no doubt that they had any intention of curbing attacks by Fatah guerrillas.[13]

Tensions between Israel and Syria mounted, with continued attacks and infiltration into Israel from Fatah base camps in Syria. In April 1967, heavy artillery fire from long-range guns in Syria was directed at farms and villages in Israel. Israel aircraft responded with attacks on the Syrian gun positions. Six Syrian MIG fighter aircraft that were sent aloft to intercept the Israeli aircraft were shot down by the Israelis. Following this encounter, Israeli officials made it known to Syria that further attacks and provocations from across the frontier would result in measures that would endanger the continued existence of the Syrian regime. Fear of a major attack by Israel prompted Syria to make an urgent plea to Nasser for assistance.[14] Nasser, bound by a mutual defense agreement with Syria signed in 1966, wasted no time in reacting to the threat to Syria. No doubt his prestige in the Arab world would have been seriously damaged if he had not demonstrated solidarity with Syria.[15]

Egypt Mobilizes for War

On May 17, 1967, Nasser mobilized the Egyptian armed forces and deployed them into the Sinai Peninsula. Within several days, he had amassed a force of one hundred thousand troops and over one thousand tanks along Israel's southwestern border.[16] On the same day that Egyptian troops marched into the Sinai, Nasser demanded the removal of the United Nations Emergency Force (UNEF), which had been in place as a peacekeeping buffer between Egypt and Israel since 1956. Reluctantly, the UN agreed to withdraw the Emergency Force, knowing that it meant there would soon be war. On May 22, 1967, Nasser raised the probability of war with Israel by again banning all Israeli shipping from passing through the Straits of Tiran, which effectively imposed a blockade of the Israeli port of Eilat and the Gulf of Aqaba. Nasser announced at a news conference that "the Israeli flag shall not go through the Gulf of Aqaba."[17] In making this move, Nasser was in effect asking for war, since he was well aware that Israel had made it clear that such an act would be a declaration of war.[18]

Arab states increased war hysteria with a stream of anti-Israeli threats. Egyptian state radio added fuel to the war frenzy, proclaiming that Egypt was ready to "launch a total war against Israel." Another broadcast announced that the war would "put an end, once and for all, to Zionist existence."[19] Broadcasts from Syria called for Arabs to "kill, crush, burn, and destroy the Zionist viper's nest."[20] Syria brought its armed forces to maximum readiness, and its Defense Minister declared, "It is high time to launch the battle for the liberation of Palestine."[21] Jordan put its armed forces on alert and, in compliance with a recent defense agreement with Nasser, agreed to a joint command with an Egyptian general over Arab forces operating in Jordan. Iraqi forces moved into position to attack through Jordan. Saudi Arabia, Kuwait, Yemen, Algeria, and Lebanon announced their readiness to dispatch troops in support of the battle to wipe out the Jewish state.[22] With all these Arab forces poised to attack, the concern among Israeli officials reached a fever pitch.

Although Israeli forces had been mobilized with the call up of thousands of reserves, Israel knew they were facing three times as many troops, three times as many tanks, and over three times as many combat aircraft as they had in their forces. Moreover, the Soviet Union and Eastern Bloc countries were aiding Egypt and Syria.[23] The United States was bringing enormous pressure on Israel to avoid being the first one to fire a shot to ignite the war.[24] Israel's leaders were faced with only a few options, the choice of which could mean survival or annihilation. If the Arabs were in fact planning to attack and launched a first strike, Israel would be at a great disadvantage. With the numerical odds stacked against them, a first strike could be devastating to Israel. A surprise attack could catch Israel's air force on the ground and severely damage this critical war-fighting capability. The enemy could gain air superiority over the battlefield, placing Israeli ground forces at greater risk. More importantly, a first strike by the Arabs would undoubtedly result in much higher combat losses for the Israelis. From the strategic viewpoint, surrounded on all land frontiers by much larger military forces, Israel's survival could only be assured if it seized the initiative and launched a preemptive first strike against the Arabs.

Israel's military commanders argued heatedly for a preemptive strike and warned that every day of delay in launching the strike would mean heavier casualties for their forces. Arab forces had grown to 328,000 troops arrayed against Israel's largely civilian army of 250,000; the Arabs had 2,330 battle tanks compared with Israel's 1,000; and Israel's 286 combat aircraft were up against 682 Arab aircraft. Faced with these odds and the movement of Egyptian, Syrian, Iraqi, Jordanian, and Lebanese forces into forward positions close to Israel's borders, Israeli leaders concluded that the very existence of the State was threatened.

Having exhausted last minute diplomatic efforts to head off the crisis, Israel could wait no longer. On Sunday, June 4, 1967, Prime Minister Eshkol called the cabinet into session, and the decision was made to go forward with a preemptive strike.[25]

Israel Launches Preemptive Strike

Early in the morning of June 5, 1967, the Israeli Air Force launched one of the most brilliantly planned and executed uses of air power in modern times. The strike force took a detour out over the Mediterranean and approached Egypt from the sea, skimming a few feet above the water so as not to be detected by air defense radar. The operation was a complete surprise and with lightening speed achieved complete success. The first wave of air strikes attacked Egypt's 15 air bases, destroying 189 planes, most of which were still parked on the runways. The initial attack also demolished 16 air defense radar sites and put six Egyptian airfields out of service. By late morning, most airfields were no longer useable. The Egyptian Air Force was essentially wiped out, having lost 147 fighter aircraft, including 90 of the latest Soviet-made MIG-21 fighter planes. They also lost 57 bombers and 32 transport aircraft. Destruction of the bombers was crucial in preventing the threat to Israel's civilian population centers. In the air campaign with Egypt, Israel lost only 19 aircraft, two in aerial combat and the rest to ground fire.[26] With complete air superiority over Egypt, Israel launched a ground offensive into the Sinai Desert and sent Egyptian forces reeling in retreat. By the end of the second day, Israeli forces were approaching the bank of the Suez Canal.[27]

Israel encouraged Jordan's King Hussein to stay out of the battle; however, acting under the provisions of the defense pact with Egypt, Jordan joined in the attack on Israel on the first day of the war. Jordanian long-range artillery began shelling Israeli towns, and Jordan's troops crossed the armistice line in Jerusalem to attack Israeli positions. By noon of the first day of the war, Jordanian aircraft attacked several Israeli towns and strafed a small Israeli airfield. In response, Israeli Air Force planes struck Jordanian airfields, and in a short time Jordan's air force was put out of action. At the same time, Israel began a ground operation to drive Jordanian forces from the West Bank back into Jordan.

A short time after the Jordanian air strikes on Israel, Syrian Air Force planes attacked Israeli positions around the Sea of Galilee and bombed an airfield in northern Israel. Israel struck back swiftly, destroying 55 Syrian fighter aircraft and two bombers, mostly on the ground at Syrian air bases. The Iraqi Air Force was next to strike an Israeli city. Israel's air force commander retaliated immediately by sending Israeli aircraft 500 miles across Jordan to strike an Iraqi airfield, where ten aircraft were destroyed on the ground.[28]

In the first two days of the war, the Arabs lost 416 aircraft. Of that number, 58 were shot down in aerial combat. Over the same time period, Israel lost 26 aircraft in action. For all practical purposes, Israel was the only one of the combatants left with an air force. This gave Israel's air force complete domination of the sky and enabled it to devote full attention to supporting the ground forces.[29] By the end of the second day, the main Egyptian forces in the Sinai had been overrun, and Israeli forces were thrusting deep into the Sinai. By the fourth day, Egyptian resistance was effectively broken. By the next day, Egyptian armored forces in the Sinai were destroyed, and Israeli forces had completed their advance to the Suez Canal. In less than five days, an Israeli force of three divisions had defeated an army of seven divisions! On this front, the Israeli Army suffered 300 killed in action, over a 1,000 wounded, and 61 tanks destroyed, while the Egyptians lost an estimated 10,000 to 15,000 soldiers and over 500 captured. As many as 800 Egyptian tanks were abandoned or destroyed. While this was going on, Palestinian Arabs began shelling Israeli settlements from the Gaza Strip. Although under Egyptian control since the 1956 war, the Gaza Strip was defended by a Palestinian division. There was bitter fighting, but the Israelis prevailed by the end of the third day.[30]

One of the main objectives in the fight with Egypt was the removal of the naval blockade of the Straits of Tiran. To accomplish this, Israel planned an air, sea, and paratroop assault on Sharm El-Sheikh, the stronghold that guarded the entrance to the Strait. When Israeli forces arrived, they found the stronghold abandoned by the Egyptians. The blockade of the Port of Eilat and the Straits of Tiran had ended.[31] With the completion of this objective, Israel had accomplished the three objectives of their operation against Egypt: first to destroy the Egyptian

Army and break its strength for the long term; second to capture Sharm El-Sheikh and end the blockade of the Straits of Tiran; and third to take and occupy the Sinai Peninsula, which was essential to maintain control of Sharm El-Sheikh. In addition to close air support, which was an important force multiplier in the ground operations, several other factors contributed to the incredible success of the Israeli Army. Officers, from company commanders, battalion commanders, brigade commanders, and down to the lowest level of command, fought at the head of their troops. The fighting spirit of the troops was at its highest. Courage and conviction were ever present, for they knew this was a fight for the life of their country.[32] While the Israelis were fighting the Egyptians, they were at the same time engaging the Jordanians and Syrians on other fronts.

The Battle for Jerusalem

Since the end of the War of Independence, Jerusalem had been divided into two separate entities. The western part of the city was mostly Jewish with approximately 100,000 inhabitants. The eastern part of Jerusalem was predominately Arab and was under the control of the Arab Legion (Jordanian Army). This part of the city included the historic Old City, which held the sacred shrines and holy places for all three major religions. The city was heavily defended by the Jordanian Army which surrounded it on three sides and controlled the approaches from each direction. Since the occupation of the Old City by Jordon in 1948, the Jewish people had been denied access to pray at their most holy place, the Wailing Wall. Shelling of Jewish settlements in the western part of the city by the Jordanians on the first day of the Six-Day War gave Israelis the opening to take back their holiest place. With the destruction of the Jordanian Air Force, Israeli aircraft were able to attack Jordanian positions around Jerusalem without resistance. On June 6, units of an Israeli infantry brigade, supported by armored forces, advanced into the center of the city where they fought a fierce house-to-house battle. By evening they had overcome the enemy resistance. During the night, a Jordanian infantry brigade attempted to reinforce their beleaguered troops that were still holding part of the city. At dawn Israeli aircraft and artillery battered the reinforcements and forced them to withdraw. When the reinforcements failed to break through, the commander of the Jordanian forces, who remained in the city, decided to withdraw. By 10:00 on the morning of June 7, a large Israeli force passed through the St. Stephen's Gate and entered the Old City. They met no organized resistance; the bulk of the Jordanian forces had withdrawn.[33]

The Fight for the West Bank

While the battle for Jerusalem was being waged, other units of the Israeli Army were engaging Jordanian forces in the West Bank. Israeli infantry and tanks attacked from several directions, breaking the Jordanian resistance. In some instances, Jordanians abandoned tanks, and troops fled on foot toward the Jordan River. In the far north, on the morning of June 7, a fierce tank battle that began on the previous day resumed. With more than half of the Jordanian armored brigade's tanks destroyed, the Jordanians withdrew toward the Damya Bridge to escape across the river back into Jordan. The Israelis moved swiftly to the east and seized control of three bridges across the Jordan. Late on the evening of June 7, Israel and Jordan accepted the United Nation's call for a ceasefire. Jordan had lost the West Bank along with extensive amounts of weapons and equipment and over 6,000 troops killed or missing. Israeli casualties on this front were approximately 550 killed and 2,500 wounded. Iraqi forces stationed in Jordan did not enter the fight.[34]

Israel takes the Golan Heights

The high tension that caused Egypt to go on a war footing was generated by Syria's urgent insistence that Israel was preparing an attack to overthrow the Syrian regime in Damascus. Syria was counting on Egypt to come to its aid in consonance with their mutual defense pact. Leading up to the outbreak of war, Syria had announced that its armed forces were at maximum readiness and declared it was high time to launch the battle for the liberation of Palestine.[35] From this bombastic language, Syria was expected to strike in force as soon as the war began. However, that was not the case. Except for the air strike mentioned previously, the Syrians took only limited action near the border with Israel. They shelled Israeli positions along the eastern front, launched several company-size probes toward two Israeli kibbutzim, and as they had done repeatedly in the past, struck Israeli villages below the Golan Heights with artillery and armored units.[36]

At first Israel was reluctant to mount a full-scale attack on Syria; however, as late as June 9, Defense Minister Dayan ordered Israeli forces to take the Golan Heights. Israeli infantry and tanks, supported by the air force, encountered heavy resistance. Syrian forces were entrenched and well fortified in very rough, steep terrain. Enemy positions were protected by multiple strands of barbwire, minefields, trenches, concrete pillboxes, machine-guns, and anti-tank barriers. Some positions were taken only with fierce hand-to-hand fighting. Israeli losses were heavy, but by the morning of June 10, the last day of the war, Syrian forces broke and began to flee, with the Israeli Air Force in pursuit. Many tanks were abandoned as the Israelis attacked. By nightfall the Golan Heights was in Israel's hands.[37]

Victory

The Soviet Union became very agitated over Israel's attack on its client state, Syria. Early in the morning of June 10, the Soviets severed diplomatic relations with Israel and threatened sanctions against Israel. Later on that day, the Soviet Union demanded that the United States pressure Israel to stop its attack on Syria or they (Soviets) would intervene, including with military action against Israel. In the face of the Soviet threats, Israel accepted the United Nations imposed ceasefire, satisfied that they had completed their objective in the Golan Heights. The war was thus over by the end of June 10, 1967. In just six days, Israel had defeated Egypt, Jordan, and Syria and captured three times the amount of territory it had at the beginning of the war (see Map 6 and 7 at end of chapter). A small state of (then) three million people had beaten Arab states with a combined population of 39 million people.[38] Victory over the Arabs left Israel with the occupation of the Sinai Peninsula, the Gaza Strip, the Golan Heights, the West Bank, and all of Jerusalem, including the Wailing Wall. In addition to restoring possession of territory with special meaning to its religious past, the captured territory gave Israel a buffer zone that decreased its vulnerability to Arab attacks. The captured territory also placed a million Palestinian Arabs under Israel's control and created thousands more refugees who had been uprooted by the war.[39]

The newly occupied territory also presented Israel with the formidable task of ruling over a hostile population of Palestinian Arabs spread over a vast territory. For that reason, and to satisfy the international community, Israel acted quickly to offer the return of most of the occupied land to its original owners but stood firm on retaining certain territories essential for security and those with religious and historical meaning. As early as June 19, Israel proposed peace with Egypt and Syria and offered to return most of the occupied territory in exchange for an end to the jihad against Israel. However, Arab leaders meeting in Sudan in September 1967 declared they would not negotiate, recognize, or make peace with Israel. Soon after that meeting, Israel's possession of the occupied territories became more complicated. The United Nations passed Resolution 242, which called for Israel to withdraw from the territories it occupied during the Six-Day War. The resolution also called for all Middle East nations to live in peace. Israel took the position that it would comply with the resolution only after the Arab states agreed to recognize its right to exist and signed a lasting peace agreement.[40] Based on the declaration of Arab states meeting in Sudan, this was not likely to be forthcoming. Israel had just lost thousands of its people fighting for its survival, and to give up all that without any assurance of being allowed to live in peace would have been folly. The Arabs states had made it clear there would be no peace or recognition of Israel. Israel would have to continue to be prepared to fight for its survival.

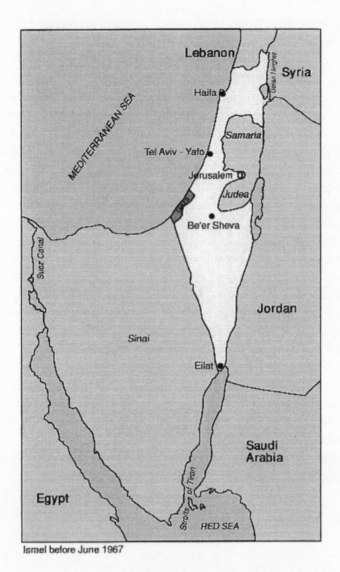

Israel before June 1967

Map 6. Israel before June 1967 and the Six-Day War
Source: Jewish Virtual Library.
A Division of the American-Israeli Cooperative Enterprise.
By Israeli Ministry Foreign Affairs
Note: <u>Gaza</u> Under Egyptian Control
<u>Judea - Samaria</u> (West Bank) Under <u>Jordan Control</u>

46

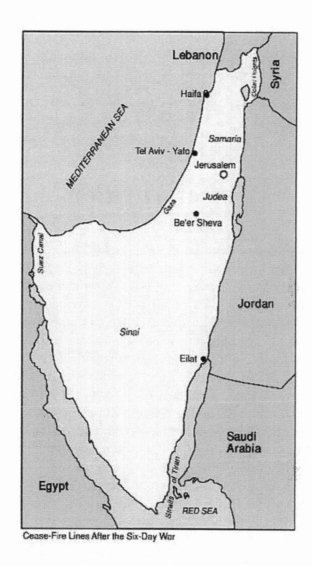

Cease-Fire Lines After the Six-Day War

**Map 7. Israel at the end of the Six-Day War
Source: Jewish Virtual Library.
A Division of the American-Israeli Cooperative Enterprise.
By Israeli Ministry Foreign Affairs**

Chapter 5

War of Attrition

The citizen soldiers of Israel were just getting back to their normal lives when Egypt renewed hostilities. Although the Egyptian Army had been devastated during the Six-Day War, Nasser had not given up the fight against Israel. Several weeks after the ceasefire between Egypt and Israel went into effect, Nasser set in motion a new strategy against Israel—a war of attrition. As the name implies, the plan was to bleed Israel economically, politically, and militarily with an endless series of limited attacks short of full-scale war. The main focus of the attacks was against the eastern bank of the Suez Canal, which Israel had occupied since the end of the Six-Day War. Nasser was bent on restoring Egypt's honor after suffering a humiliating defeat during the Six-Day War. His immediate objective was to retake the eastern bank of the Suez Canal and the Sinai Peninsula, which were lost during the war. The first attack of the War of Attrition was initiated on July 1, 1967, when Egyptian forces ambushed an Israeli patrol along a narrow dyke on the Suez Canal. An Israeli armored infantry company engaged the Egyptians, and while under artillery and armored fire from the Egyptians on the west bank of the Suez Canal, they drove off the Egyptian forces. This was the first of many engagements with the Egyptians who regularly directed tank and artillery fire at Israeli patrols on the eastern bank of the Canal.[1]

On July 14, the Egyptians opened fire on small Israeli boats in the Canal near the ceasefire line. This triggered a major tank and artillery battle across the Canal. Israeli and Egyptian air forces joined in the fight, and in the air battle that unfolded, seven Egyptian fighters were shot down by the Israelis. The Israelis lost nine men killed and 55 wounded before the artillery dual ended. There was a lull in the fighting across the Canal until September 1967 when Egyptians opened fire on Israeli ships passing through the Israeli sector of the Gulf of Suez. The fighting spread to artillery duels all along the Canal. Several towns on the Egyptian side of the Canal were caught in the fighting and had to be evacuated, creating a large population of refugees. On October 21, the Israeli destroyer, *Eilat,* in international waters off the coast of Port Said was attacked with surface-to-surface missiles. Three missiles fired from an Egyptian ship anchored inside Port Said harbor struck and sank the *Eilat.* Of the 199 Israeli crew members on board, 47 were killed and 90 were wounded. Four days later, Israel responded with a vengeance. They launched a massive artillery barrage along the southern end of the Suez Canal, striking Egyptian refineries, petroleum depots, and petrochemical plants. Fires raged for days, destroying everything in its path. The damage was in the millions. Following this encounter, another period of relative calm settled in, interrupted by sporadic outbreaks of artillery fire and air battles, until the fall of 1998.[2]

Nasser Escalates the War

By September 1968, Nasser was feeling much bolder. The Soviets had moved into Egypt, introducing thousands of advisors who essentially reorganized the Egyptian Army. At the same time they replaced most of the equipment lost in the Six-Day War with the latest in tanks and aircraft. With a stronger military posture, Nasser was prepared for an escalation in the war of attrition. In early September 1968, he deployed 150,000 troops along the Egyptian side of the Suez Canal. Then on September 8, he launched a massive barrage against the Israelis on the eastern bank of the Canal. Over a thousand artillery pieces, mortars, and tanks concentrated their fire at the Israelis from one end of the eastern bank to the other. Israeli losses were 28 killed and wounded. Nasser boasted of a great victory. Several weeks later, the Egyptians again opened up with a heavy barrage of artillery, coordinated with the insertion of a commando unit on the Israeli side of the Canal. The attack left the Israelis with 49 killed and wounded. Out-gunned by the massive infusion of Soviet weapons, Israel decided on a new strategy. On October 31, 1968, it sent a commando force by helicopter 220 miles inside Egyptian territory, where they attacked bridges on the Nile and an electric transmission station. Egypt got the message and reduced its attacks across the Canal.[3]

During the respite in shelling, Israel began the construction of fortifications along their side of the Suez Canal to protect its troops from attacks by Egypt. The new line of defense, known as the Bar-Lev line, was completed in March 1969, just in time for renewed fighting. Egypt resumed the war with massive barrages at Israel's new fortifications. The weakness of the fortifications soon became apparent; they provided a stationary target for the Egyptians gunners. Artillery barrages increased in frequency and continued without letup. Israel fought back with counter fire and sent troops on raids into Egyptian territory, but this did little to reduce the intensity of the Egyptian attacks. In December 1969, the U.S. Secretary of State, William Rogers, proposed a peace plan that required Israel to return to the pre-1967 borders (see Map 6). Israel rejected this plan, viewing it as a danger to its security and real peace.[4]

Israel Strikes Back

As the war along the Suez Canal continued, the Israelis embarked on an aggressive new strategy to stop the Egyptian attacks. They unleashed their air force in a massive bombing campaign on Egyptian positions along the Suez Canal. This resulted in a temporary letup in shelling of Israeli positions; however, the Egyptians resumed attacks as soon as they recovered. The limited success of this strategy led Israel to escalate its efforts to silence the attacks from across the Canal. They began sending their air force to attack targets deep inside Egypt, with the objective of forcing Nasser to reposition his forces away from the Suez Canal. The Egyptians sent up their air force fighters to challenge the Israelis. In one air battle in July 1969, five Egyptian fighters were shot down by the Israelis. In another air combat engagement on September 11, 1969, the Israeli Air Force shot down 11 Egyptian aircraft with the loss of only one Israeli aircraft. Israel's deep penetration air operations lasted from January through April 1970, including several thousand air missions. They proved successful in reducing the frequency of attacks along the Canal and in decreasing Israeli casualties. However, Israel drew intense international criticism when bombing mistakes accidentally caused the death of a number of civilians, including school children.[5]

Growing Soviet Involvement

International pressure, along with the growing intervention by the Soviet Union in Egypt, caused Israel to curtail its cross-border air operations. In early 1970, the Soviets began upgrading the older Egyptian Air Force fighters to the latest MIG-21s. At the same time, they began providing Egypt with one of the most sophisticated air defense systems using SA-2 and SA-3 surface-to-air missile (SAM) batteries. The Soviets also operated the SAM batteries and took part in downing Israeli aircraft. One of the Soviet officers claimed credit for shooting down five Israeli aircraft. As Soviet involvement grew, and the number of air battles increased, Israel's air force began encountering MIG-21 fighters flown by Soviet pilots. In one air battle, an Israeli patrol was jumped by eight MIG-21s, possibly flown by Soviet pilots. Five of the Soviet-made aircraft were shot down. No Israeli aircraft were lost.[6]

In the midst of growing anti-war sentiment among the Israeli people, the government became more amenable to peace initiatives. In July 1970, the second American Rogers Plan was accepted by both Israel and Egypt. The Plan included a ninety-day ceasefire along the Suez Canal and a freeze on the military posture on both sides of the Canal. The Rogers Plan also included the return of the UN special envoy, Dr. Jarring, who was charged with negotiating with both parties to achieve a peaceful settlement based on UN Resolution 242. However, before the Jarring mission could get underway, Egypt violated the ceasefire agreement. On the same day the ceasefire took effect, Egypt and its Soviet suppliers deployed 42 SAM air defense systems to forward positions along the western bank of the Canal. This ended any meaningful progress of the Jarring mission.[7]

In September 1970, Egypt's President Nasser died. He was replaced by Anwar el-Sadat, who immediately pressed for negotiations with Israel for the return of the land Egypt had lost during the Six-Day War. Sadat was receptive to Dr. Jarring's proposal to open indirect talks with Israel. On this basis, indirect talks resumed in January 1971. Sadat offered a plan that included Israel's partial withdrawal from the Sinai to a position 48 kilometers east of the Suez Canal. He also promised to commit to a six-month ceasefire. Israel's Prime Minister Meir refused to accept Sadat's proposal without a full peace treaty.[8]

In February 1971, Dr. Jarring suggested a new peace plan that called for Sadat to enter into a peace agreement with Israel and for Israel to withdraw from Egyptian territory back to the pre-1967 border. Sadat demanded a specific commitment from Israel to withdraw from the Sinai Peninsula and Gaza Strip. He also insisted on settlement of the Palestinian refugee problem and acceptance of a UN peacekeeping force. In late February 1971, Israel rejected Dr. Jarring's latest proposal. Soon, thereafter, Washington undertook a new peace initiative but was unable to convince Israel to accept even a limited withdrawal from the Sinai. In July 1972, Sadat sought to improve relations with the United States and gain assistance for a settlement with Israel. As a gesture of his sincerity, he expelled 15,000 Soviet advisers from Egypt. This was to no avail, for Israel refused to relinquish any land without full recognition by the Arabs. With negotiations deadlocked, Israel turned its attention to the escalating problem with the PLO.[9]

The PLO Intensifies Attacks

Following Israel's occupation of the Gaza Strip in 1967, the PLO set out to turn the Palestinian population against Israel. The PLO launched a campaign of terror against the Palestinians who had taken jobs with the Israelis. They organized secret terrorist cells that carried out attacks against the Israelis and any uncooperative Palestinians. In July 1971, Israel began a concerted military operation to end the violence in Palestine. Many resistance fighters were either killed, arrested, or deported. After a seven-month campaign, the uprising was put down. However, the Israelis were still faced with attacks on other fronts.[10]

Along the Jordanian border, there were hundreds of attacks against Israeli forces and civilians in the West Bank by Jordan's army, the Iraqi Army (stationed in Jordan), and the PLO. Soon after Israel occupied the West Bank during the Six-Day War, the PLO took advantage of the large Arab population residing there to recruit fighters and establish a sympathetic staging base for attacks on Israel. The Israelis stepped up their efforts to root out the terrorist base camps in the West Bank, and in time forced them to move their camps to the east side of the Jordan River. This did not put an end to the PLO attacks across the Jordan into Israel. The PLO shelled Israeli patrols and villages and struck a school bus, killing and wounding many children. In response, Israel's armed forces, equipped with tanks and infantry backed by close air support, mounted a major offensive against the PLO base camps on the east side of the Jordan River. The Israelis destroyed the main base camps, killing 200 PLO combatants and capturing 150. Israel suffered 28 killed and 69 wounded and the loss of four tanks and one aircraft.[11]

Israel's attack east of the Jordan River was successful in driving the PLO units farther east into Jordan and higher into the mountains. There they set up training and operational camps near Jordanian villages, where they could use the civilians as shields from Israeli attacks. However, the shelling and rocket fire into Israel continued, and major artillery duels flared up frequently. Several times the long-range guns of the Iraqi forces stationed in Jordan assisted the PLO in shelling Israeli villages. The Israeli Air Force was called in to counter the Iraqi artillery. The Iraqi guns were silenced, with major damage to their equipment and heavy casualties to their crews. The PLO power base continued to grow in Jordan, and following an attempted assassination of Jordan's King Hussein by the PLO, it was branded a danger to the internal security of Jordan. In September 1970, the Jordanians reacted forcefully with a sweeping campaign to drive the PLO out of Jordan. The PLO shifted its main base of operations to Lebanon. Conflict along the Jordan front diminished, but now Israel had a new front to contend with on its northern frontier, which in the years ahead would become a major threat to its security.[12]

Meanwhile, the situation was relatively quiet on the Egyptian front. Egypt's Sadat had imposed a strict ceasefire along the Suez Canal. Israel, feeling somewhat secure, focused its attention on settling thousands of new immigrants and rebuilding its economy. As Israel was to find out, the relative calm on the Egyptian front belied Sadat's true intentions.

Chapter 6

1973

Yom Kippur War

Nasser's War of Attrition did not convince Israel to end its occupation of the east bank of the Suez Canal or any of the Sinai Peninsula. Sadat's diplomatic efforts were also unsuccessful in changing Israel's policy of refusing to negotiate with the Arabs until they recognized Israel as a legitimate state. Sadat was determined to achieve two objectives:

(1) restore the honor of Egypt after the humiliating defeat at the hands of Israel during the Six-Day War in 1967 and

(2) regain possession of the Sinai Peninsula that was lost to the Israelis during the Six-Day War.

Sadat made several attempts at diplomacy to achieve these objectives. Soon after becoming the President of Egypt, he surprised his own people, as well as the international community, with an offer of a peace agreement with Israel—the first Arab leader ever to do so. However, as a condition of this offer, Israel would have to withdraw from the Sinai Peninsula and all other Arab territories it had captured during the 1967 War, including the West Bank, the Golan Heights, and East Jerusalem. Israel was also expected to resolve the Palestinian refugee problem. Israel turned down this proposal. It was not willing to return to prewar borders, which were viewed as indefensible and likely to invite more incursions by the Arabs. It is worthy of mention that not long after the 1967 War, Israel made a proposal to Egypt and Syria to withdraw from the Sinai Peninsula and Golan Heights, with minor border modifications, in exchange for genuine peace treaties. The answer to this offer came at the Arab summit in Sudan where peace with Israel was rejected.[1]

Sadat Prepares for War

In February 1971, Sadat proposed a partial withdrawal of Israeli forces to several passes 20 to 30 miles from the east bank of the Suez Canal. For this he was willing to sign a peace agreement with Israel and reopen the Suez Canal to shipping. Moshe Dayan was in favor of this move, but Sadat's initiative was rejected by Golda Meir, then Prime Minister of Israel. She was unbending in her insistence on keeping defendable borders. With the failure of his proposal of a partial withdrawal, Sadat concluded that war with Israel was the only way he could achieve his goals, and he ordered his generals to begin preparing for war. He was reported to have asserted that he was willing to sacrifice a million of his soldiers to get back the Sinai.[2] Sadat's ultimate goal was to launch a full-scale, all-out war with Israel to take back all the Arab lands Israel had occupied during the Six-Day War. However, the Soviet Union had refused to provide Egypt the long-range fighter-bombers needed to penetrate deep into Israel to strike its airfields, air defense systems, and command and control facilities. Sadat thought these aircraft were necessary to prevent Israel from achieving air superiority like they did during the Six-Day War. Egypt also wanted the Soviets to provide long-range, strategic retaliatory capability in the form of Scud missiles to strike the heart of Israel in the event of a full-scale war. The Soviet Union refused to provide these weapons to Egypt, fearing such action might harm their recent overtures for detente with Washington.[3]

Deception and the Soviet Buildup

Without long-range aircraft and Scud missiles, Sadat concluded he could not proceed with an all-out war with Israel. He scaled back his war plans to encompass a limited strike to push the Israelis back from the east bank of the Suez Canal. In gaining a foothold on the east bank and part of the Sinai, he hoped to acquire the leverage to force Israel, with the help of the international community, into negotiations for the return of the Sinai. He instructed his generals to prepare for a limited war against Israel and directed them to implement an elaborate, covert deception campaign to prevent Israel from detecting their preparations for war. The cleverly designed deception plan was intended to lull Israel into a false sense of security. The plan included a strict ceasefire along the Suez Canal to lower tensions and reduce the threat level between the two enemies on each side of the Canal. From late 1972 into the fall of 1973, the Egyptians conducted a series of mobilizations and deployments along the Canal. They were intended to give the impression that their army was conducting routine training exercises, which were harmless and of no threat to Israel. Egypt went so far as to assemble a special staff to spread misinformation, such as weaknesses in the Egyptian Army and lack of equipment.[4] This was right out of the playbook of the former Soviet Disinformation Directorate of the KGB, and considering the heavy influence of Soviet advisors that had been in Egypt for years, it is not a far reach to suspect Soviet participation in this program. Although Sadat had expelled thousands of Soviet advisors in the summer of 1972, many of them had returned to provide technical assistance with the newly provided weapons and to help Egypt plan its attack across the Suez Canal.

In addition to their campaign to catch Israel off guard, Egypt had to come up with a new strategy to combat the expected counterattack by Israel's tank corps and infantry and prevent Israel from gaining control of the airspace over the battlefield. That combination of Israeli forces had devastated Egypt's forces during the Six-Day War. This is where the Soviets came in with a crash program to upgrade Egypt's and Syria's air defense systems. The Soviet Union supplied both of these countries with the latest air defense systems, including SA-2, SA-3, and SA-6 surface-to-air missiles (SAM) and ZSU-23 self-propelled anti-aircraft (AAA) guns. With these weapons, the Soviet advisors constructed two of the most dense, sophisticated air defense systems anywhere in the world, comparable to the one they and the Chinese installed and operated in North Vietnam, which accounted for shooting down hundreds of U.S. aircraft.[5] The SA-6 was especially troubling to Israel's Air Force, for neither they nor the United States had developed counter measures for this missile system. As one of the latest and most sophisticated systems in the Soviet inventory, the SA-6 was a very real threat to Israeli pilots. It used several different frequencies for tracking the target and rapidly switched between them to prevent detection and evasion by the pilots.

The SAM and AAA umbrella gave the Egyptians and Syrians a good chance to limit Israel's control of the airspace over the battlefield, but defeating the Israeli ground forces was another matter. Once again the Soviets entered the picture. They provided the Egyptian and Syrian armies with thousands of Soviet-made anti-tank weapons, including RPG-7 shoulder-fired rocket propelled missiles, Sagger missiles, and missile-carrying armored vehicles.[6] The Sagger anti-tank missile uses a wire data link, optically guided to the target by the operator. It is quite accurate in the hands of a trained soldier for a range of up to 3,000 yards. The Sagger is similar to the U.S. BGM-71 anti-tank, wire-guided missile.

The Soviet Union also supplied Egypt with the pontoon bridges, boats, ferries, and other equipment required for the assault across the Suez Canal. The Egyptian Army practiced canal crossings numerous times, which, along with mobilizations and exercises, were intended to deceive the Israelis. These activities and the buildup of SAMs and artillery on the western bank of the Canal did not go unnoticed by Israel, but the Mossad, Israel's intelligence service, was convinced that the preconditions required to enable Egypt to embark on a war were not present. However, Israel soon became aware that one of those preconditions, the delivery of long-range, ground-to-ground Scud missiles, had been achieved by early summer 1973. The Scud missiles had a range of 180 miles and could be used against civilian targets in Israel.[7] The Scud missiles were used against U.S. forces and Israeli civilian targets by Iraq during the first Gulf War.

The Syrian Front

The increased buildup of SAMs, artillery pieces, and armored forces on the Golan Heights was also observed by the Israelis, but they were convinced that Syria would not go to war without Egypt. Israel's intelligence estimates were also clouded by a confrontation with Syrian aircraft in mid-September 1973. Syria scrambled fighters to intercept an

Israeli reconnaissance aircraft photographing Soviet ships approaching Syrian ports. Israeli fighters covering the Recon aircraft joined the fray and shot down 13 Syrian fighter aircraft without the loss of any Israeli aircraft. This engagement gave Syria an excuse for its increased deployment of forces on the Golan Heights.[8]

Unknown to Israel, Sadat had met with Hafez Assad, President of Syria, and reached an agreement for a simultaneous surprise attack on Israel, with Egyptian forces attacking in the south across the Suez Canal and Syria launching an attack on the Golan Heights in the north. Sadat and Assad also sought help from other Arab states. Promises were secured from Saudi Arabia and Qatar for financial aid. Saudi Arabia, Algeria, Libya, Morocco, Sudan, and Iraq obligated troops and aircraft for use in the coming war with Israel. Two squadrons of Mirage fighter aircraft from Iraq and Libya were deployed to Egypt in readiness for war. Sadat considered the use of oil as a weapon and met with King Feisal of Saudi Arabia to lay the groundwork for imposing an oil embargo on Western powers.[9]

The Attack Nears

Although there were numerous indicators that Egypt was preparing for war, in most cases they were ignored by the Israelis or passed off as Egyptians preparing for another exercise. That was just what the Egyptians wanted them to think. Egypt's campaign of deception had been successful beyond Sadat's expectations. It was also a colossal failure of Israel's intelligence service, which would have far reaching consequences. As the Egyptian forces began maneuvers along the Suez Canal in the first days of October 1973, some of the Israeli forces at the fortifications on the east bank of the Canal began reporting an increase in activities, such as movement of troops, armored vehicles, and artillery into forward positions. Surface-to-air and surface-to-surface missile batteries were being fully manned. Earth moving equipment was in operation in what appeared to be preparation for crossing and positioning of bridges. Minefields were being cleared on land, and underwater mines were being detonated. However, civilians and soldiers on the Egyptian side of the Canal went about their daily routine, with some soldiers fishing and walking along the banks without battle gear. This casual activity was another aspect of Egypt's grand scheme of deception. At this juncture, it was just four days from the surprise attack scheduled for October 6. Still, the Israelis had not foreseen that war was imminent. No action had been taken to mobilize the reserves, although as a precaution Israel forces in the Southern Command were placed on a higher state of alert along the Canal.[10]

Israel's defense concept was driven by its relatively small population and the financial burden of maintaining a large military force on active duty. The concept depended on having sufficient warning of an impending attack, based on solid intelligence information, to mobilize its reserves. While the reserves were responding to the call to duty, it was believed that the active duty army would be able to hold off the attacking forces until the reserves were in place. Its air force, which maintained a large active force, would assist in holding back the enemy until the reserves were fully mobilized. Since Israel maintained a large, well-trained reserve force, this concept had merit, as long as the Israeli military and civilian leadership received timely and accurate intelligence. Unfortunately, this was not the case on the eve of the Yom Kippur War.

Sadat chose to strike on October 6 for two reasons that complimented his deception plan. For one, the date was within the window of the Moslem holiday period of Ramadan, which was a time when the Arabs would not be expected to start a war. That date was also chosen for another reason. It fell on Yom Kippur, the most sacred day in the Jewish calendar, a time when Israel would least expect a war to begin. It was a time when the whole country traditionally came to a standstill. Yom Kippur, also known as the Day of Atonement, is a complete Sabbath. No work can be performed on that day. It is a complete 25 hour fast during which Jewish people observing the day refrain from eating and drinking, even water. Radio and television stations are shut down. On this day the people are usually at home or at the synagogue. This was not a day that the Israelis expected to be interrupted by a war. The Egyptian's counted on Israel being lulled into a complete sense of security on this day. They knew it would be the worst time for Israel to initiate a full-scale mobilization, and any delay in Israel's mobilization of reserves would give them more time to gain a foothold on the east side of the Canal before the Israelis could organize a counterattack.[11]

On October 3, the Mossad received information that Soviet ships were abruptly leaving Egyptian and Syrian ports, and Soviet civilians were suddenly being flown out of Cairo and Damascus. Israel's Chief of Staff, Elazar, was alerted to these movements with a warning that the Mossad believed war was imminent. The military chief of intelligence, General Zeira, disputed Mossad's conclusion. He considered the information too vague to act upon. Defense Minister Dayan agreed. Thus no action was taken. On October 5, it was clear that Egyptian and Syrian armies were massing along Israel's border. Syrians were moving heavy artillery forward, Soviet advisors were leaving, and Egyptian reconnaissance teams were infiltrating across the Suez Canal. Chief of Staff Elazar placed the active army on the highest state of alert, but there was still no decision to mobilize the reserves. He was convinced he could expect sufficient warning in time to order a general mobilization. The military chiefs still held the belief that the active force could hold off any offensive by Egypt and Syria. High level Israeli officials were hesitant to order a full mobilization, because several months earlier they had reacted to erroneous information and wasted a fortune on an unnecessary mobilization. They were also hesitant to call for an all-out mobilization fearing they would be blamed for inciting a war.[12]

War Breaks Out

Before dawn on October 6, 1973, Israel's Director of Military Intelligence, General Zeira, received information from a purported highly reliable source that the war would begin on that day at six o'clock in the evening, with simultaneous attacks by Egypt and Syria. In reality, the time of the attack had been set for two o'clock in the afternoon of October 6, several days before the planned attack. This raises questions about the reliability of the source that had passed the information to Israel's Director of Intelligence. Israel's cabinet met soon after word of the impending war was received. As improbable as it might seem, at a time when their very existence was threatened, a heated argument erupted over what to do next and the extent of mobilization that should be undertaken. Chief of Staff Elazar insisted on full mobilization and supported a preemptive strike on Syria's airfields and SAM sites; however, Defense Minister Dayan was only willing to mobilize two divisions (approximately 20,000 troops). The cabinet authorized call up of only 100,000 reservists. The issue was finally raised to Prime Minister Meir, who decided on full mobilization but disapproved the preemptive strike on Syria. It was just one hour before two o'clock, the actual hour of the attack, when the Chief of Staff was able to issue the general mobilization order. Just 30 minutes before the scheduled attack, Cairo Radio announced that the Israelis had launched a raid on Egyptian installations on the Red Sea coast. As two o'clock approached, Egypt announced that its troops were crossing the Suez Canal in retaliation.[13] This thinly veiled attempt to blame Israel for starting the war could not have played well in most Arab capitals and the Soviet Union, since they had all received advanced notice of the planned attack on Israel. However, it undoubtedly worked on the streets of these countries to raise the level of hate for the Jews.

In the years since the Six-Day War, the Egyptian Army had undergone extensive expansion and modernization. All of the equipment lost in the previous war had been replaced by the Soviet Union, along with massive increases in additional equipment. The Soviets had done the same for Syria. In 1973 the Egyptian armed forces consisted of 1.2 million troops, half of which were deployed along the western bank of the Suez Canal in preparation for the impending war. They were equipped with 2,200 tanks, 2,300 artillery pieces, and 150 SAM batteries. The Egyptian Air Force included 400 combat aircraft, 60 transport planes, and 150 helicopters, augmented by six squadrons of fighter aircraft from Iraq, Libya, and Algeria. The five infantry divisions deployed on the western bank of the Suez Canal were supported by three mechanized divisions and two armored divisions. Adding to this firepower, 160 tanks were imbedded in each of the five infantry divisions. On the northern front, the Syrian forces manning the Golan Heights numbered 185,000 troops, augmented by 100,000 soldiers from Iraq, Jordan, and other Arab countries. This included three infantry divisions (one made up mostly of Moroccan troops) and two armored divisions, supported by 1,500 tanks, 1,000 artillery and mortar guns, 50 SAM batteries, and 265 combat aircraft.[14]

Against this formidable array of troops and weapons, Israel's active duty armed forces consisted of 75,000 troops. Of this number, two-thirds of the active duty force consisted of conscripts undergoing training during their first hitch and reservists on active duty tours. With full mobilization, the armed forces could grow to 350,000. The army was equipped with an assortment of British, United States, and captured Soviet tanks, many of World War II vintage, for a total of approximately 2,000 tanks. The mainstay of Israel's artillery arm consisted of World War II American self-propelled 155 howitzers, Israel-produced Soltam guns mounted on Sherman tank chassis, and some Soviet pieces captured in the 1967 War, for a total of 575 artillery guns. For air defense, Israel had 1,000 anti-aircraft guns and 75 U.S.-made SAMs. The Israeli Air Force was equipped with 360 combat aircraft, including U.S.-made F-4 Phantoms and A-4 Skyhawks and older model French-made Mirage fighters.[15] The hard facts were that to make full use of all these weapons, Israel had to mount a full-scale mobilization with all the units manned and ready to fight. Egypt and Syria did not have the same limitations. They had been planning and getting ready for the attack on Israel for many months. More importantly, they had the crucial element of surprise.

Israel's mobilization of reserves was just getting underway when the sirens signaled the beginning of the attack. Reservists from ages 18 to 55 were required to report for immediate duty. Israel had practiced calling up the reserves many times and had devised an effective recall system that was surprisingly effective even on a major holiday like Yom Kippur. The cabinet meeting in Prime Minister Meir's office was still in progress when word came that the Arabs had launched attacks on both fronts. At 2:05 p.m. the first wave of 240 Egyptian aircraft attacked across the Suez Canal, hitting Israeli surface-to-air missile batteries, anti-aircraft guns, artillery batteries, radar stations, command posts, strongholds along the east bank, and airfields in the Sinai. The aircraft strikes were quickly followed by a massive artillery barrage against the entire Israeli front along the Suez Canal. As many as 2,000 artillery guns and mortars rained down 10,500 shells on the Israeli fortifications in the first minute. Katyusha and Frog missiles joined in and struck Israeli defenses. In addition to this massive bombardment, Egyptian tanks, positioned high on ramparts on the western bank, fired across the Canal.[16]

At approximately 2:20 p.m., the Egyptian aircraft completed their bombing runs and departed the airspace over the Suez Canal, leaving behind 40 aircraft after an encounter with Israeli Air Force fighters. It was then time for the Egyptian assault troops to begin crossing the Canal. Five Egyptian divisions (approximately 10,000 to 12,000 troops each) were poised to swarm across using rapidly prepared bridges, pontoons, and boats of various types. In a well-planned and rehearsed operation, during the first hour 20 infantry battalions (14,300 troops) with light weapons crossed the Canal. By 5:30 p.m. of the first day, 32,000 Egyptian troops had crossed and opened bridgeheads two miles inside the Sinai. At dusk hundreds of Egyptian commandos were dropped by helicopter behind Israeli lines; however, this threat was minimized when 14 helicopters carrying commandos were shot down by the Israeli Air Force. By midnight, the Egyptians had completed eight heavy bridges that could carry tanks and four light bridges for troops and light vehicles to use in crossing the Canal. This opened the door for Egyptian forces to pour across the Suez Canal.[17]

Israeli forces facing this overwhelming Egyptian invasion consisted of a thin line of 450 Israeli soldiers and 91 tanks, tasked with defending 16 Bar-Lev fortifications and four strongholds along a stretch of 110 miles of the eastern bank of the Canal. A second line of defense located a few miles behind the Bar-Lev fortifications was equipped with 200 Israel tanks, 12 artillery batteries and mortars, six antiaircraft batteries, and two surface-to-air missile batteries. The Israeli forces on the northern front in the Golan Heights were no better off. Only 200 Israeli infantrymen manned ten strongholds along a forty-mile front that faced three Syrian divisions with 40,000 men. Israel's 177 tanks and 11 artillery batteries on this front were opposed by 1,400 Syrian tanks and 115 artillery batteries, supported by SAM systems and Syria's air force. The Syrian plan was to mount a breakthrough before Israeli reserves could join the battle. The Syrian attack began simultaneously with the Egyptian attack in the south. Syria sent 60 aircraft to bomb Israeli targets in the Golan Heights and at the same time unleashed a massive artillery bombardment against Israeli positions. There were no major land barriers in the Golan Heights like the Suez Canal in the south, to prevent Syria from launching a massive armor and infantry assault against Israeli forces. Just as the main assault began, a Syrian commando unit attacked and captured Mount Harmon, a key observation and electronic listening post used by the Israelis.[18]

The Israeli forces in the northern part of the Golan were attacked by a Syrian infantry division, an armored brigade, and a Moroccan infantry brigade. However, the main thrust of the Syrians was toward the rolling hills of the central and southern Golan. There the Israeli 188th Brigade with 57 tanks met two Syrian infantry divisions and elements of an armored division with 600 tanks. The vastly outnumbered Israelis fought valiantly, but by Sunday morning the 188th Brigade was almost completely destroyed. By afternoon the few remaining Israeli tanks put up a last ditch fight, but all were wiped out. By mid-day, 90 percent of the Israeli officers leading the fight against the Syrian advance were killed or wounded. These incredibly brave warriors were credited with holding off the Syrians long enough for the reserves to mobilize and begin reaching the front.[19]

This was the first time since becoming a state that Israel's very existence hung in the balance. The Arab armies were not the same as they had been in previous wars. Their armies, especially Egypt's, had made major improvements in the way they trained their officers and in the quality of their soldiers. The complex planning that had gone into the preparation for the surprise attack on Yom Kippur demonstrated a significant improvement in military competence. There is little reason to doubt that the thousands of Soviet advisors, who had been integrated into the Egyptian and Syrian military infrastructure, had a lot to do with these improvements. This is born out by a number of instances where Soviet military doctrine was evident in the 1973 war. Of equal importance was the enormous supply of arms and up-to-date weapons systems supplied by the Soviet Union. The highly sophisticated air defense systems built by the Soviets in Egypt and Syria gave these two armies a crucial edge in control of the airspace over the battlefield. Israel's tank forces in previous conflicts had been unbeatable; however, the thousands of modern anti-tank weapons provided to the Arab troops and used at all levels of the battlefield caused a much higher kill rate of Israel tanks. In order to turn the tide of the battle on both fronts, Israel had to develop new tactics to fight the anti-tank weapons and defeat or destroy the enemy surface-to-air missile batteries. As the war progressed, these tactical challenges would prove to be crucial in the outcome of the war.

The Egyptians Cross the Canal in Force

By early morning of October 7, the Egyptians had succeeded in sending 90,000 troops, 850 tanks, and 11,000 vehicles across the Suez Canal. Four hours later another infantry division and an armored brigade had crossed. The Bar-Lev fortifications and strong points were close to being overrun. Israeli tanks at the spearhead of the fight against the Egyptians at the bridgehead were hit hard by Egyptian Sagger missiles. Sixty percent (153 Israeli tanks) were put out of action in the opening phase of the fighting. Several Israeli tank brigades were sent forward to help defend the fortifications. One brigade was driven back with the loss of all except 20 of its tanks. Another Israeli tank brigade encountered advancing Egyptian tanks, and with only two tanks still able to fight, held off 50 Egyptian tanks all night and the rest of the next day. A third Israeli tank brigade moved forward to cover the passes on a 35 mile front. On this broad front, the brigade faced two Egyptian infantry divisions, a mechanized division, and an armored division, with a total of 650 tanks. The Egyptians outnumbered this Israeli brigade six-to-one in tanks. When the Israeli brigade began advancing toward the Suez Canal late Saturday afternoon, it had 100 tanks. By early Sunday morning it had only 23 tanks left.

On October 8, the third day of the war, the Israelis resorted to one of their proven tactics from previous wars and mounted a major counterattack on the Egyptians, with the aim of throwing them off balance before they could consolidate their positions on the eastern bank. This time it did not work. The counterattack was beaten back with heavy losses. The widespread use of anti-tank weapons by the Egyptians took a heavy toll on Israeli equipment. It was also a blow to the morale of the Israeli troops, who received a blunt awakening at the toughness and spirit of the Egyptian soldiers. However, the Egyptians had little time to enjoy their success, for the Israeli forces were quickly being reinforced by the reserves. After the fourth day of fighting, the Israelis succeeded in stabilizing the front with the Egyptians. However, on the fifth day, the Egyptians launched five separate attacks in the Sinai. An

Israeli armored division, led by General Ariel Sharon, outmaneuvered the Egyptians and destroyed 50 of their tanks. On the northern front, by the sixth day the Syrians were being driven back, and the Israelis were able to transfer some of their forces from the Golan Heights to the fight in the south. Meanwhile, some in the Egyptian High Command had visions of expanding their drive into the Sinai Peninsula beyond the goals they had set in the beginning[21]

Sadat had originally directed the generals to mount a war with limited objectives, including crossing the Suez Canal and penetrating only a few miles into the Sinai. However, Syria was urgently calling for Egypt to increase its attacks on Israel to relieve the pressure on its front. With Sadat's approval, the Egyptian Army mounted an attack to drive deeper into the Sinai. This was the break the Israelis were waiting for. As the Egyptian forces moved further into the Sinai, they left behind the protective cover of their air defense SAMs. The Egyptians launched three separate attacks on the morning of October 14, with hundreds of artillery guns and fighter-bombers attacking Israeli positions. A major tank battle reminiscent of the great armor battles of World War II ensued. The Egyptian troops and armor were exposed to relentless pounding by the Israeli Air Force. They were also hit by Israeli tanks that were dug into protected positions. The Egyptians were thrown back with heavy losses. The battle was a major turning point in the war, which saw 260 Egyptian tanks destroyed with the loss of only 20 Israeli tanks. This gave Israel the opportunity to go on the offensive. The Israelis, with their well-known strategy of taking the battle to the enemy, hastily put together a bold, risky plan to deliver a surprise blow to the Egyptians. [22]

The Israelis Counterattack

The Israeli plan to seize the offensive, developed by General Sharon, consisted of Israeli forces crossing the Suez Canal to the west bank to attack the Egyptians from the rear. The objective was to catch the Egyptians off guard, cut off their forces that had crossed to the eastern bank, and destroy the SAM sites on the west bank to clear the way for the Israeli Air Force to dominate the airspace. The Suez Canal crossing, code named Operation Gazelle, was planned to take advantage of a gap between Egypt's Second and Third armies. The initial crossing and establishment of a bridgehead on the west bank of the Canal, spearheaded by a brigade of Israeli paratroops, took place just ten days after the war began. In the next few days, the Israelis fought many engagements with Egyptians in an effort to keep open the corridor to the staging area where the crossing was to take place. On October 17, the Israelis encountered an Egyptian armored brigade with 96 tanks at a crossroad leading to the staging area. By late afternoon, 86 of the Egyptian tanks had been destroyed, and a large number of Egyptian armored personnel carriers and supply vehicles were put out of action. Four Israeli tanks were lost when they ran into a minefield. As the battle progressed, an Israeli infantry battalion, supported by tanks, took up the fight against an Egyptian stronghold known as the Chinese Farm. The Egyptians had established fortified defensive positions and poured withering fire into the Israelis throughout the night. The Israelis took heavy casualties and by morning had lost all of the battalion's 60 tanks and 120 crewmen.

While the Israelis fought to build bridges for crossing the Canal, the Egyptians launched a major air and artillery attack to smash this effort. Egyptian fighter planes struck before Israeli aircraft could intervene. The Egyptians threw everything they had at the Israelis. Artillery guns, mortars, and rockets rained thousands of rounds onto engineers who were constructing the bridges, killing 100 and wounding many more. By the afternoon of October 17, a pontoon bridge had been completed, and two brigades of tanks had crossed by dawn of October 18. By early morning of October 19, a massive prefabricated bridge, towed many miles by Israeli tanks, reached the crossing and was soon ready to carry large numbers of tanks and troops. The Israelis poured more and more forces across the Suez Canal, where they destroyed Egyptian rear bases, artillery positions, and SAM sites on the west side of the Canal. As they pushed forward, they effectively put the Egyptian air defense system out of action as far inland as nine miles. By October 21, the Israelis had effectively isolated the Egyptian Third Army on the eastern bank and had cut it off from its rear headquarters and supply bases. Although faced with the possible annihilation of the Third Army, Sadat still refused to move any of his forces on the eastern bank back to the west side. However, he finally decided it was time to call on the Soviet Union to exercise its influence at the UN to broker a ceasefire.[24]

On the northern front, the Syrian attack had been broken and was in full retreat. Of the 1,400 Syrian tanks that had attacked the Israelis, most of them were out of action by the fifth day of fighting, along with many of their supply vehicles, armored personnel carriers, and fuel vehicles. Israel had scored a major victory against Syria. The Israeli 17th Brigade, equipped with 40 to 50 tanks, destroyed 200 Syrian tanks along a major road. As the Syrians retreated, they left behind 867 tanks in the Israeli-controlled Golan Heights. While the Syrians were being driven back, armed forces from two other Arab states arrived to assist them. A brigade from Jordan that engaged the Israelis was rendered ineffective when the Israelis knocked out 14 of its tanks, killing 27 and wounding 50 Jordanian soldiers. The other armed force coming to Syria's aid was an Iraqi expeditionary force consisting of 500 tanks, 700 armored personnel carriers, and 30,000 troops. As they joined the fight, the Iraqis encountered several Israeli armored brigades, and in one battle 25 Iraqi tanks were knocked out. Another Israeli brigade struck the Iraqis from the rear and put 20 more of their tanks out of action. The Israelis did not sustain any loses in these two actions. Bolstered by their successes and the arrival of reserve units, the Israelis drove the combined forces of Syria, Jordan, and Iraq out of the Golan Heights and carried the fight onto Syrian soil.[25]

The question then arose over how far the Israelis should penetrate into Syrian territory. The Israeli leadership was reluctant to drive all the way to the Syrian capital, knowing that the Soviet Union might intervene to defend Damascus. Prime Minister Meir made the decision to push on to a depth of 12 miles, where a strong defensive line could be established. The Syrian High Command was becoming desperate as the Israelis drew closer to its capital, Damascus. The Israeli Air Force struck Syrian targets almost at will, including airfields, power stations, oil storage facilities, and other strategic targets. Not unexpectedly, President Assad of Syria turned to the Soviet Union for help. Moscow announced that it would not stand idly by while the Israelis attacked Syria and made it known that an elite force of Soviet airborne troops had been put on alert to respond in the defense of the Syrian capital. All the while the Soviets kept up the airlift of arms to Syria and called for other Arab states to join in the battle.[26]

In the first few days of the Syrian invasion of the Golan Heights, Israeli Air Force pilots took great risks to provide close air support for the outnumbered Israeli ground forces. The Israeli Air Force losses were high as a result of pilots deliberately penetrating SAM air defenses in order to strike the advancing Syrian forces. In this action, along with later attacks on targets inside Syrian territory, Israel lost 50 fighter aircraft. During the action over the northern front, Syrian aircraft rose to engage the Israeli fighters. The Syrians lost 222 aircraft over this front, of which 162 were downed in aerial combat with the Israelis. On the southern front, the Israeli Air Force was a major force in destroying the Egyptian ground forces when they advanced beyond their surface-to-air missile umbrella. Major air battles took place between Egypt and Israel, with as many as 40 to 50 aircraft engaged in aerial combat at once. The Egyptians downed five Israeli aircraft, while 172 Egyptian aircraft were shot down by the Israelis. During the war, Egypt and Syria lost a combined total of 514 aircraft. Israel lost a total of 102.[27]

With the tide of the war clearly turning in Israel's favor on both fronts, the Soviets concluded that it was time to end the war. They realized the risk of even greater defeat of their Arab clients if the war were allowed to continue. There was also concern for Sadat's political survival at home in the face of defeat. The Soviet Union promised Sadat to guarantee a ceasefire, and with that he agreed to an immediate ceasefire. On October 19, Henry Kissinger flew to Moscow to negotiate a ceasefire, and from there he traveled to Tel Aviv to obtain Israel's agreement. The UN Security Council met on October 22 and passed Resolution 338, calling for a ceasefire by the evening of that day. However, on October 23, the Israelis, seeking to improve their negotiating position, launched a major assault on the Egyptian Third Army, which was still isolated on the east bank of the Suez Canal. This Egyptian force of 45,000 men and 250 tanks, cut off from supplies and reinforcements, was in danger of being decimated by the Israelis. Under growing pressure from the Soviet Union, the United States, and two UN resolutions, Israel agreed to halt its advance on the Third Army and accepted a second ceasefire.[28]

The War Ends

The Yom Kippur War ended on October 25. Militarily, Israel was the victor, but Sadat gained in stature for having crossed the Suez Canal and stood up to the Israelis. The war was costly in many ways. Israel lost much of the prestige and confidence it had gained from the Six-Day War victory. Its government fell into a deep crisis, as the people demanded accountability for being caught off guard and unprepared. Political fallout led to the resignation of Prime Minister Golda Meir and the Minister of Defense, Moshe Dayan. Several high ranking intelligence officers were relieved from their posts. The war cost Israel 2,687 lives and 7,251 wounded. The army also took heavy losses of equipment, including 400 tanks. The Egyptian casualties amounted to 12,000 dead, 35,000 wounded, and 8,400 taken prisoner. The Egyptian Army took heavy losses of equipment, including 1,000 tanks. Much of the damaged Egyptian equipment was recovered by the Israelis and put to use in their army. On the northern front, the war cost Syria 3,100 killed, 6,000 wounded, and 370 were taken prisoner. The cost to the Iraqi Army was 278 killed and 898 wounded. Jordan lost 23 killed and 77 wounded. The Syrians lost 1,150 tanks; 200 Iraqi and 50 Jordanian tanks were destroyed.[29]

On January 18, 1974, the chiefs of staff of the Israeli and Egyptian armies finalized the terms of an agreement to end the war. Israel agreed to withdraw its forces from the west bank of the Suez Canal. On the eastern bank, Egypt occupied a 19 mile zone next to the Canal and Israel assumed control to the east of that zone. A UN buffer was placed between the Egyptian and Israeli zones. Egypt and Israel were each allowed to keep 7,000 solders, 30 tanks, and 36 artillery guns in their zones.[30]

Syria accepted the ceasefire on October 22 but did not sign a ceasefire agreement with Israel. Syria refused to negotiate directly with Israel. In response to Israel's continued occupation of Syrian territory captured during the war, Syria began a war of attrition, with unprovoked artillery and small arms fire against Israel. At times small-scale clashes of infantry units were sparked by the Syrians. The strategy of these clashes was to inflict casualties on the Israelis and force them to negotiate on terms favorable to Syria. No real progress was made on a lasting end to hostilities until the U.S. Secretary of State, Henry Kissinger, negotiated an agreement that was signed on May 31, 1974. Israel relinquished several strips of land previously occupied by Syria, and a demilitarized zone, patrolled by a UN observer force, was established. The UN zone was supposed to prevent another surprise attack on Israel, similar to the one launched by Syria at the beginning of the recent war. The agreement between Israel and Syria, implemented in June 1974, marked the final end of the Yom Kippur War (see Ceasefire Map 8 at end of chapter), but it did not herald a new era of peace. It was in essence the beginning of a new kind of war that had no defined front lines and no clearly identifiable enemy combatants.[31]

Israel did not have long to wait for the new war to begin. On the same day in April 1974 that Prime Minister Meir stepped down, a group of Palestinians from Habash's Popular Front attacked a town in northern Israel and killed 18 civilians, including 8 young children. A month later in May, Palestinians from another terrorist group seized a school in a northern Israeli town and took 100 children hostage. Israel refused to yield to the terrorist's demands to release Palestinian prisoners and stormed the school to free the hostages. The operation cost the lives of 22 children.[32]

Another weapon of a different type emerged during the Yom Kippur War. The Arab oil-producing nations instituted an oil embargo against the United States and Western nations that had aided Israel. The Arabs intended to use the embargo to force the U.S. and West to put pressure on Israel to withdraw from territories captured during the 1967 War.[33] The long lines at the gas pumps and sharply rising prices were a stark reminder of the power the Arab states wield and the high stakes that the Middle East oil is destined to play on the global stage. It also served as a warning for the United States to strive for energy independence.

Yom Kippur War Cease Fire Lines
(October 24, 1973)

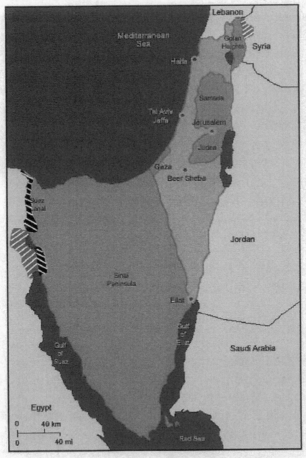

Map 8. Source: Jewish Virtual Library.

Israeli territory before the Six-Day War

Under Israel control after Six-Day War

Held by Egyptian Army

Held by Israeli Army

Chapter 7

War in Lebanon

The Arab oil embargo of 1973 impacted many countries around the world and gave rise to increased pressure on Israel to accede to Arab demands for the establishment of a Palestinian state in the West Bank and Gaza Strip. In essence this would have been a return to the pre-1967 borders, which Israel rejected until the Arab states agreed to end their ongoing war of annihilation. Although the Arab states that took part in the Yom Kippur War initially made some impressive gains against the Israelis, the outcome of the war convinced them they could not succeed in destroying Israel militarily. Soon after the Yom Kippur War ended, the Palestinian National Council (PNC) met in Cairo to plan alternative approaches for destroying Israel. Yasser Arafat, who was a key spokesman at the Cairo gathering, boldly proclaimed that the Ramadan Campaign (Yom Kippur War) was only the beginning of the Arab nations' drive against Israel, which would end in Tel Aviv.[1] On June 8, 1974, the PNC adopted a plan that encompassed a three-stage strategy for Israel's destruction. The text of this plan, known as the PLO's Phased Plan, was essentially a road map for the liberation of all of Palestinian territory by armed struggle (terrorism), the implementation of a PLO-controlled state over all of Palestine, and the eventual elimination of Israel entirely.[2] The complete text of the Phased Plan may be seen in Appendix B.

Several key events took place following the adoption of the Phased Plan that furthered the influence and power of the PLO. At the 1974 Arab summit in Morocco, the PLO was recognized as the sole representative of the Palestinian people. Later that same year, the PLO received UN recognition.[3] This strengthened Arafat's authority over Palestinians in southern Lebanon where he had set up a base of operations after the PLO was driven out of Jordan. This became a staging base from which attacks could be launched on Israel and terrorists dispatched for operations outside the region. While the sectarian strife between Lebanon's Christian Maronites and the region's Muslim majority grew in the 1970s, Lebanon deteriorated into a battleground of warring factions, which led to the Civil War of 1975-81. The instability and lack of a functioning central government gave Arafat the freedom to establish a PLO state-within-a-state in southern Lebanon.[4]

With an unchallenged base of operations in Lebanon, Arafat was free to increase the number and size of operations within and outside Israel. While the shelling of settlements in northern Israel continued, the PLO gained notoriety on the international stage with a rash of terrorist attacks in the 1970s. In May 1972, the Black September faction of the PLO took over a Sabrena flight from Brussels to Tel Aviv and demanded release of 317 Palestinian prisoners. An Israeli commando unit stormed the aircraft and released the passengers. In that same month, three Japanese members of the Red Brigade, working for the PLO, opened fire with machine guns after landing at Lod airport in Tel Aviv, killing 27 passengers and wounding 78. In September 1972, a PLO group took 11 athletes of the Israeli Olympic team in Munich hostage. All members of the Israeli team were killed in a rescue attempt by German Special Forces. Then there was the hijacking in June of 1976 of an Air France airliner carrying 256 passengers from Tel Aviv to Paris that was diverted to Entebbe, Uganda, where the passengers and crew were held hostage. A daring raid by Israeli commandos freed the hostages. One Israeli officer was killed during the operation, and one elderly Israeli woman who was left behind in an Ugandan hospital was subsequently murdered.[5]

PLO Raids

Meanwhile, during most of the 1970s, the PLO relentlessly shelled northern Israel and carried out cross-border raids from southern Lebanon, striking unsuspecting Israeli civilians. On May 15, 1974, a group of 11th grade Israeli students on a field trip to the Golan

Heights were attacked by three terrorists at a school where they were staying the night. Some of the students escaped, but the rest were held hostage. An elite Israeli unit stormed the school just as time ran out for negotiations. As many as 26 Israelis, including 21 children, were killed by the terrorists, all of whom were eliminated by Israeli commandos. In November of that same year, Palestinian terrorists struck the Israeli town of Beit Shean, killing four and wounding 20 civilians. A month later, terrorists threw a grenade into a cinema in Tel Aviv, injuring 51 civilians. In March of 1975, eight terrorists attacked a hotel in Tel Aviv, taking hostages who were held for two days until they were rescued by Israeli commandos. During the rescue operation, eight hostages were murdered and 11 were wounded. Seven terrorists were killed, and one was captured. In July of that year, a bomb was set off at a main square in Jerusalem, killing 13 and injuring 65 civilians.[6]

The year 1978 saw one of the most brutal attacks on Israeli civilians. In that attack, 13 members of the Fatah faction of the PLO landed on the Mediterranean coast of Israel south of Haifa, where they seized a taxi and two civilian buses. The Israelis took out 11 terrorists; however, before the terrorists died, they set fire to one of the buses, and most of the passengers, including many children, were burned alive or killed by terrorist gunfire. The attack took 35 innocent lives and injured 100. In 1979, four Fatah terrorists took an Israeli family hostage in an apartment at a coastal resort town. Three Israeli civilians and a policeman lost their lives, and two of the terrorists were killed. Another attack on that same town later that year took the lives of three Israelis.[7]

Throughout the 1970s and early 1980s, the PLO and several of its factions continued to carry out attacks in Israel and abroad. Hundreds of innocent lives were taken, not all of whom were Israelis, all in the name of the PLO Charter that declared armed struggle as the only way to liberate Palestine. While Israel struggled to defend against the threat from PLO terrorists, it also exchanged views with Egypt for peace and normalization of borders. In September 1975, following months of negotiations moderated by Secretary of State Henry Kissinger, the two nations signed the Sinai II Agreement. The agreement returned part of the Sinai Peninsula to Egypt and prompted a mutual commitment by the two parties not to use force or threat of force against each other.

Building on the Sinai II Agreement, following lengthy negotiations, President Sadat and Prime Minister Begin signed the Camp David Accords in Washington, D.C. on September 17, 1978. The Accords established the framework for a formal peace treaty between Egypt and Israel and laid the groundwork for giving the Palestinians autonomy over the West Bank and Gaza Strip. It also included Israel's complete withdrawal from the Sinai Peninsula and assured Israel freedom of navigation in the Gulf of Suez and Suez Canal. On March 26, 1979, Egyptian and Israeli leaders gathered in Washington for the formal signing of the peace treaty. Arab states were quick to condemn Sadat for making peace with the "enemy," and most of them severed diplomatic relations with Egypt. The PLO rejected the proposal to give the Palestinians autonomy over the West Bank and Gaza Strip. They would only accept complete independence. Unfortunately, Sadat's quest for peace and Palestinian independence was rewarded with his assassination by Muslim extremists on October 6, 1981, the anniversary of the beginning of the Yom Kippur War in 1973.[8]

While Israel was engaged in peace talks, attacks by PLO factions in Lebanon accelerated. Israel responded with a massive military offensive against the PLO bases in southern Lebanon, pushing as far north as the Litani River, approximately 40 kilometers inside Lebanon. Under intense pressure from the UN and the United States, Israel finally withdrew its forces from Lebanon in June 1978. They were replaced by a UN Interim Force (UNIFIL) which did little to prevent the PLO forces from reoccupying their bases in southern Lebanon or from continuing their attacks on Israel.[9]

Strike on Iraq's Nuclear Facility

In the mean time, a new threat emerged from an old enemy who had taken part in every war between the Arabs and Israel. As early as 1976, Iraq's leader, Saddam Hussein, had brokered a deal with France for the development of a nuclear reactor for Iraq. Israeli experts predicted that Iraq would be able to produce a nuclear weapon within nine years. As the reactor project progressed, Israeli leaders concluded that their very existence would be at risk if Iraq or any other Arab state were to obtain nuclear weapons. Israel put forth its best effort at diplomacy to persuade France to end the project. When that failed, Israel decided that military action was the only other option, otherwise the entire Israeli population would be in danger of annihilation. Timing of the strike was critical, because if the reactor became operational, it would not be possible to attack without the risk of spreading a radio active cloud over populated areas in Iraq. With that in mind, the date for the attack was set for June 7, 1981. The air strike by Israeli fighter-bombers was executed flawlessly, and the target was destroyed without the loss of any Israeli aircraft. Israel was quickly condemned by the UN and other nations, including the United States.[10]

In hindsight, the United States and coalition forces should be very grateful for Israel's destruction of Iraq's nuclear program. If Saddam had been left alone to acquire nuclear weapons, the outcome of the Gulf War in 1991 could have been a disaster for the United States and coalition forces. Even more foreboding is the probability that the U.S. and coalition nations would have decided that the loss of life in a war with a nuclear Iraq would have been far too prohibitive. It is also noteworthy to consider where the world would be today if Iraq had become a nuclear power. With nuclear weapons in the hands of a madman, who would have stopped Saddam from seizing control of the Middle East oil? Fast forward to the present day where Israel is confronted with the same dilemma, only this time with Iran and its nuclear ambitions and the Iranian leaders' frequent threats to wipe Israel off the map.

War Erupts in Lebanon

In the spring of 1981, the Lebanese Christians, who had been supported by Israel, were close to being wiped out by the PLO Muslim fighters and the Syrians who had occupied Lebanon since 1976. The Christian Phalangist leader, Bashir Jemayel, appealed to Israel for help. From Israel's perspective, a victory over the Christian forces would have given the PLO and Syria almost complete control over Lebanon. Israel considered this an unacceptable risk to its national security. Accordingly, a decision was made to lend air force support to the Lebanese Christians. In this engagement, the Israeli Air Force shot down two Soviet made helicopters that were supporting Syrian forces. The Syrians used this air engagement as an excuse to move surface-to-air missile batteries into east Lebanon and the Beqa'a Valley. This posed a serious threat to Israel's air operations over many parts of Lebanon.[11]

In July 1981, the PLO launched a massive bombardment with long-range artillery and rocket fire, striking 33 towns and villages in northern Israel. Normal activity came to a halt for the inhabitants of these locations. Israel retaliated with bombings of PLO targets throughout Lebanon. After ten days of fighting, a ceasefire was arranged by U.S. Ambassador Habib. The PLO agreed to discontinue operations on Israel's northern border; however, instead they mounted numerous operations inside Israel from across the Jordan River. Jewish targets abroad were also fair game. The PLO attacked Jewish people in various parts of Europe, including the assassination of an Israeli diplomat in Paris. In all, there were 240 PLO attacks against Israel during the ceasefire. Israel's leaders reached the conclusion that the PLO had to be driven out of Lebanon if peace were to prevail for its people. The breaking point came with the shooting of Israel's ambassador to Britain on June 3, 1982, by a rouge faction of the PLO and the discovery by British police of a list of prominent Israelis marked for assassination. Prime Minister Begin wasted no time in ordering air strikes against the PLO targets in southern Lebanon and near Beirut. The air strikes were followed two days later with a major ground offensive by Israeli forces against PLO positions in Lebanon.[12]

Operation Peace for Galilee, Israel's operations plan for the incursion into Lebanon (see Map 9 at end of chapter), was at first intended to have the limited objective of driving the PLO out of southern Lebanon and put them out of range to fire on Israel. However, as the operation progressed, the objective changed to include driving the PLO entirely out of Lebanon. Israeli forces advanced rapidly and linked up with the Christian Phalange forces on the outskirts of Beirut. The Israelis were under orders not to fire on the Syrians unless they first attacked. However, the Israeli advance into the eastern sector of Beirut was blocked by Syrian forces, and the PLO in that sector had taken up positions behind the Syrians. As the Israelis advanced, the Syrians opened fire to prevent their forces in Beirut from being cut off from reinforcements. This gave the Israelis reason to return fire. As the battle ensued, Israeli ground units called for air support; however, the Syrian surface-to-air missile systems put the Israeli pilots at great risk. Israel's cabinet was persuaded to give permission for its air force to destroy the Syrian missile batteries. In one major air operation, 96 Israeli fighter aircraft knocked out 17 of the 19 missile batteries and damaged the remaining two. The Syrian Air Force sent up as many as 100 of the latest version of Soviet fighters to intercept Israeli aircraft. In the massive air battle that ranged over Lebanon's skies, Syria lost 29 aircraft without any Israeli losses. In the first week of air combat over Lebanon, the Israelis shot down a total of 96 Syrian fighter planes without a single loss of their own.[13]

With uncontested skies over the battlefield, the Israeli ground forces were free to drive back Syrian armored forces all along the eastern front. In the western sector, the PLO held out at a village 11 miles south of Beirut, which was the home of PLO camps, headquarters, and weapons storage. The Israeli forces took the village after heavy fighting. In the central sector, the Israelis fought fierce tank battles with the Syrians, who were determined to keep Israeli forces from taking a strategic highway that linked Beirut with Damascus. Back in the eastern sector, the Israeli forces broke through the Syrian defenses and advanced east to engage a Syrian armored division. In this battle, the Syrians lost 150 tanks. While the Syrians were being driven back in the central and eastern sectors, they attempted to move reinforcements into Lebanon. One Syrian armored brigade was decimated by the Israeli Air Force as they crossed into Lebanon. At the same time a Syrian armored division equipped with the massive T-72 tanks, the latest in the Soviet Union's inventory, pushed into Lebanon's Beqa'a Valley. An Israeli armored division with the new Israeli-made battle tank, the Merkeva, engaged the Syrian division and took out nine of its T-72 tanks.[14]

PLO Expelled from Lebanon

As the Israeli forces gained the upper hand against the Syrians, Israel called a unilateral ceasefire on June 11, 1982, which the Syrians agreed to honor. Israel made it clear that the ceasefire did not apply to PLO forces, since it was still Israel's objective to drive Arafat and all his followers out of Lebanon. The ceasefire ended a few hours after it began, when the Syrians moved to block the Israelis from reaching east

Beirut. The Israelis broke through the Syrian defenses, linked up with the Christian forces in east Beirut, and soon after surrounded west Beirut. A second ceasefire between Israel and Syria was negotiated on June 12 by U.S. Ambassador Habib. Israeli forces continued to bombard the PLO insurgents who were holding out in Beirut with artillery fire and air strikes. For almost two months, Israeli forces maintained a siege of the PLO in Beirut and occasionally launched limited attacks on the PLO along the perimeter of the city. Meanwhile the Lebanese government and Ambassador Habib pressed Arafat to leave Beirut and Lebanon. Arrangements were eventually made with other Arab states to give the PLO a safe haven. A multinational force oversaw the evacuation of the PLO from Beirut. By the end of August 1982, Arafat had moved his headquarters to Tunisia, while most of his army was evacuated to other Arab countries. At the same time, Syrian troops withdrew to eastern Lebanon, where they were firmly in contol.[15]

The expulsion of the PLO from Lebanon did not live up to Israel's expectations of peace on its northern border. Civil strife in Lebanon flared up and hampered the formation of a stable government there, and Syria gave every indication that it had no plans to withdraw its forces from Lebanon. In late August, the Lebanese parliament elected Bashir Jemayel as president of Lebanon. This was a promising sign, since Jemayel had been on good terms with Israel and was believed to be able to put together a strong central government. Just days before he was to take office, Jemayel was assassinated. Syria was suspected of having a hand in this murder. Several days after Jemayel's murder, his brother, Amin, was elected to take his place as President of Lebanon. He was known to have close relations with Syria but not as favorably disposed toward Israel.[16]

Partial Withdrawal by Israel

Israel began withdrawing its forces to new positions south of Beirut as the multinational force of U.S. Marines and French and Italian troops took their place. Israeli forces that remained in Lebanon were caught up in renewed civil strife, which increased demands by Israeli people to pull all of their forces out of Lebanon. Israel officials moved quickly to negotiate with the Lebanese government for an arrangement that would assure Israel's security on the northern border. On May 17, 1983, an agreement, brokered by U.S. Secretary of State George Shultz, was signed by Israel and Lebanon. The agreement gave Israel a security buffer in southern Lebanon and called for the withdrawal of all foreign troops from Lebanon. Not unexpectedly, Syria quickly condemned the agreement and made it clear it had no intention of withdrawing from Lebanon. Not long after that, the Lebanese government also nullified the agreement. With the agreement essentially abolished, Israel was bound by security interests to limit its withdrawal from Lebanon to the Awali River, approximately 25 miles south of Beirut.[17]

Arafat Returns to Lebanon

In July 1983, Arafat returned to Lebanon. He immediately encountered an armed rebellion against his leadership, mainly from one of the PLO's largest factions, Al Fatah. The turmoil was exacerbated by fighting within Lebanon, which saw the Syrians in Lebanon up against the Phalange forces, various elements of Muslims in northern Lebanon battling each other, Christians locked in combat with the Druze Muslims, and Libyan and Iranian units entrenched in the Beqa'a Valley. The long arm of Syria, whose objective was to bring all of Lebanon under its control, intensified the chaotic situation in Lebanon. The growing aggressiveness of the Syrians, spurred on by the Soviet Union's delivery of large quantities of their latest weapons to replace Syria's battle losses and the rapid introduction of 4,500 Soviet advisers into Syria, was even more troubling. The Syrians lost no time in deploying some of the newly received weapons to confront the Israelis in Lebanon. One of the new weapons was the Soviet SA-5, a long-range surface-to-air missile that could reach out 185 miles to hit targets in the skies over Tel Aviv. The SA-5 sites in Syria were manned by Soviet troops. The Soviet Union was clearly intent on using Syria as a base for expanding its influence in Syria and the Middle East.[18]

Arafat Leaves Again. Chaos Returns

Arafat's return to Lebanon was short lived. He was unable to gain control of the various PLO factions, and Syria had thrown its support behind the anti-Arafat forces. His demise was due largely to his

81

failure to support a military strategy over a political one. Arafat was pressured by Syria and the Fatah to leave Lebanon. Arrangements were made for Greek ships to transport Arafat and 4,000 of his followers to Tunisia and several other Arab countries. This was Arafat's second forced removal from Lebanon. The continued viability of the PLO was thus in doubt. However, for the time being, the future of Lebanon was essentially in the hands of the Syrians and the remaining PLO dissidents. Under these conditions, Israel had no choice but to keep a foothold in southern Lebanon to prevent that area from being used for cross-border attacks.[19]

In an effort to facilitate its eventual withdrawal from Lebanon, Israel set out to create a strong central Lebanese government. As part of this effort, Israel took steps to form the South Lebanon Army (SLA), which was to support the central government. However, this did little to prevent attacks on Israeli forces in Lebanon. Attacks on Israeli installations and the SLA increased sharply, with an average of 15 to 20 strikes a month. In one such incident, a Shiite suicide bomber struck an Israeli headquarters inside the security zone, killing 60 people and wounding 32 Israelis and 12 Palestinians. The organization claiming responsibility for this attack was the Lebanese National Resistance Front (LNRF), which was dedicated to driving the Israelis out of Lebanon. This group was believed to be supported by Syria. Iranian-backed Shiites were also engaged in terrorist operations against the Israelis in Lebanon. Pressures were mounting in Israel to pull its forces out of Lebanon. As of May 1983, Israel's casualties in Lebanon amounted to 480 killed and 2,600 wounded. Israel had lost 50 tanks compared to 350 to 400 Syrian tank losses. Syrian casualties consisted of 480 killed and 1,000 wounded. PLO losses included 1,000 dead and 6,000 prisoners in the hands of the Israelis.[20]

Israeli Forces Pull Back

In April 1985, the Israeli forces pulled back to a security zone that was three to twelve miles north of the Lebanese border. In June of that year, the Israeli government directed a complete withdrawal of its forces from Lebanon. Israel continued to support the SLA with weapons, ammunitions, and funds. However, the SLA came under heavy attacks by various Shiite militias. The militias were intent on taking control of southern Lebanon from the SLA. As the intensity of attacks increased, Israel could not accept hostile forces on its northern border again and once more found it necessary to redeploy its forces into the security zone in southern Lebanon.[21]

Hezbollah Emerges in Lebanon

While the various Shiite organizations pressed their attack on the SLA and Israeli forces, they also fought with each other for control of southern Lebanon. One organization, Hezbollah, "the party of Allah," emerged as the leader and the primary organization in the south. Hezbollah is a Lebanese Muslim terrorist organization established with the support of Iran and Syria. Hezbollah's ideology is radical Shiite Islam patterned after Iran's spiritual leader, Ayatollah Khomeini, now deceased. As a Shiite jihad organization, Hezbollah is dedicated to a fanatical and relentless struggle against Israel until the liberation of Jerusalem, the annihilation of Israel, and the establishment of an Iranian-style Islamic theocracy in Lebanon. It is intensely hostile toward the United States and is fervently committed to ending U.S. presence and influence in the Middle East. Hezbollah's choice of tactics to achieve its aims is the use of terrorism in a strategy of asymmetrical conflict (unconventional, guerrilla warfare) with suicide bombers as key weapons in their arsenal.[22]

With massive funding and support from Iran and Syria, Hezbollah grew from a small group of Shiite guerrillas in the Beqa'a Valley and southern Lebanon into an organization with military and civilian capabilities far beyond those of other terrorist organizations in the Middle East and the world. From the outset, 2,000 elite military men from Iran's Revolutionary Guard Corps (IRGC) arrived in Lebanon to assist Hezbollah in setting up and running training camps in Beqa'a Valley and other areas in Lebanon. Training focused on how to conduct assassinations, kidnappings, suicide bombings, and guerrilla warfare. Hezbollah built a sweeping media network to use in a very sophisticated information and propaganda campaign. Under the stealth hand of the Revolutionary Guard, Hezbollah established its own radio station, a satellite television station, Al-Manar, and a vast Internet presence. It has its own photographers who are embedded with its forces to film attacks on the Israelis and the SLA. Al-Manar is operated professionally and is very popular in Lebanon and throughout the Middle East, the entire Arab-Muslim world, and abroad. This extensive communications capability has become an important tool in the battle for the hearts and minds of its audience and the propagation of Iranian-style radical Islamic ideology. Although Hezbollah rose to preeminence during the first Lebanon War, it is still a major force for terrorism today. In forthcoming chapters, it will be revealed as a major player in Israel's struggle for existence.[23]

As Israel wound down its incursion into Lebanon, the prospects for peace were not hopeful—Israel's northern border was still vulnerable, a civil war was raging in Lebanon, Hezbollah was on the rise, and there was growing unrest in the Gaza Strip and the West Bank.

Lebanon

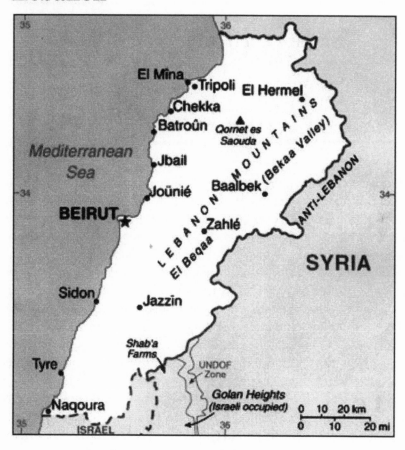

Map 9. Source: CIA World Fact Book

Chapter 8

First Intifada

The war in Lebanon did not end with a ceasefire or armistice as with previous wars between the Arabs and Israel. In essence, it has never ended. Although marked by various levels of intensity, Israel's northern border with Lebanon has continuously been under the threat of terrorist attacks, up to and including the present day. When the terrorists could not penetrate the security zone in southern Lebanon, guarded by Israeli and SLA forces, they tried to go around and attack from the sea. In one incident, two members of a terrorist group from Lebanon flew over the border in motorized hang gliders and attacked an Israeli military camp. They killed an officer and woman in a vehicle near the camp, then broke into the camp where they killed five soldiers and wounded six others before they were eliminated by Israeli troops. The number of cross-border raids increased to such an intensity that Israel was forced to respond with force. In May 1988, Israel launched a major operation inside the security zone and deep into Lebanon to strike Hezbollah's forward bases. The operation captured arms caches, but most of the terrorists fled farther north and did not stay to fight.[1]

Violence Erupts in Refugee Camps

With threats from Hezbollah by land, sea, and air on its northern frontier, as well as an economy that had not recovered completely from previous wars, Israel's attention was turned away from what was going on in the Palestinian territories. In a few years, the Palestinian population density had increased dramatically, to 650,000 in the Gaza Strip, to 900,000 in the West Bank, and 130,000 in East Jerusalem. In 1987 many of the Palestinians still lived in poverty stricken, overcrowded, and unsanitary conditions. In the Gaza Strip, 200,000 were living in eight crowded and run down refugee camps operated by the United Nations. The largest camp in the Gaza Strip, Jabalya, housed 60,000 people. In the West Bank, 90,000 lived in 19 refugee camps run by the United Nations. Moreover, 700,000 Arabs lived within the State of Israel. The territories were inhabited by a very young population, with 60 percent born since 1967.[2] In the camps, there was very little hope for young or old to escape to a better life. In the 1970s Israel launched a program to build modern apartments and houses near the camps for Palestinian families; however, the PLO warned Palestinians not to accept the offer. Nonetheless, some 8,000 Palestinian families moved to the new housing between 1976 and 1978, but most of the refugees continued to live in the overcrowded camps.[3]

The squalid conditions in the camps and the lack of hope for a future created an environment that was seething with hate and despair. It was a ticking time bomb, ready to explode with the slightest nudge. The incident that sparked the uprising was fed by a rumor without a basis. On December 8, 1987, four young Palestinian laborers from the Jabalya refugee camp were killed when an Israeli vehicle struck the car that was transporting them. A rumor spread rapidly among the Palestinians that the four young people had been killed deliberately in retaliation for the stabbing of an Israeli two days before. On the day following the accident, thousands of angry mourners turned out to pay their respects when the four bodies were carried down the road to the cemetery in Jabalya. Soon after the funeral, large-scale riots broke out in Jabalya and quickly spread throughout the Gaza Strip. In the next few days, rioting spread to the West Bank and East Jerusalem. This was the beginning of an *intifada*—a popular uprising or in Arabic "shaking off" Israeli rule. There are reasons to believe the uprising was spontaneous, but there are also reasons to assign the cause to the growing movement of Islamic fundamentalism. In the territories, there was a multitude of organizations ready to harness the discontent and use it to further their jihad against Israel. This included Arafat's Fatah movement, the Syrian-backed PLO groups, the Palestinian Communist Party, the Damascus based Popular Front for the Liberation of Palestine (PFLP), the Democratic Front for the Liberation of Palestine (DFLP), the Palestinian Liberation Army (PLA), and the two main groups in the Gaza Srip, the Muslim fundamentalist Islamic Jihad and the Muslim Brotherhood. The latter two were quick to mobilize support for the rebellion.[4]

The Palestinian Islamic Jihad

The terrorist group known as the "Palestinian Islamic Jihad" (PIJ) was formed in 1979 by the Islamic fundamentalist, Fathi Shaqaqi, and other radical Palestinian students in Egypt who had split from the Palestinian Brotherhood in the Gaza Strip, which they deemed too moderate. The PIJ is committed to the creation of an Islamic Palestinian state and the destruction of Israel through *jihad* (holy war).

The Egyptian government banished the PIJ to the Gaza Strip after learning of its close relations with the radical Egyptians who assassinated President Anwar Sadat in 1981. The PIJ began its terrorist campaign against Israel in the 1980s and carried out several terrorist attacks against Israelis in the Gaza Strip. In 1988, the faction's leader, Shaqaqi, was expelled to Lebanon, where he reorganized the faction and established close ties with Hezbollah and the Iranian Revolutionary Guard unit stationed in Lebanon.[5]

The PIJ leader, Shaqaqi, was killed in 1995 in Malta, allegedly by Israeli agents. This did not end the PIJ's terrorist activities, one of which was a suicide bombing in downtown Tel Aviv in March 1996 that killed 20 civilians and wounded more than 75. Since September 2000, the PIJ has been responsible for scores of suicide and car bombings, killing 25 Israelis and wounding almost 400. The PIJ is based in Damascus, Syria, where it receives financial backing and other support from Syria and Iran. The PIJ's goals include the destruction of the State of Israel by means of an armed and uncompromising Jihad and the establishment of a religious Islamic Palestinian state in its place.[6]

Hamas Emerges

The other organization that moved quickly to exploit the unrest in the Palestinian territories was an offshoot of the Muslim Brotherhood called the Islamic Resistance Movement. This group is known by the acronym, HAMAS, which in Arabic stands for "zeal."[7] A brief introduction to Hamas follows:

> Hamas was founded in 1987 with the beginning of the first violent Palestinian insurrection (intifada) against Israel in the Gaza Strip and the West Bank.... At the top of its priority list, Hamas put the eradication of the State of Israel through the use of terrorist strategy and tactics.
>
> Hamas's ideology states that the Palestinian problem is religious and therefore can never be solved by political compromise, and that the land of Palestine, "from the river to the sea," is consecrated to Islam (by wakf—by the Supreme Muslim Council). It cannot be given up, not even a part of it, especially not Jerusalem.
>
> Hamas is utterly opposed to a political settlement with Israel. It has opposed any agreements the Palestinian Authority (PA) or PLO [have] reached with Israel, particularly the Oslo accords [to be discussed later]....
>
> The perpetration of terrorist acts against Israel is central to its ideology. As long as Palestinians live under the "occupation" (including within Israel) they must "resist" through jihad (holy war), by which they mean an armed insurrection against the State of Israel.... [8]

Although Hamas's covenant was written in 1988, senior Hamas leaders have affirmed that they are still committed to the ideology of the original charter. Since the early days of the intifada, Hamas steadily gained support of Palestinians in the Gaza Strip and to a lesser degree in the West Bank. In 2006 Hamas won a majority of seats in the Palestinian Authority legislative election. It has since taken complete control of the Gaza Strip and has become a significant threat to the security of Israel. Today, Hamas represents the main terrorist organization within the Palestinian territories and is committed to destroying Israel through a holy war (jihad).[9] For example, on March 30, 2007, Hamas spokesman, Ismail Radwan, delivered a hate-filled sermon calling for the "liberation of Palestine" through terrorism. The sermon, which included a call to slaughter the Jews, was broadcasted on Palestinian television, controlled by Abu Mazen, Chairman of the Palestinian Authority.[10]

The Iranian-backed terrorist group, Hamas, continues to pose a grave danger to Israel with its continued dedication to violence and extremist ideology. Hamas terrorists fired thousands of rockets into Israel almost immediately after Israel withdrew from the Gaza Strip. Hamas continues to this day to smuggle weapons into Gaza through tunnels and via coastal waters.[11] Hamas's support of the intifada was only the beginning of its holy war against Israel. This terrorist organization will be a threat to Israel's very existence for many years to come; therefore, it is important to get to know this radical Islamic menace, its ideology, goals, objectives, radical thinking, strategy and tactics, and plans for an Islamic state in all of Palestine—after driving out the Jews. Hamas's 1988 Covenant, which has not changed since its inception, is a good place to begin. Excerpts from the covenant of the Islamic Resistance Movement (Hamas) are quoted below. Additional articles are included in Appendix C.

> **Article 1.** The path of the Islamic Resistance Movement [Hamas] is the path of Islam, from which it draws its principles, concepts, terms, and worldview with regard to life and man. It turns to [Islam] when religious rulings are required and asks [Islam] for inspiration to guide its steps.
>
> **Article 2.** The Islamic Resistance Movement [Hamas] is the branch of the Muslim Brotherhood in Palestine. The Muslim Brotherhood is a global organization and the largest Islamic movement in modern times....
>
> **Article 6.** The Islamic Resistance Movement is uniquely Palestinian.... It acts to fly the banner of Allah over all of Palestine....

Article 7. Muslims who adopt the path of the Islamic Resistance Movement [Hamas] and act to support it, to adopt its positions and to strengthen its holy war are spread over the face of the earth, making the movement universal....

The Islamic Resistance Movement [Hamas] is one link in the chain of holy war in its confrontation with the Zionist invasion....

Article 11. The Islamic Resistance Movement [Hamas] believes that the land of Palestine is a religious Islamic endowment for all Muslims until Resurrection Day. It is forbidden to relinquish it or any part of it or give it up or any part of it....

Article 13. There is no solution to the Palestinian problem except jihad. Regarding the international initiatives, suggestions and conferences, they are an empty waste of time and complete nonsense....

Article 14. That being the case, the liberation [of Palestine] is the personal duty of every Muslim, wherever he may be.... [12]

As Hamas gained strength and began exerting control over the uprising (intifada), Arafat attempted to direct the movement from his headquarters in Tunis. He began funneling money and instructions to PLO operatives inside the territories to keep the insurrection going. Arafat's second in command at his headquarters in Tunis, Abu Jihad, pressed for an escalation of the intifada. He was known to have boasted that he was commanding the uprising. Abu Jihad was assassinated by an elite commando team at his home in a suburb of Tunis on April 16, 1988. Unofficial reports credit the commando raid to a joint Mossad and Israel Defense Forces' special unit with naval and air support. The elimination of the PLO's key insurrection organizer was intended to be a blow to the intifada.[13]

Violence Spreads

Unfortunately, Israel's expectations of a let up in the rioting with the removal of Abu Jihad did not occur. Instead, the assassination breathed new momentum into the intifada.[14]

Palestinians continued to use every weapon available to them to attack and disrupt the Israelis. They lashed out at any Israeli, military or civilian, with rocks, knives, and firebombs. They blocked roads with burning tires, furniture, trees, and any other material available. The riots had become well organized and directed. Israeli forces were hard pressed to control the rioting. Early attempts to quell the rioting met with very little success. There were a few instances in which Israeli troops fired live ammunition; however, that quickly ended. Rubber and plastic bullets were tried, but they proved to be ineffective. Clubs were issued to the troops, but they were criticized for being too brutal. Israel resorted to many other methods to quiet the rioting, such as cutting off telephones and electricity, extending curfews on towns and villages, demolishing homes, closing schools and universities, and arresting and deporting militants. In the first year of the uprising, 311 Palestinians were killed. Palestinians killed six Israeli civilians and four Israeli security personnel.[15]

Violence spread outside the territories and into Israel proper. In October 1988, an Israeli bus was fire-bombed, killing five Israelis, including a mother and three children, and wounding four others. Surprisingly, the PLO denounced the attack. In July of that year, a bus traveling from Tel Aviv to Jerusalem was attacked by an Arab passenger. He jumped the driver and turned the bus into a steep abyss. Sixteen passengers were killed and 25 were injured. The attacker, a member of the Gaza-based Islamic Jihad, was arrested. In September 1989, a Palestinian was stopped from carrying out an attack on a bus similar to the one previously cited. In February 1990, two Israeli soldiers were abducted and murdered by Hamas terrorists in two separate incidents.[16]

The most devastating incident of violence occurred in October 1990 at the Temple Mount in Jerusalem when 19 Palestinians were killed, over 200 Palestinians were injured, and 11 Israelis were injured. The incident was at first instigated by an extremist Jewish group that announced they were going to march on the Temple Mount on the Jewish holiday Sukkot. Fear of a Jewish takeover of the al-Aqsa Mosque, the third holiest shrine of Islam, located at the entrance to the Temple Mount, ignited anger among Palestinians. Over 3,000 Muslims converged on the Temple Mount while 20,000 Jewish worshipers gathered at the Western Wall for holiday prayers. The angry Muslims unleashed a hail of heavy rocks on the Jews below at the Wall. Police reinforcements reacted to augment those on site and used live ammunition, rubber bullets, and tear gas against the dissidents, causing untold numbers casualties. Palestinian organizers were quick to use the incident to escalate the intifada. The Palestinian United National Command (UNC) declared that every Israeli soldier and settler in Palestine were targets and should be eliminated. The Fatah urged the use of weapons and knives. Hamas proclaimed that all Jews were targets for killing.[17] The Palestinian practice of praising those who were killed in the uprising as martyrs and heroes added fuel to an already explosive atmosphere. To further stoke acts of terrorism, the PLO gave monetary rewards to families who offered their sons and daughters for martyrdom.[18]

The Second Front

While the Israelis were occupied with the rebellion in the territories, terrorist organizations in Lebanon, predominantly Hezbollah seized the opportunity to open up a second front on Israel's northern border. They launched rockets and armed attacks into Israel's security zone in southern Lebanon. They tried numerous attempts to penetrate Israeli territory, at times coming very close to reaching Israeli settlements. They began using suicide bombers and improvised explosive devices (IEDs) against Israeli troops. On October 19, 1988, a Hezbollah suicide bomber in a car loaded with explosives detonated the charge close to an Israeli military convoy, killing eight soldiers and wounding seven. A few months later an Israeli commando force raided a village in southern Lebanon and captured the commander of Hezbollah forces in that area along with two of his staff. Attempts to exchange these captives for three Israeli soldiers held by Hezbollah were unsuccessful. Syria's failure to rein in Hezbollah in Lebanon led to a further increase in hostilities. Israel launched artillery and air strikes against several Shiite villages in southern Lebanon. Hezbollah retaliated with massive rocket attacks against Israeli towns near the Lebanese border. Casualties of Israeli troops increased with each passing year.[19]

Iraq Threatens

The year 1990 found Israel confronted with problems on multiple fronts. There was the insurrection in the territories that was spilling over into Israeli cities; hostilities on the border with Lebanon were on the rise with encouragement by Syria from behind the scene; 185,227 new Jewish immigrants had arrived from Russia; and on top of all this, Iraq began making threats against Israel. In April of that year, Saddam Hussein, the ruthless leader of Iraq, threatened to wipe out half of Israel with chemical weapons. The fact that he had used chemical weapons before to kill thousands of his own people, the Kurds, made this threat even more menacing. At a parade in Baghdad, Saddam stood with Yasser Arafat and pledged to help liberate Palestine. Arafat added that Iraq's long-range missiles would be used to liberate Palestine. In June of 1990, Saddam threatened to launch his missiles against Israel if they bombed any Arab country. These threats became even more foreboding when on August 2, 1990, Saddam invaded neighboring Kuwait.[20]

The United Nations passed 14 resolutions calling for Iraq to withdraw from Kuwait. The United States began deploying armed forces into the Gulf region and forming a coalition of concerned states. Saddam attempted to link his invasion of Kuwait with the Arab-Israeli conflict. He proposed the unconditional withdrawal of Israel from the occupied territories of Palestine, Syria, and Lebanon. Only after these conditions were met would he consider discussing Kuwait. The U.S. denied any linkage, as did Israel. However, this worked against President Bush's efforts to pull together a coalition that included the Arab states. He overcame the biggest stumbling block, Syria's President Assad, with a commitment to make a determined effort to promote the peace process once Kuwait was liberated. The final UN Security Council resolution set January 15, 1991, as the deadline for Iraq to withdraw from Kuwait. If Iraq failed to comply, the UN resolution authorized member states to use all necessary means to liberate Kuwait. On January 16, 1991, the coalition forces launched a massive assault to drive the Iraqis out of Kuwait.[21]

Two days after the coalition struck, Saddam Hussein began firing Scud missiles into Israel's cities. On the first strike, five missiles hit Tel Aviv and three landed on Haifa. Saddam was gambling that Israel would strike back, and that would likely cause the Arab member states to withdraw from the coalition. The decision by Israel's cabinet not to strike back was razor thin, with Prime Minister Shamir casting the deciding vote. The United States rushed Patriot missile systems to Israel to help defend against the Scud missiles, but this system had only limited effectiveness against the incoming Scud missiles.[22] In just over a month, Iraq fired 39 Scuds into Israel. The missiles hit mostly in Tel Aviv and Haifa; however, a few landed in the West Bank and desert. These attacks caused the direct death of two Israeli civilians and wounded 259. Four Israelis suffered heart attacks, and seven deaths were the result of incorrect use of gas masks. The missiles damaged 332 Israeli homes, 6,142 apartments, 23 public buildings, 200 stores, and 50 automobiles. The continuous threat of incoming missiles each day of the war had a significant psychological impact on the Israelis. There was always the fear that Saddam would use deadly nerve gas in the missiles. Consequently, each Israeli citizen had to carry a gas mask for the duration of the war.[23]

The Gulf War ended on March 6, 1991, enabling Israel to back off of the war footing and high state of readiness it had been on since the beginning of the war. Many of the Arab countries sided with the United States' efforts to drive Iraq out of Kuwait; however, Arafat chose to support Saddam's invasion of Kuwait. He paid heavily for this decision, with the loss of several of his Arab contributors, including Saudi Arabia and Kuwait. By the end of the Gulf War, the intifada had begun to lose momentum, but it was still smoldering under the surface. One of the factors that shifted the focus of Israel and the Palestinians away from the insurrection was the beginning of several peace initiatives that arose soon after the conclusion of the Gulf War.

Chapter 9

Al-Aqsa Intifada

The 1990s were characterized by peace initiatives laced with terrorist attacks by those who opposed any agreement with Israel. Soon after the first Gulf War, the United States took the initiative to sponsor peace talks between Israel, Arabs, and Palestinians. These talks, known as the Madrid Peace Conference, opened on October 30, 1991, in Madrid, Spain, with representatives of Israel, Jordan, Syria, Lebanon, and the Palestinians in attendance. The conference succeeded in establishing the framework for bilateral talks between Israel, Arabs, and Palestinians and multilateral talks about common interests and conflict prevention. The three-day conference did not result in the development of a peace agreement; however, it was significant in bringing about direct peace talks between Israel and its neighbors for the first time since 1949. Bilateral talks did, in fact, begin in Washington between Israel and others who attended the Madrid Conference. However, the discussions soon became bogged down. In December 1992, an Israeli soldier was kidnapped and murdered by Palestinians. Israel responded by expelling 415 Islamic fundamentalists from occupied territories to Lebanon. In retaliation, the Palestinian and Arab delegations in Washington suspended participation in the talks.[1]

The Oslo Accords

Bilateral talks in Washington resumed four and a half months later when the Arabs ended their suspension, but the talks soon drifted into a stalemate. Meanwhile, "unofficial" secret talks were taking place in Oslo, Norway, between Israeli and PLO representatives.

After several meetings in Oslo, official representatives of Israel and the PLO entered into negotiations, and a bilateral agreement, known as the Oslo Declaration of Principles (DOP), was accepted by both sides in August of 1993. Three weeks later, the declaration was signed by PLO Chairman Arafat and Israel's Prime Minister Rabin at the White House. The declaration spelled out the arrangements for the interim self-government by the Palestinians; the establishment of the Palestinian Authority to administer the territories; the transfer of power in the West Bank and Gaza Strip to the Palestinians; the withdrawal of Israeli troops from Gaza and part of the West Bank in the second year of an interim period; and free general elections. The interim or transitional period, which was not to exceed five years, would culminate in a final status agreement for a permanent Palestinian state.[2]

As a follow on to the Oslo Accords, Yasser Arafat sent a letter to Prime Minister Rabin declaring that the PLO was committed to the peace process and renounced the use of terrorism and other acts of violence. He also declared that the articles of the PLO Charter that denied Israel the right to exist were no longer valid. In a reply to Arafat, Rabin confirmed Israel's decision to recognize the PLO as the sole representative of the Palestinian people.[3] The Cairo Agreement of May 4, 1994, outlined the initial withdrawal of Israel's defense forces from the Gaza Strip and Jericho in the West Bank and the creation of the Palestinian Authority (PA). Problems with self-rule were not long in coming. There were numerous breaches of the Oslo agreement by Palestinians. Smuggling of weapons into Gaza continued unabated. Wanted terrorists were protected by the Palestinian Authority. In short, the Palestinian Authority failed to meet its commitments to crack down on terrorist groups.[4]

Peace is Threatened

There were those on both sides who opposed the peace process. On February 25, 1994, a Jewish settler and members of an extreme right group opened fire on Muslim worshipers at the main Mosque in Hebron. Twenty-nine Palestinians were killed by gunfire and more died in the stampede that resulted. Hamas retaliated on April 6 and 13, 1994, with suicide bombers who blew themselves up, killing 13 Israeli civilians and wounding dozens more. In October of that year, Hamas militants killed two Israelis and injured 13 others in Jerusalem. Two days later they kidnapped an Israeli soldier. The kidnappers demanded the release of 200 prisoners in exchange for the soldier's life. Israel first thought the PLO was holding the soldier in Gaza, but that proved to be incorrect. They discovered that the soldier was being held by another group near Jerusalem. A rescue attempt by the Israelis resulted in the death of the soldier and an Israeli officer. Ten days after this incident, the bombing of a bus in Tel Aviv by a Hamas suicide terrorist killed 22 and injured 42 Israeli civilians.[5]

The peace process was threatened again in January 1995, when two Islamic Jihad suicide bombers blew themselves up in a busy Israeli bus station, killing 22 and wounding 63 Israeli soldiers and civilians. Israel's leaders first considered suspending ongoing peace talks, but in the end they decided not to give in to the terrorist's efforts to sabotage the talks. Still, the attacks did not stop. On April 9, 1995, two suicide attacks in the Gaza Strip killed seven Israeli soldiers and one civilian and wounded 45 others. On July 24 of that year, six Israelis were killed and 32 wounded in a suicide bombing of a bus near Tel Aviv. Again, on August 21, a suicide bomb was detonated in a bus in Jerusalem, killing four and wounding 106.[6]

Despite the relentless violence, the peace process moved forward. On September 28, 1995, the Oslo II Agreement was signed in Washington by Rabin and Arafat. It broadened and superseded the 1994 Cairo Agreement. It dealt with the transition to Palestinian autonomy, including Israel's departure from Palestinian-populated areas in the West Bank and Gaza Strip and the provision for Palestinians to elect a newly established Palestinian Legislative Council. The West Bank was divided into three sections based on the responsibility for security, either Israel or the PLO.[7]

On November 4, 1995, Israel was rocked by the assassination of Prime Minister Rabin by a right-wing zealot in Tel Aviv. In February 1996, Shimon Peres, Rabin's successor, announced elections to be held in Israel in May 1996. Two weeks after the announcement, there were nine days of terrorist attacks, possibly to test the new Israeli Prime

Minister or in retaliation for Israel's killing of Hamas's suicide bomb maker mastermind, Yehiye Ayyash. Whatever the reason, Islamic fundamentalist terrorists struck with vengeance. On February 25, 1996, a suicide bomber detonated himself on a Jerusalem bus, killing 24 and wounding over 70 civilians. On the same day, a Palestinian blew himself up killing one person and injuring dozens. A week later, an attack on a Jerusalem bus killed 19 and wounded 10. The next day, 14 Israelis died and over 100 were injured when a suicide bomber blew himself up at a busy mall. Although too late for the Israeli victims of the suicide bombers, Arafat finally acted. He outlawed Hamas's military wing and began to round up Hamas and Islamic Jihad militants.[8]

The Northern Front Erupts

While Israel struggled to implement Oslo II and cope with a storm of suicide bombers, the northern front erupted. Hezbollah opened up with rocket fire from across the border in Lebanon, striking Israeli settlements in Galilee in northern Israel. On April 2, 1996, Israel struck back with a major military offensive designated "Operation Grapes of Wrath." The objective of the operation was to damage Hezbollah's infrastructures and exert pressure on Syria to restrain Hezbollah. Another aim was to destroy Hezbollah's Katyusha rocket launchers, positioned in the heart of Lebanon's population centers. During the operation, Israeli forces returned Hezbollah rocket fire but mistakenly hit a UN civilian shelter with artillery fire, killing more than 100 hiding there. The incident caused a surge of rage and condemnation from Arab and Western nations, which resulted in a ceasefire and the end of the operation.[9]

An understanding between Israel, Syria, and Lebanon was brokered by the United States. The purpose of the understanding was to end cross-border attacks from either side. Specifically, Hezbollah and other groups in Lebanon were not to attack Israeli territory with rockets or any other type of weapon. The parties committed not to fire on civilian targets or use civilian population centers as launching bases for attacks. This provision was meant to stop Hezbollah from imbedding military weapons in populated areas, which they had done in the past. However, Hezbollah interpreted this provision as applying only to Katyusha rocket fire; therefore, it did not ban them from staging and locating military operations in civilian areas. Nevertheless, the understanding was signed in Washington by all parties on July 12, 1996. An international monitoring group, made up of military representatives from France, Lebanon, Israel, and the United States, was established to identify and resolve violations to the understanding.[10]

Violence Shifts to Jerusalem

The northern front had been quiet for only a few short weeks when there was another outburst of violence, this time in Jerusalem. In September 1996, Netanyahu, the newly elected Prime Minister of Israel, ordered the excavation of an exit at the northern end of an ancient tunnel that ran close to the holy al-Aqsa Mosque in the Old City of Jerusalem. This move resulted in violent riots and clashes between Palestinian demonstrators and Israeli security forces, which spread from East Jerusalem to Bethlehem and throughout the Gaza Strip. In one Israeli settlement, demonstrators attacked a Jewish religious school. Six Israeli soldiers were killed at that site. Israel was forced to resort to stronger defensive measures that included the use of helicopters and tanks as a show of force. The rioting subsided in three days, but the death toll during that brief interval had risen to 84 Palestinians and 15 Israeli soldiers.[11]

In January 1997, Prime Minister Netanyahu focused on resolving the issue of redeploying Israeli soldiers from Hebron. For some time Israel had justified retaining control of Hebron because of continuing Palestinian violence there. A protocol was signed by Netanyahu and Arafat on January 17, 1997, which set in motion Israel's withdrawal from Hebron, which was the last remaining Palestinian city in the West Bank under Israel's control.[12] With that settled, the Prime Minister took the bold step of authorizing the construction of 6,500 housing units on land southwest of Jerusalem. This tract was still under dispute between Israel and the Palestinians, and the decision to build a Jewish settlement there enraged the Palestinians. For this and other reasons, relations between the Palestinians and Israel deteriorated to a new low. They reached the breaking point on July 30, 1997, when a Hamas suicide bomber blew himself up in Jerusalem killing 14 and injuring

160 Israelis. Arafat was blamed for failure to prevent terrorist attacks. Netanyahu responded by tightening security measures and freezing the implementation of Oslo II.[13]

Renewed Peace Efforts

In 1998 U.S. President Clinton hosted a summit between Netanyahu and Arafat in an effort to get the peace process back on track. On October 23, 1998, after almost ten days of negotiations, the agreement, known as the Wye River Memorandum, was signed by Netanyahu and Arafat. The memorandum stressed the need for the Palestinian side to uphold its security obligations. Arafat made a commitment to prevent acts of terrorism and hostilities against Israel. He also reaffirmed his pledge of 1988 to nullify the provisions in the Palestinian Covenant that denied Israel's right to exist. In return, there was to be a phased turnover of land to the Palestinians. The Wye Memorandum did not give the peace process new momentum, mainly because Arafat did not uphold his commitments. In a move that put a damper on the peace process, Arafat announced he was going to unilaterally declare a Palestinian state. Netanyahu promptly halted the implementation of the Wye agreement until Arafat renounced his plans to declare a state and halted all violence.[14]

Another attempt to breathe new life into the peace process was sponsored by Egyptian President Mubarak at a meeting in the Egyptian resort town of Sharm el-Sheikh in September 1999. Arafat and the new Prime Minister of Israel, Ehud Barak, met to reaffirm their commitment to the Oslo peace process. The resulting memorandum addressed the delay in implementation of the Oslo Accords, Palestinian compliance with security obligations, prisoner release, economic issues, and established a new deadline of September 13, 2000, for the completion of peace talks.[15]

Meanwhile, efforts to bring about a peace agreement between Syria and Israel were fostered by the Clinton administration at a summit in Washington with Assad of Syria and Israel's Barak in attendance. The initial meeting in December 1999 held out some hope, and another meeting was convened near Washington on January 3, 2000. However, this meeting failed to overcome the differences involving the Golan Heights and the Sea of Galilee. Later, Barak offered to withdraw from the Golan Heights if Assad would give up access to the Sea of Galilee. President Clinton met with Assad in Geneva to present Barak's last offer. Assad rejected the offer and insisted he had no intension of giving up access to the Sea of Galilee. With the collapse of negotiations with Syria, Barak turned his attention to the withdrawal of Israel's troops from the security zone in southern Lebanon, where they had guarded the border since 1982. In July 2000, Israeli troops withdrew from the Lebanon security zone under a hail of mortar and rocket fire by Hezbollah.[16]

One of the most significant efforts to settle the Israeli-Palestinian conflict was driven by Prime Minister Barak, who pressured the Clinton administration to broker another summit meeting in Washington. In July 2000, Arafat and Barak met with President Clinton at Camp David. Barak was determined to achieve peace, once and for all. He offered a number of concessions:

(1) withdrawing all Israelis from the entire Gaza Strip and 95 percent of the West Bank;

(2) eventually creating an independent Palestinian state in those areas;

(3) dismantling all Israeli settlements in the areas given to Palestinians;

(4) granting Palestinian rule over East Jerusalem and most of the Old City (except the Jewish Quarter); and

(5) resolving the refugee problem with a program that included $20 billion to settle claims of refugees, to be used to compensate refugee households and countries that would accept and rehabilitate refugees. Arafat rejected Barak's offer in its entirety without making a counter offer. President Clinton interceded with a similar proposal that included a few modifications favoring the Palestinians, but Arafat abruptly ended the talks, commenting that

there was no point in continuing efforts to reach an agreement. The summit ended in failure.[17]

The Intifada Begins

Following the failed talks, widespread violence broke out in the Gaza Strip, the West Bank, and Israel proper. There are conflicting views on what started the uprising, which became known as the al-Aqsa intifada. It is often suggested that this intifada was triggered by Ariel Sharon's visit to the Temple Mount in Jerusalem. According to reports, "On September 28, 2000, Ariel Sharon, leader of Israel's Likud minority party, went to visit the Temple Mount, Judaism's holiest place, which Muslims have renamed *Haram al-Sharif* and regard as Islam's third holiest place."[18]

Palestinian spokesmen claimed that "the violence was caused by the desecration of a Muslim holy place—*Haram al-Sharif*—by Sharon and the 'thousands of Israeli soldier' who accompanied him." They said, "The violence was carried out through unprovoked attacks by Israeli forces, which invaded Palestinian controlled territories and 'massacred' defenseless Palestinian civilians, who merely threw stones in self-defense."[19]

The Israelis contend that "Sharon did not attempt to enter any mosques, and his visit of only 34 minutes was conducted during normal hours when the area is normally open to tourists. Palestinian youths—eventually numbering around 1,500—shouted slogans in an attempt to inflame the situation. Some 1,500 Israeli police were present at the scene to forestall violence."[20] [The Palestinian security chief had refused to do anything to prevent violence during Sharon's visit.]

As the day of Sharon's visit wore on, there were outbreaks of stone throwing in the vicinity of the Temple Mount which injured 28 Israeli policemen. There were no reports of Palestinian injuries on that day.[21]

The true cause of the uprising is best described by Palestinians in their own words and deeds: "On September 29, the voice of Palestine, the PA's [Palestinian Authority] official radio station sent out calls 'to all

Palestinians to come and defend the al-Aqsa Mosque.' The PA closed its schools and bused Palestinian students to the Temple Mount to participate in the organized riots."[22]

The Palestinian Authority's Communications Minister, Imad Falouji, admitted it was not Sharon's visit to the Temple Mount that caused the uprising. Several months after the beginning of the intifada he said, "Whoever thinks that this [war] started as a result of Sharon's visit to al-Aqsa [Temple Mount] is in error. It was planned since Arafat's return from Camp David [in July] where he firmly stood up to Clinton and rejected the U.S. terms."[23]

At the beginning of the al-Aqsa intifada, the majority of the Palestinian population was no longer under Israeli rule. An elected Palestinian Authority (PA) had been established; Israel had transferred 98 percent of the Palestinian population to the PA, including the entire Gaza Strip; and Israel had withdrawn its military forces and administration from all major Palestinian cities in the West Bank. In those locations, the PA had taken over security and civil administration.[24] In view of these facts, Sholomo Gazit, former head of Israel's Military Intelligence, in *The Arab-Israeli Wars,* drew the following conclusion about the reason for the al-Aqsa intifada: "Hence the goal of the Palestinians' violent struggle was not to free themselves from [Israeli] occupation, but to strengthen their position in the political negotiations with Israel."[25] He described the uprising in this way: "Almost from the first, this intifada was a war, using firearms and explosive charges. Two striking aspects were the large quantities of weapons available to the Palestinian militants (of much higher quality than before) and the inexhaustible supply of explosives."[26]

In dealing with the al-Aqsa intifada, Israel was faced with combating multiple terrorist organizations, which were receiving funding and other support from Saudi Arabia, Iran, and Syria. Weapons were smuggled across borders and through tunnels to terrorists groups in the Gaza Strip and the West Bank. Weapons also came by sea. For instance, "In 2002 the Israeli Navy intercepted the 'Karin A,' a ship carrying 50 tons of advanced weaponry and rockets supplied by Iran and Hezbollah that were destined for Gaza to supply Palestinian terrorist groups."[27]

In many ways, the terrorist organizations had become proxies of Iran and Syria. In the Palestinian arena at the beginning of the al-Aqsa intifada, there were seven Palestinian terrorist organizations pitted against Israel. On the northern front, Hezbollah carried out attacks in support of the Palestinian groups and provided them with weapons and funds.

Asymmetric warfare is not new, but rarely if ever has there been a conflict where a small state like Israel has been confronted with an alignment of many terrorist groups sponsored by several large states. It is nearly impossible for a small state to survive when it does not have defense in depth (geographical separation from enemies) and is faced with multiple threats on every front. Yet, that has been the conditions under which Israel has had to live since it became a Jewish state. To make matters worse, the terrorists attacking Israel have often used suicide bombers as their weapon of choice. Such attacks are difficult to stop and usually kill and maim innocent civilians. Similarly, the rockets and mortars fired into Israel's schools, homes, and markets are meant to strike terror into the hearts of the civilian population. The aim of the terrorists is to drive the Israelis out of the Holy Land.

Terrorist Organizations

A brief look at the terrorist organizations aligned against Israel reveals the enormity of the threat Israel has faced for many years and must contend with today.

> **Fatah—Tanzim/Al-Aqsa Martyrs' Brigade**. Tanzim, the military arm of Fatah, spearheaded the violent confrontation during the first intifada, and in the years leading up to the al-Aqsa intifada, it expanded and became more powerful. Its primary goal was the elimination of Israelis from Palestine. When the violence broke out in September 2000, Fatah was essentially an arm of the Palestinian Authority, from which it derived funding as well as from other sources including Hezbollah and Iran. As the violence spread, Fatah took an active part in terrorist operations with attacks in Gaza and the West

Bank. Fatah was responsible for a number of suicide bombings within Israel. Between 2002 and 2004, Fatah operatives carried out eight suicide attacks, killing 83 Israeli civilians and wounding many more.[28]

Hamas—The Islamic Resistance Movement. This terrorist organization sprang into existence in the early days of the first intifada in 1987 and grew rapidly in strength and influence. Its ideology is along the lines of Islamic fundamentalism as practiced by the Muslim Brotherhood.... [Hamas has become even more powerful today, and it is important to know the dangers that this organization poses for Israel and the region.]

[Hamas] advocates the destruction of the State of Israel as its main goal and perpetrates acts of terrorism against Israel as the primary tool for advancing that goal....

Hamas claims that the land of Palestine, 'from the [Jordan] river to the Mediterranean Sea' is consecrated to Islam and none of it can be given up, especially Jerusalem. Thus Hamas denies the possibility of any political settlement with Israel and objects to all agreements between the PA/PLO and Israel, and totally rejects the Oslo accords....

Terrorism is one of the main tenets of Hamas ideology... Hamas has an operational-terrorist infrastructure (Izzedine al-Qassam Battalions) in the Gaza Strip, the West Bank, and abroad...During the [al-Aqsa intifada] confrontation, Hamas was the leading organization in the armed insurrection and responsible for an enormous number of terrorist attacks....[29]

Some of Hamas's more prominent attacks against Israel include:

1. A suicide bombing attack at the Dolphinarium in Tel Aviv (June 1, 2001); 21 Israeli civilians murdered, most of them teenagers.

2. A suicide bombing attack at the Sbarro Restaurant in Jerusalem (August 9, 2001); 15 Israeli civilians were murdered.

3. A suicide bombing attack at the Park Hotel in Netanya during the Passover Seder (March 27, 2002); 30 Israeli civilians were murdered.

4. A suicide bombing attack in Rishon Le'tzion, 7 miles south of Tel Aviv along the coast (May 7, 2002); 16 Israeli civilians murdered.

5. A suicide bombing attack at a major intersection in Jerusalem (June 18, 2002); 19 Israeli civilians murdered.

6. A suicide bombing attack on the Number 2 bus in Jerusalem (August 19, 2003); 23 Israeli civilians murdered.[30]

The Palestinian Islamic Jihad (PIJ). The PIJ has an extremist Islamic ideology which calls for the destruction of the State of Israel as a means of bringing about an Islamic revolution in the Arab world . . . Shaqaqi [the founder] and his followers…were impressed by the Islamic revolution in Iran (1979). [It] is under the Iranian patronage. The PIJ was prominent during the first violent confrontation (1987-1993). After the Oslo Accords, to which they objected fiercely, the PIJ perpetrated suicide bombing attacks as a means of sabotaging any effort to come to a solution. During the [al-Aqsa] violent confrontation, the PIJ joined Hamas and Fatah to perpetrate terrorist attacks against Israel….[31]

Prominent PIJ terrorist attacks [2002-2003] against Israel include:

1. A suicide bombing attack on a bus in Wadi 'Ara in the northern part of Israel (March 20, 2002); 7 Israeli civilians murdered, 30 wounded.

2. A suicide bombing attack on a bus at the Yagur junction near Haifa (April10, 2001); 8 Israeli civilians murdered, 15 wounded.

3. A car bomb with a single terrorist exploded next to a bus at the Megiddo junction in the northern part of Israel (June 5, 2002); 17 Israeli civilians murdered, 50 wounded.

4. A car bomb with two terrorists exploded next to a bus at the Karkur junction near Hadera, 28 miles north of Tel Aviv (October 21, 2002); 14 Israeli civilians murdered, 50 wounded.

5. A shooting attack near Hebron, 18 miles south of Jerusalem (November 15, 2002); 12 Israeli civilians returning from prayers killed, 16 wounded.

6. A suicide bombing attack at the Maxim Restaurant in Haifa (October 4, 2003); 21 Israeli civilians murdered, including 6 members representing 3 generations of the same family.[32]

The Popular Front for the Liberation of Palestine (PFLP). The PFLP is a Marxist organization which advocates armed insurrection. It perpetrated show-case, media-oriented attacks, particularly the hijacking of planes, to bring the Palestinian cause to public attention ... The PFLP's political leadership resides in the PA-administered territories and Syria.... During the al-Aqsa violent confrontation the PFLP called for an armed insurrection and perpetrated a number of terrorist attacks....[33]

Some of its more prominent attacks include:

1. Hijacking of 3 planes belonging to Western countries (September 6, 1970). Three commercial airliners were hijacked and blown up after the passengers were evacuated. An attempt to hijack an

Israeli (EIAI) airliner was foiled. Three days later another Western airliner was hijacked as well.

2. A suicide bombing attack at the West Bank village of Karnei Shomrom (February 16, 2002); 3 Israelis murdered, 25 wounded.

3. A suicide bombing attack at a bus station at the Geha Junction in Tel Aviv (December 25, 2003); 3 Israelis murdered.[34]

The Democratic Front for the Liberation of Palestine (DFLP). The DFLP, which belongs to the PLO, initially had a radical Marxist–Leninist ideology and cooperated with other radical left-wing organizations (some of them underground). It supports armed insurrection against Israel and began its terrorist activities in 1973...Hawatmeh [the leader] and other senior members of the DFLP are based in Syria and maintain a small organizational terrorist wing in the Gaza Strip. During the al-Aqsa violent confrontation the DFLP confined its activities to a small number of terrorist attacks in the Gaza Strip....[35]

Some of DFLP's most prominent terrorist attacks against Israel include:

1. Terrorist attack on the northern border town of Ma'alot (May 15, 1974); 25 Israeli civilians murdered, many of them children.

2. Attack on a private residence in the town of Beit Shean (November 19, 1974); 4 Israeli civilians murdered.

3. A wagon rigged with a bomb which exploded in the Jerusalem (November 13, 1975); 7 Israeli civilians murdered.[36]

The Popular Front for the Liberation of Palestine—General Command (PFLP-GC). The PFLP-GC was established in April 1968...mostly around a nucleus of former Syrian army officers . . . Since its inception the PFLP-GC has advocated armed insurrection. Although the organization has no particular ideology, it has certain Marxist characteristics . . . The PFLP-GC, under Syrian influence, opposed the Oslo accords and advanced the continuation of the armed insurrection.... The organizational-terrorist infrastructure and bases are located in Syria and Lebanon....[37]

Its (PFLP-GC) prominent attack against Israel include:

1. Blowing up a Swissair plane (February 21, 1970); 47 murdered. An attack on a bus of children from Avivim, a moshav [a small agricultural community] near the Lebanese border (May 21, 1970); 12 Israeli civilians murdered, 9 of which were children. 25 civilians wounded.

2. An attack in Kiriyat Shmonah in the far north of Israel (April 11, 1974); 18 Israeli civilians murdered.

3. The kidnapping of 3 Israeli soldiers in 1982 who were exchanged on May 20, 1985, for 1,150 Palestinian prisoners.... [38]

The Popular Resistance Committee (PRC). The PRC is a terrorist organization active in the Gaza Strip. The organization was founded in September 2000, at the beginning of the current [al-Aqsa intifada] violent confrontation....[39]

Since its inception, the PRC has been attacking Israel:

1. The PRC (and its operational-terrorist wing, the Salah al-Din Brigades) is responsible for a large number of attacks against Israelis in the Gaza Strip, both civilians and soldiers. Some of the more prominent attacks include the following:

    a. Large explosive charges meant for Israeli tanks which killed three Israeli soldiers on February 14, 2002; three more [killed] on March 14, 2002; and one on September 5, 2002.

    b. Attacks on civilian targets in the Gaza Strip: a side charge was detonated at a bus full of children as it passed near Kfar Darom, an Israeli settlement in the Gaza Strip, on November 20, 2003, killing two; shots were fired at a bus carrying airport workers near the Rafah terminal, at a Palestinian city in the south of Gaza, on October 8, 2000, wounding 8 Israeli civilians; shots were fired at a car on the road from Kerem Shalom to the Rafah terminal, killing the woman driver.

c. Mortar attacks on Israel targets in the Gaza Strip, including civilian villages, some within a very short period of time: three on the same day (April 28, 2001) against Moshav Netzer Hazani (five young people wounded, one of them seriously; another (April 29, 2001) against the village of Kfar Dorom; and one (May 7, 2001) against the village of Atzmona.

2. The PRC was apparently behind the attack on the American convoy at the Beit Hanoun in the northern part of the Gaza Strip (October 15, 2003). Two side charges were detonated, blowing up a vehicle and killing three security personnel who were accompanying the American cultural attaché.

3. PRC terrorists have various weapons at their disposal: small arms, explosives (commercial and homemade), mines, hand grenades, and anti-tank rockets and mortars. The PRC has recently (July 2004) begun launching homemade Nasser 3 rockets at Israeli villages close to the Gaza Strip.... [40]

Hezbollah. Since its inception in 1982, Hezbollah has conducted a terrorist campaign aimed at promoting the radical Shiite-Islamic doctrine conceived by Iran's leader, Ayatollah Khomeini, who died in 1989.... [41] The basic objective of this organization is "the consistent and relentless struggle against Israel until the 'liberation of Jerusalem' and the annihilation of Israel are achieved.... [42] [This terrorist organization will be covered in more depth in the next chapter about the Second Lebanon War.]

The forgoing introduction to the numerous terrorist organizations Israel has had to defend against, many of which are still active today, was presented here to show the scope and nature of the threats. One very important lesson to take from this is that these terrorist organizations all have one thing in common: The destruction, annihilation, and extermination of Israel. They will not hesitate to kill every Israeli man, woman, and child to accomplish this goal.

Peace Initiatives Resume

Returning to the al-Aqsa intifada, there is considerable disagreement on how long this uprising lasted. It is accepted that it began in September 2000. Some suggest that it lasted until the end of 2005. There are some who believe it never ended. For the purposes here, it lasted until September 29, 2006, which marked six years from the outbreak of the intifada. As incredible as it might seem, peace initiatives continued throughout those years of confrontation:

Taba [Egypt] Conference—January 22-27, 2001. In the midst of the Second [al-Aqsa] intifada, and as a follow-up to the Camp David Summit, the Israelis and Palestinians met for a final attempt to come to an agreement on a Palestinian state. Israel offered 94 percent of the West Bank in addition to Israeli land, culminating in an offer of 97 percent of the total land area requested by the Palestinians. The "right of return" was also considered. However, the conference ended again in a standstill....[43]

The Arab Peace initiative—March 28, 2002. Leaders of Arab nations came together at the Beirut Summit, where Saudi Arabia proposed a plan for peace between Israel and the Palestinians. The plan called for Israel to withdraw completely to pre-1967 borders; supported the "right of return" for all Palestinian refugees and their descendents; and the creation of a Palestinian state with East Jerusalem as its capital. The Arab states in attendance pledged not to exercise military action to end the hostilities and stated that if Israel agreed to the aforementioned stipulations without modification, the Arab countries would in return consider the Arab-Israeli conflict to be over and would normalize relations with Israel. Israeli Foreign Minister Shimon Peres responded to the initiative on behalf of Israel, stating that Israel viewed the plan as encouraging, but that the agreement must be discussed directly with the Palestinians and that no accord could come to fruition unless terror activities ceased, a condition not mentioned in the Arab Initiative.[44]

President Bush's Vision for the Middle East—June 24, 2002. In a Rose Garden Speech, President George W. Bush outlined a new plan for peace between Israel and the Palestinians, with the possibility of a sovereign Palestinian state established in the near future. The policy called for new Palestinian leadership (specifically acknowledging the corruption and unwillingness to stop terrorism that characterized Arafat's regime) and a reformulated democratic government for the Palestinians. The president also called upon the Palestinians, as well as the other Arab states supporting or tolerating terrorism, to cease those activities. The plan focused mainly on the impediments to the peace process posed by the Palestinians....[45]

Roadmap for Peace—April 30, 2003. Based upon President Bush's speech on June 24, 2002, and principles of the Oslo Accords, this plan was supervised by the International Quartet: the United States, the European Union, the Russian Federation, and the United Nations. It called for serious alterations in the Palestinian government and resulted in the appointment of the Palestinian Authority Prime Minister, Mahmoud Abbas. The Roadmap, which charted the progress toward a final-status agreement through a series of benchmarks relating to security and political progress, is still considered to be the official blueprint towards peace between Israel and Palestinians....[46]

Peace Summit at Aqaba—June 4, 2003. Sharon and Abbas met in Jordan to reaffirm their commitment to the Roadmap. Sharon promised withdrawal of Israeli troops from Palestine areas, and Abbas pledged an end to the intifada and the Palestinian culture of hate against Israel. The prospects of the summit were shattered August 19, 2003, after Palestinian terrorists carried out a suicide bombing in Jerusalem. As a result, on September 1, 2003, the Israeli cabinet decided to wage war against Hamas and other terrorist groups, and halted the diplomatic process with the Palestinian Authority until it proved it was taking concrete measures to stop terrorism.[47]

Fourth Herzliya Conference—December 18, 2003. At this conference, Prime Minister Sharon presented a plan for Israel's unilateral disengagement from the Gaza Strip and northern Samaria [West Bank] in exchange for peace. The Israeli cabinet approved the plan on June 6, 2004, and the Knesset [Israel's Parliament] approved it on October 25, 2004. The disengagement plan, a major sacrifice for peace, called for evacuating nearly 9,000 Israeli residents living in Gaza and the West Bank. Israel also proposed the disengagement plan in the hope that it would stimulate progress in the peace process on the Palestinian side.[48]

Sharm el-Sheikh Summit I—February 8, 2005. Sharon met with PA President Abbas, Egyptian President Hosni Mubarak, and King Abdullah of Jordan to announce the implementation of Israel's disengagement from the Gaza and parts of the West Bank. Abbas and Sharon agreed upon a ceasefire. Sharon expressed his hope that the disengagement would foster a step forward in the Roadmap for Peace.[49]

Gaza and West Bank Disengagement—August 15-23, 2005. In an effort to relieve the security threats against Israelis living in Gaza and to try to put the Israeli-Palestinian peace talks back on track, Israel pulled all of its citizens out of the Gaza Strip and the northern West Bank. This dramatic move cost Israel approximately $2 billion and included the evacuation of the roughly 9,000 Israelis living in the affected areas. The evacuation also included exhuming and transferring all graves in the Gaza to Israeli territory. On September 12, 2005, the last Israel Defense Forces' soldier departed the Gaza, marking an historic step toward peace by Israel. The disengagement did not have a significant effect on the peace process.[50] Just days after the disengagement began, some Hamas leaders called for a continuation of terrorism:

1. At a rally in Gaza, Ismail Haniya, a high-ranking Hamas official, stated that the Israeli withdrawal was the result of the Qassam rockets [made by Palestinians] launched by his organization. He added that Hamas would continue its strikes against Israel "everywhere, on the sea and on land and underground, by means of rockets and mortars." He repeated Hamas's claim that the organization would not give up its weapons and that the topic

was not open to negotiation (Hamas's Al-Aqsa Radio, August 22, 2005).

2. Sa'id Siyam, a member of Hamas's political office, called for "an application of the Gaza Strip model in the West Bank" and for the "armed resistance" to be transferred to the West Bank after the Israeli withdrawal had been completed (Qudsnet Internet site, August 23, 2005).[51]

Terrorist Attacks Continue

Attempts at ceasefires did not have a marked impact on peace or the end of terrorist attacks. On March 17, 2005, the Palestinian Authority and associated terrorist organizations reached an agreement for a lull in the conflict with Israel. The "lull" did not result in an end to the terrorist attacks:

> According to the terrorist organizations' interpretation, this [the lull] was not a complete stop of violence but a temporary reduction in the magnitude of the confrontation, valid only through 2005...While it drove Hamas to embrace a restrained policy of terrorist attacks, the Palestinian Islamic Jihad and other insubordinate terrorist elements strove to derail the lull in order to provoke an escalation of the Israeli-Palestinian conflict....
>
> In 2005, the Palestinian Islamic Jihad spearheaded the effort to undermine the lull and render obsolete the Sharm el-Sheikh agreement, with the guidance of its Damascus-based leadership and the support of Syria and Iran. By derailing the lull and escalating the conflict, the organization sought to position itself as the leader of the struggle against Israel, creating a belligerent alternative for the Hamas movement, which lowered its profile of terrorist attacks in the wake of the lull. Thus, the Palestinian Islamic Jihad joined forces with insubordinate terrorist organizations that also strove to

escalate the conflict [such as the Popular Resistance Committees and insubordinate Fatah factions].

The primary tool used by the Palestinian Islamic Jihad in its attempts to derail the lull was suicide terrorism, the organization's "specialty."...The deadly suicide bombing attacks perpetrated by the organization resulted in the reemergence of a dynamic that has been visible throughout the history of the Israeli-Palestinian conflict: multi-casualty terrorist attacks amidst Israeli populations intensified the Israeli security force's counter-activities [targeted killings, arrests, closures, air strikes on terrorist targets, artillery fire on rocket launching sites]....

Syria and Iran, two state sponsors of terrorism, under pressure by the international community [to end attacks], nonetheless urged the [terrorist] organization to continue the strategy of undermining the lull. The two countries had interests in diverting attention to the Israeli-Palestinian conflict and making it clear to the U.S. that they were able to disrupt its Middle East policy....[52]

While the Islamic Jihad took the lead in undermining the lull, Hamas carried out a restrained policy of involvement in terrorist attacks. However, it did not completely end its perpetration of terrorist attacks against Israel:

Two prominent terrorist attacks perpetrated by the [Hamas] movement were a suicide bombing attack in Beersheba...and the abduction and murder of Sasson Nuriel [an Israeli businessman]. Moreover, Hamas played a central part in the escalation of Qassam rocket fire from the Gaza Strip, the most significant of which took place in July, on the eve of the disengagement... In addition, Hamas extended behind-the-scenes assistance to terrorist activity conducted by other terrorist organizations, mainly the Popular Resistance

116

Committee, as a means to perpetrate terrorist attacks without being directly associated with Hamas.[53]

The six years of confrontation that characterized the al-Aqsa intifada resulted in the death of many Israelis and Palestinians and severely affected the economies of both sides. Although Israeli troops were better trained, mainly for conventional war, they have been confronted with unconventional, asymmetrical warfare since the 1982 Lebanon War. Terrorists engaged in this type of conflict usually have the element of surprise, and those opposing them are often at a disadvantage because they are not able to make effective use of modern weapons of war. The Israeli troops and police encountered almost every form of attack, ranging from single suicide bombers, to angry and violent mobs, and to bands of terrorists infiltrating from every possible direction. The assailants were armed with pistols, assault rifles, machine guns, grenades, and Molotov cocktails. Some had acquired modern rockets and mortars, with ranges capable of striking many Israeli cities. The rules of engagement for Israeli troops prohibited the use of weapons except in life-threatening situations. At times they have had to defend themselves by firing rubber bullets and live ammunition.[54]

Many of the attacks on Israel during the al-Aqsa intifada, especially suicide bombers and rocket attacks, were difficult to prevent. Consequently, casualties were high, especially among civilians:

> Throughout the course of the confrontation, 26,159 terrorist attacks [were] perpetrated against Israeli targets, leaving 1,060 Israelis dead and 6,089 wounded.[55]

> Suicide bombings contributed disproportionably to the number of casualties. Of the attacks, 147 were suicide bombings [as of December 31, 2005] carried out by 156 male and 8 female suicide bombers. Some 450 of the other suicide bombing attacks were foiled at various stages by the Israeli security force.... The objective of most of the 147 suicide bombing attacks was to indiscriminately kill Israeli civilians. The [suicide]

attacks killed 527 Israelis and wounded approximately 3,350...."[56]

The lull in the terrorist attacks came to an abrupt end when Hamas openly urged a renewal of the confrontation with Israel:

> On Friday, July 15, 2005, a Qassam rocket attack was carried out against Israeli towns in the western Negev and the Gaza Strip, in which Hamas terrorists took part. On that very day, *Radio Sawt al-Aqsa* broadcasted a non-scheduled and unannounced belligerent sermon full of incitement by an unidentified preacher. *Radio Sawt al-Aqsa* is affiliated with Hamas and operates from the Gaza Strip alongside additional local radio stations affiliated with the terrorist organizations.
>
> The sermon, accompanied by verses from the Quran, repeatedly called upon all the Palestinian organizations to unite in order to resume the violent confrontation with Israel [the intifada] on the basis of a united political program, without surrendering any stretch of Palestinian land and without acknowledging the State of Israel. At the end of the sermon, the preacher addressed [the U.S. war in Iraq] the Iraqi people and wished them victory, saying: "We [Hamas] are with Iraq and with the people of Iraq; we are against America and against Britain. Thus, jihad continues and the intifada continues, and the next breakthrough is going to take place in Jaffa...." (*Radio Sawt al-Aqsa*. July 15, 2005).[57]

As 2006 approached, Israel again became the target of suicide bombings, and a war with Hezbollah in Lebanon was on the verge of breaking out.

Chapter 10

Second Lebanon War

As the al-Aqsa intifada entered its sixth year, it was foreshadowed by several events that were to have far-reaching implications for Israel and the region. First, the nature of the attacks by Palestinian terrorist groups in the Gaza Strip gradually shifted from suicide bombings to unleashing heavy bombardments of rockets and mortars into Israel. This transition in strategy was partly due to Israel's counterterrorism actions, the newly constructed wall along the border with Gaza and the availability of new technology for rockets and other armaments.[1] On the political stage, in January 25, 2006, Hamas won a landslide victory in the elections for the Palestinian Authority's Legislative Council. Hamas won 74 of the 132 council seats. Its main rival, Fatah, the leader of the Palestinian national movement, was defeated, winning only 45 seats. Hamas thus gained control of the Palestinian Authority and soon after seized complete control over the Gaza Strip in a bloody coup. Israel now shared a border with a duly-elected, radical Islamic terrorist movement.[2]

Hezbollah Gains Strength

In another arena, Israel's complete withdrawal from southern Lebanon in 2000 created a vacuum that Hezbollah and other terrorist groups were eager to fill. During the six years between 2000 and 2006, Hezbollah continued to carry out terrorist attacks against Israel, although on a somewhat reduced scale. Hezbollah's operations included abducting Israeli soldiers and attacking Israeli outposts and patrols with mortars, anti-tank fire, and small arms fire. Its operatives placed roadside charges to interdict Israeli patrols and fired Katyusha rockets into Israel, just as they did on May 28, 2006, when they fired eight 122-mm rockets into Mount Meron in northern Israel. Hezbollah encouraged an escalation of the Palestinian terrorism campaign against Israel and supplied arms and funds for carrying out attacks.[3]

In the years leading up to the Second Lebanon War, Hezbollah embarked on a massive buildup of its military forces, with the unprecedented assistance and backing of Iran and Syria. Vast amounts of high-quality, advanced weapons and ammunition were smuggled into Hezbollah's base camps. Hezbollah was propelled from a terrorist and guerilla operation into an organization with capabilities equal to or surpassing those of a state. The upgrade of Hezbollah's military infrastructure had the following objectives:

1. Gaining strategic resilience, meaning:

    a. In the offensive aspect, the ability to conduct a sustained campaign against Israel in order to inflict massive, continuous damage to civilian population, including on the Israeli home front.

    b. In the defensive aspect, the ability to mount a coordinated, well-planned defense against a ground assault by the Israelis, allowing the organization to maintain its survivability, power, and status.

2. Creating a balance of terror, which would deter Israel from initiating another confrontation while allowing Hezbollah to continue perpetrating attacks on Israel without provoking a full-scale war.

3. Establishing Hezbollah's power and status on the internal Lebanese scene, where it was a revolutionary force striving to establish the dominance of the Shi'ite community and radically change the existing traditional government system and the pro-Western orientation of the Lebanese regime.[4]

These objectives clearly reflected Hezbollah's intention to wrest control of Lebanon from the Lebanese government. While Hezbollah embedded itself in Lebanon and its political power structure, it did not stray from its true aspirations of the Islamic revolution and armed struggle against Israel. Since its formation, Hezbollah has stayed faithful to Khomeini's revolutionary ideology, and its leadership has remained religiously and politically loyal to the leader of the Islamic revolution in Iran, now Ali Khamenei.[5] The main goals of Hezbollah's charter (or program) are summarized below:

1. The destruction of the State of Israel including "liberating Jerusalem" and eliminating Israel.

2. The establishment of an Iranian-style Shiia theocracy in Lebanon, following the Iranian model.

3. The eradication of Western influences in Lebanon and the greater Middle East.[6]

The following abstract gives a more succinct insight into Hezbollah's doctrine:

> Since its inception in 1982, Hezbollah conducted a terrorist campaign aimed at promoting the radical Shiite-Islamic doctrine conceived by Iran's spiritual leader, Ayatollah Khomeini, who died in 1989. The basic principles of the doctrine, which reflect the fundamental identity of Hezbollah as a Shiite jihad organization, are
>
> (1) the consistent and relentless struggle against Israel until the "liberation of Jerusalem" and the annihilation of Israel are achieved and
>
> (2) intense hostility toward the United States, along with efforts to force its presence and influence out of the Middle East. In order to achieve these goals, Hezbollah has placed the use of

terrorism against its enemies at the focal point of its strategy of asymmetric conflict, with the weapon of suicide as one of its key components. In Hezbollah's view, the United States and Israel have no adequate response to such weapons.[7]

Iran and Syria Increase Support for Hezbollah

Iran and Syria regarded Lebanon as their front line against Israel and have been eager to advance Hezbollah as their strategic proxy. They embarked on an unprecedented program to upgrade Hezbollah's military capabilities and assist in planning and organizing Hezbollah's deployment in southern Lebanon, along the lines of Iranian military doctrine. Under the direction of an elite unit of the Revolutionary Guard, known as the Jerusalem (Quds) Force, the Iranians provided financing (more than $100 million annually), training in Iran and Lebanon, state-of-the-art weapons, and intelligence about Israel. Most troubling for Israel was the long-range missiles supplied to Hezbollah that have the capability of striking targets deep inside Israel, as far as 210 km (120 miles). These rockets cannot be aimed with precision, which places civilian populations at greater risk.[8]

On the eve of the Second Lebanon War, Hezbollah's arsenal had risen to over 20,000 rockets with various ranges. These can be divided into three types:

1. Rockets made by the Iranian arms industry: Rockets with ranges of 25 to 85 miles. These rockets were the source of the strategic threat posed by Hezbollah to the civilian population of northern and central Israel.

2. Rockets produced by the Syrian arms industry: Large, heavy 220mm and 302mm rockets with a range of 42 to 60 miles. The 220mm rockets, equipped with metal pellets, like those that struck the city of Haifa.

3. Short range, 122mm rockets made by Iran, Russia, and China: Russian and Iranian 122mm HE (i.e. high explosive) fragmentation

rockets, 122mm Chinese long-range Grad rockets, and 122mm Chinese cluster rockets. Most of the rockets fired at Israel by Hezbollah have been various types of 122mm projectiles.[9]

4. Other advanced arms and ammunition provided to Hezbollah:

    a. Upgraded Iranian-manufactured anti-tank missiles with a special warhead that can penetrate armor: Some with a range of 3,000 meters (1.86 miles) that can penetrate 400 mm (16 inches) armor; an Iranian version of the U.S. TOW (wire guided missile), with a range of 3,750 meters (2.33 miles) that can penetrate 550 mm (22 inches) steel armor.

    b. Chinese-made coast-to-sea missiles, with a range of 65 nautical miles. This type of missile hit an Israeli missile boat off Israel's coast at the outbreak of the Second Lebanon war, killing four crewmen.

    c. Unmanned air vehicles (UAVs), developed by Iranian industry, including reconnaissance and attack versions carrying warheads.

    d. Motorized hang gliders, some with a range of 100 km (62 miles).

    e. Russian-made SA-7 [shoulder-fired, heat-seeking anti-aircraft missiles] and SA-14 [improved version of the SA-7].[10]

The forgoing array of modern weapons was in the hands of Hezbollah at the outset of the Second Lebanon War. As a prelude to the war, a volley of eight Katyusha rockets was fired deep into Galilee from Hezbollah-controlled territory in Lebanon. The Israeli Air Force responded immediately, striking two bases belonging to the Popular Front for the Liberation of Palestine (PFLP), a pro-Syrian terrorist organization known to operate in collaboration with Hezbollah. The confrontation escalated into heavy exchanges of fire along the Israeli-Lebanese border following a sniper attack by Hezbollah. Israel returned fire, and Hezbollah opened up with artillery and more sniper fire. Israel responded with strikes by fighter aircraft and artillery fire, targeting 20 Hezbollah strongholds along the border. The day ended with a ceasefire arranged by the UN Force in Lebanon.[11]

The Second Lebanon War Begins

The Second Lebanon War began in the morning hours of July 12, 2006. Hezbollah terrorists crossed into Israel from Lebanon. They attacked Israeli forces and civilian communities along the Israeli-Lebanese border. The terrorists ambushed Israelis in two jeeps patrolling along the northern border with Lebanon. The terrorists set off explosive charges and fired anti-tank missiles at the two Israeli vehicles, killing three soldiers and wounding two. Two others Israeli soldiers were abducted by the attackers. Simultaneously, Hezbollah unleashed a massive barrage of rockets on population centers and army posts in northern Israel. An Israeli ground force entered Lebanon in pursuit of the abductors; however, as they crossed into Lebanon their tank was hit by a large explosive charge. The tank was severely damaged, and its four crew members were killed. Later, Israeli infantry and armored forces crossed into Lebanon to recover the tank and came under heavy Hezbollah fire. One Israeli soldier was killed and three were wounded.[12]

On July 13, the second day of the war, the Israeli Air Force struck Hezbollah targets in Lebanon, including headquarters, bases, training camps, installations, posts, and arms depots. They also attacked Hezbollah's TV station and transmission tower in south Beirut. Lebanese targets were not immune from attack. Runways and fuel storage tanks were hit at the Beirut international airport, and an airport in northern Lebanon was targeted.[13] The effectiveness of Israel's war fighting in Lebanon was severely handicapped by Hezbollah's practice of using Lebanese civilians as human shields. Hezbollah constructed a broad military infrastructure within densely populated areas in Lebanon. It was designed to minimize Hezbollah's vulnerability to Israeli attacks. Hezbollah launched thousands of rockets at Israeli cities from positions in close proximity to Lebanese residences and public institutions.[14] Massive salvos of rockets rained down on Israeli cities every day of the fighting. In the 34 days of the war, Hezbollah fired 4,000 rockets into Israeli territory. In all, 53 Israelis were killed by rocket fire alone. Most of the victims were residents of Israel's large cities as far south as Haifa. During the war, Hezbollah's advanced anti-tank weapons were used effectively against Israeli ground forces.[15]

In the course of the war, Israeli forces succeeded in destroying much of Hezbollah's stockpile of long-range rockets, including 309 rocket launchers and inflicting extensive damage to the organization's military headquarters and infrastructure. Israel's aim in the war was to break Hezbollah's military power and reduce its hold on Lebanon, especially in the south. In the aftermath of the war, there was considerable internal criticism of Israel's military performance during the war. However, the ceasefire agreement set forth in UN Security Council Resolution 1701 appeared to have satisfied most of Israel's objectives. Three Lebanese army brigades were transferred to southern Lebanon, and the UN force in southern Lebanon was expanded. Together, these troop deployments pushed Hezbollah further away from the Israeli-Lebanon border. Nonetheless, Hezbollah still had the capability to fire rockets into Israel. With Iran and Syria supplying weapons and pouring large sums of money into its military infrastructure, Hezbollah's military capabilities could be easily rebuilt. One glaring omission from the UN Resolution was the absence of the requirement for the disarmament of Hezbollah or the designation of an authority to enforce an embargo on supplying it with new weapons—meaning that Hezbollah would be free to continue its jihad against Israel.[16]

There is a lesson for Israel and the United States in events leading up to the Second Lebanon War, which is that weakness in the face of terrorists is a fatal mistake. In October 2000, Hezbollah kidnapped three Israeli soldiers during an attack on an Israeli patrol near the border with Lebanon. Hezbollah's leader, Nasrallah, viewed Israel's response to this attack to be weak and feeble. He was amazed by the passive voices in Israel that called for restraint. This, along with Israel's action to pull out of the security zone in Lebanon, reportedly gave Nasrallah the impression that the Israeli people were fearful of being drawn back into another quagmire in Lebanon. As a result, Hezbollah was undeterred in keeping tensions alive with limited attacks on Israel. However, much to Nasrallah's surprise, the abduction of two Israeli soldiers on July 12,

2006, crossed the line, causing Israel to abandon its policy of restraint. The limited response expected by Hezbollah turned into a full-fledged war.[17]

The war took a heavy toll on Israel's civilian population and economy. A total of 159 Israelis lost their lives during the war and 4,262 were wounded. Approximately 530 Hezbollah guerrillas were killed by Israel's armed forces. During the war, one million Israeli civilians were forced to live in bomb shelters, and 350,000 to 500,000 were displaced from their homes. Some 6,000 Israeli homes were hit by rockets. The estimated cost of damage to Israel's economy was $1.6 billion. The total cost of the war was estimated to be $5.3 billion. For a small country with a population of about seven million, this is an enormous financial burden.[18]

Hezbollah Continues Protracted War

In 2006 Hezbollah stepped up its efforts to direct and support terrorist organizations in the Palestinian territories to improve its own capabilities for terrorist operations against Israel. In the first half of 2006, Hezbollah increased the number of its undercover terrorist cells in the territories by 150 percent. At the beginning of the Second Lebanon War, there were approximately 80 of these cells operating in the territories, split between the Gaza Strip and the Judea and Samaria areas in the West Bank. Hezbollah was intent on encouraging Palestinian terrorist groups to pursue their armed struggle against Israel and duplicate the Hezbollah-Lebanese model. Hezbollah went so far as to increase the cash award for a suicide bombing from $20,000 to $100,000. Hezbollah's assistance to Palestinians included smuggling high-quality weapons, military training, financial aid, intelligence, and propaganda. To further its capabilities, Hezbollah set up its own terrorist apparatus in Israel and the Palestinian territories and began recruiting Israeli Arabs to carry out terrorist attacks. Given these efforts to strengthen the Palestinian terrorists, it is not surprising that at the height of the war in Lebanon, Hezbollah urged Palestinian terrorist organizations to attack Israel to open a second front in parallel with the Lebanon-Israeli front. This did not prove to be very successful because Hamas was somewhat preoccupied with forming a new government in the Gaza Strip, and

Israel's counterterrorism operations had been successful in curtailing Hamas's actvities.[19]

As the Second Lebanon War receded, Israel was faced with terrorist organizations on several fronts, most notably Hamas and Hezbollah, each of which had sworn to annihilate Israel and each with growing arsenals of modern weapons and military capabilities supplied by Iran and Syria. Israel was in essence in the midst of an asymmetric conflict not too dissimilar from America's experiences in Vietnam, Iraq, and Afghanistan. Lessons from those wars tell us that this kind of conflict is one of the hardest to win, especially when the enemy is driven by a fervent ideology and based in nearby settlements. For the Israelis, their homes, their cities, and their whole country continue to be the front lines in the battle against terrorism.

The war with Hezbollah terrorists in Lebanon had barely receded when another conflict began looming in the Gaza Strip, where Hamas was preparing to exploit its new arsenal of rockets and mortars supplied by Iran.

Chapter 11

Gaza Operation

Following the Second Lebanon War, Hezbollah was content with licking its wounds and rebuilding the infrastructure and weapons stores that had been destroyed by Israeli forces. Accordingly, as 2007 rolled around, the northern front was relatively quiet. However, this was not the case in the south where Hamas was consolidating its hold on the Gaza Strip. Following its overwhelming victory over the Palestinian Legislative Council in January 2006, Hamas carried out a bloody coup in the Gaza Strip in June 2007, eliminating over 200 of its Fatah rivals. The Palestinian Authority's military and political power was neutralized, leaving Hamas free to set up a radical Muslim entity in the Gaza Strip, named Hamastan. Almost overnight, the Gaza Strip became an autonomous entity, governed by Hamas with the authority to control and direct its own internal and foreign affairs. With the backing of Iran and Syria, Hamas was also capable of conducting a terrorist campaign against Israel without constraints. The formation of an independent jurisdiction, divorced from the Palestinian Authority in Judea and Samaria (West Bank), confronted Israel with a new set of circumstances. Abu Mazen (Mahmoud Abbas), the leader of the PA, now represented only the Palestinians in Judea and Samaria. This meant there was no longer a single Palestinian Authority for Israel to deal with.[1]

Hamas Military Buildup

The rise of an autonomous terrorist regime in Israel's backyard created a national security vulnerability that was very difficult to defend against. This is doubly true when that entity is committed to radical Islam, jihad, and the eradication of the State of Israel through the use of terrorism. Added to this security nightmare was an unlimited amount of modern weapons, training, and funding provided to Hamas by Iran and Syria. The Syrian regime provided a safe base of operations for Palestinian terrorist organizations and allowed their leaders to establish their headquarters inside Syria. Secure in this setting, Hamas was able to plan and conduct terrorist activities from Syrian territory. Hamas maintained a close relationship with Iran and held regular meetings with Iran's senior leadership. It also conducted activities in a number of other countries, including Lebanon and Saudi Arabia, where it received extensive financial and other support. Hamas's tentacles reach into the Arab-Muslim world and European countries through its affiliates and Islamic foundations. There, the activities include spreading propaganda and raising funds—in some cases from Hamas-affiliated "charity associations."[2]

When Hamas came into power in Gaza, it embarked on an accelerated military buildup, with Iran and Syria as the main suppliers. The buildup included:

1. Increasing the size of its forces, which in 2008 was estimated at 20,000 armed operatives directly subordinate to Hamas or who could be integrated into its force in an emergency.

2. Reorganizing its forces into semi-military formations.

3. Carrying out large-scale training operations in the Gaza Strip and beyond, primarily in Iran and Syria.

4. Acquiring advanced weapons, especially improved rockets and advanced anti-tank weapons of the types used by Hezbollah.

5. Improving command and control of the forces deployed throughout the Strip.

6. Preparing the ground for defense, including underground systems for fighting and concealment throughout the Gaza Strip.

7. Developing powerful IEDs and placing them near roads and various locations where fighting against the Israelis was expected.[3]

This buildup increased the threat to Israel. It improved Hamas's capability to carry out complex terrorist operations, such as mass-casualty attacks; it increased the scope, accuracy, range, and force of rockets; it increased the threat to Israel's armored forces; and it increased the capability of Hamas's surface-to-air missiles to destroy Israeli aircraft.[4] The obvious question a reasonable observer might raise is—why does a small entity like Hamas need to embark on a massive buildup of military weapons? The medium to long-range surface-to-surface rockets and mortars that can reach many Israeli cities in Israel are obviously meant for offensive purposes. Most likely, each of them will one day land on Israeli schoolyards, malls, residences, and military bases. There are no other adversaries in the region for Hamas to attack, so again, why the massive military buildup? Just as inexplicable, why have Iran and Syria been spending millions of dollars to prop up Hamas?

Hamas's rise to power brought with it a sharp increase in the rocket and mortar attacks on the Israeli cities and settlements in western Negev region. (See Map 10 at end of chapter for rocket threat from the Gaza Strip.) In 2006 there were 1,423 terrorist attacks in Negev, of which 946 were rocket strikes and 455 were from other kinds of attacks, such as suicide bombings, etc. In 2007 there was a total of 2,319 attacks, of which 896 were rocket hits, 740 were mortar fire, and 683 were other types of attacks.[5] The people in the villages and settlements of the western Negev region were bombarded with rockets from Gaza, lasting as long as 24 hours a day for many days. In May 2007, rocket fire continued for ten consecutive days with a total of 170 hits in the Negev city of Sderot and nearby settlements. Hamas and the Palestinian Islamic Jihad claimed credit.[6] On September 3, 2007, nine rockets were fired at Sderot early in the morning, coinciding with the beginning of the school year. One rocket landed close to a kindergarten school. Another peak period of attacks took place in the first half of December 2007, with a barrage of 66 rockets aimed at western Negev towns and villages. There was also intensive mortar fire with a total of 68 shells fired during the same period.[7]

Another Peace Initiative

While Hamas and other terrorist organizations in the Gaza Strip stepped up their attacks on Israel, efforts were underway at a conference in Annapolis, Maryland, to breathe new life into the peace process. The peace conference, which began on November 27, 2007, was sponsored by the Bush Administration. It brought together Palestinian Authority President, Mahmoud Abbas, and the Prime Minister of Israel, Ehud Olmert, for bilateral meetings, with the United States as the mediator. Building on the Road Map from earlier negotiations, the Annapolis conference had as its objective the final peace settlement to establish a homeland for Palestinian people as part of a two-state solution. Just as they did with the Oslo Accord, Hamas and other Palestinian terrorist groups opposed the Annapolis Conference. Large demonstrations against the conference erupted in Gaza and in Judea and Samaria in the West Bank. Hamas referred to the conference as "the shame and disgrace meeting." Hamas and Iran's Ayatollah Khamenei called for a boycott of the conference. The president of Iran, Ahmadinejad, denounced the conference. The Iranian government hosted a convention of ten Palestinian representatives in Tehran to reject the Annapolis meeting. The conference ended with a pledge to continue the bilateral discussions in the months ahead.[8]

The year 2008 was a peak period of rocket and mortar shelling against Israel. Despite a six-month lull agreement, a total of 3,278 rockets and mortar shells landed in Israeli territory in that year. The explosion in the amount of fire was accompanied by a significant increase in the range of the rockets to a distance of 40 km (25 miles), which brought a number of additional Israeli cities under the threat of attack. The improved rockets smuggled into the Gaza Strip also increased the size of the warheads and amount of fragmentation. The improved mortars also had a greater range and were more accurate.[9] The first month of 2008 saw a sharp escalation in fighting, with the Israeli Air Force carrying out an intensive counterattack on January 15 against squads of mortar launchers in the Gaza Strip. Eighteen Palestinians were killed, mostly Hamas operatives. Hamas retaliated with a massive barrage of rockets at Israeli cities and villages in western Negev. About 60 rocket strikes were recorded along with 40 mortar hits.[10]

On February 27, 2008, there was a new round of escalation by Hamas. On that day a total of 50 rockets were fired at villages in western Negev. Nineteen more were fired into the villages the next morning. One of them hit near Sapir College in western Negev killing one student. Five long-range rockets were fired at the coastal city of Ashqelon; one hit a hospital helipad, and two landed near the power station that provided power to the Gaza Strip. In five consecutive days, 180 rockets were fired.[11] On May 14, another long-range rocket was fired at Ashqelon. It hit a shopping mall located in the center of the city. The rocket struck the top floor where a medical clinic was located. About 100 people were wounded, seven critically, including a mother and her two-year old daughter.[12]

Not all the terrorist attacks on Israel were by rockets and mortars. Suicide bombings, shootings, stabbings, and IEDs were still in the terrorist's arsenal of terror. A few examples follow:

- January 24, 2008: Two terrorists entered the Mekor Hayim High School south of Jerusalem and stabbed two students. The terrorists were killed by two councilors in the room.

- February 4, 2008: A 73-year-old woman was killed and 40 people were wounded when a suicide bomber blew himself up in a shopping center in the southern city of Dimona. A second bomber was shot by a police officer who noticed him reaching for his explosive belt.

- March 6, 2008: a Palestinian terrorist armed with a Kalashnikov assault rifle attacked a center of religious Zionism in Jerusalem. He shot eight students to death and wounded ten others.

- April 9, 2008: Two Israeli civilians were killed and two wounded when Palestinian terrorists attacked an Israeli-controlled border crossing.

- July 2, 2008: An Arab resident of Jerusalem deliberately drove a bulldozer into pedestrians and vehicles in central Jerusalem, overturning and flattening a number of busses and cars. Three people were killed and 66 injured in the attack.

- July 22, 2008: Sixteen people were wounded when a man drove a bulldozer into a bus and four other vehicles in central Jerusalem.[13]

A Lull in Fighting

There were daily rocket and mortar attacks from Gaza and counter-strikes by Israel over the first few months of 2008, until an Egyptian-brokered lull in the fighting became effective in June of that year. The lull arrangement included a halt to terrorism from the Gaza Strip, cessation of Israeli counter-activities in the Gaza, and opening the crossings between the Gaza Strip and Israel. It was also supposed to include Egyptian-sponsored negotiations for the release of the captured Israeli soldier, Gilad Shalit. Hamas was reluctant to exercise its authority over other terrorist organizations in Gaza; consequently, the lull arrangement was violated with sporadic fire on Israel. Moreover, there was no progress in negotiations for release of Gilad Shalit. From the beginning of the lull, Hamas accelerated its training activity and military buildup, and it continued full-scale activities to smuggle weapons and ammunition into the Gaza Strip, all for the purpose of increasing its readiness for a future confrontation with Israel.[14]

The lull resulted in about four months of relative calm, but near the beginning of November it began to break down. On the night of November 4, 2008, Israeli forces foiled a plot by Hamas operatives to abduct Israeli soldiers through a tunnel under the Gaza Strip's security fence. Seven Hamas terrorists were killed and a number were wounded. Six Israeli soldiers were wounded. Hamas responded with a massive rocket and mortar barrage. Another violation of the lull took place on November 12, when Israeli soldiers killed four Hamas operatives who were laying an IED near the border security fence. The terrorist organizations again fired dozens of rockets and mortars into Israeli territory. On November 14, the Israeli Air Force launched counter-strikes, attacking a terrorist squad in the Gaza Strip that was preparing to fire rockets. In reprisal, 17 rockets and seven mortars shells were fired at Israeli towns and villages. Between November 4 and 16, Hamas fired a total of 91 rockets and 38 mortars into western Negev population centers. Several other terrorist organizations in the Gaza Strip joined Hamas in firing rockets and mortars, including the Palestinian Islamic Jihad (PIJ), the Democratic Front and the Popular Front.[15]

The Lull Ends

Senior Hamas spokesmen publicly claimed that their intension was not to end the lull but to respond to Israeli violations. A few days later, they announced their readiness to continue the lull until December, but they claimed they could not impose a ceasefire on other terrorist organizations in Gaza. Not unexpectedly, the erosion of the lull continued with sporadic rocket and mortar fire.[16] There was an abrupt escalation of mortar fire on November 28, 2008. An Israeli patrol opened fire on a group of terrorists placing an IED near the security fence. One operative was killed and four were wounded. Terrorist organizations reacted immediately by launching 17 mortar shells from the northern Gaza Strip. One shell landed in an Israeli military base, wounding eight soldiers, one of them critically. Hamas claimed responsibility.[17] Israel countered by keeping the Gaza Strip crossings closed. Hamas exploited the closing with a propaganda campaign that exaggerated the suffering it caused to the Gazans. At one point, Hamas shut down the main power plant in Gaza, causing blackouts throughout, including hospitals. Israel was blamed for the power failure, and Hamas claimed several deaths were the result of the power outage.[18]

The final days of the lull were met with several bombardments of rockets and mortars, with dozens fired from the Gaza Strip into Israel territory during the first few weeks of December 2008. The Israeli Air Force retaliated with attacks on terrorist targets in Gaza, striking rocket launchers, weapons stores, and workshops manufacturing weapons. A number of the rocket launchers were located in Jabaliya, the main refugee camp in Gaza.[19]

On Friday, December 19, 2008, Hamas unilaterally announced an end to the lull arrangement. The announcement was accompanied by dozens of rockets launched into Israel's population centers by terrorist organizations in Gaza. Concurrently, Hamas initiated an anti-Israel campaign, excusing its attacks on Israel as merely defending themselves and reacting to Israel's aggression.[20] This was an attempt to influence world opinion, while at the same time enlisting Arab-Muslim support for terrorist groups in the Gaza Strip. Hamas's Al-Aqsa TV and Hezbollah's Al-Manar TV broadcast vicious anti-Israeli, anti-Semitic propaganda, and incitement to violence. Hamas representatives in Lebanon and Jordan called for the slaughter of Jews, the murder of Jews in Palestine, and the destruction of the State of Israel. The Gaza Operation was about to begin.[21]

Before moving on to the operation in the Gaza, it is noteworthy to review the events that led to a full-scale conflict between Israel and Hamas and other terrorist groups in the Gaza Strip. The paper, *The Operation in Gaza*, dated July 29, 2009, by the Intelligence and Terrorism Information Center, Tel Aviv, Israel, provides the most succinct and accurate background of the events leading up to the confrontation with Hamas and other terrorist organizations in the Gaza Strip:

> Israel has been engaged in an ongoing armed conflict with Hamas and the other Palestinian terrorist organizations since the massive outbreak of armed terrorist violence and hostilities in October 2000, which the Palestinians have termed the Al Aqsa Intifada [See Chapter Nine]. The terrorist attacks have included suicide bombings in the heart of Israeli cities, shooting attacks of vehicles, murder of families in their homes, and unrelenting rocket and mortar fire on Israeli towns and villages—all told resulting in the death of more that 1,100 Israelis, the wounding of thousands more, and terrorizing millions....
>
> For eight years, Hamas, a terrorist organization avowedly dedicated to the destruction of Israel, has launched deliberate attacks on Israel civilians, from suicide bombings to incessant mortar and rocket attacks. Since October 2000, Hamas and other terrorist organizations

unleashed more than 12,000 rocket and mortar rounds from the Gaza Strip at towns in Southern Israel. Even though Israel withdrew from the Gaza Strip in August 2005, the attacks continued. Israel made repeated diplomatic efforts, including appeals to the UN Security Council to end the violence, but the attacks continued. The deaths, injuries, and—as Hamas intended—terror among the civilian population, including children, were intolerable, particularly as Hamas increased the range and destructiveness of its attacks....

Israel is a sovereign State, with a moral and legal obligation, and an inherent right under international law, to protect its citizens from terrorism. No nation is required to submit to terrorist attacks. Every nation has a right and obligation to stop them. After exhausting other options, that is what Israel sought to do in its operation in Gaza, between December 27, 2008, and January 17, 2009 (the "Gaza Operation," also known as "Operation Cast Lead")—to eliminate the weapons and the infrastructure that Hamas had used to launch attacks against Israeli civilians on thousands of occasions, and to prevent those attacks from recurring....

Hamas has launched terrorist attacks on Israel's civilian population as a weapon of choice in order to achieve its strategic goals—to disrupt negotiations between Israel and the Palestinian Authority and to prevent a peaceful resolution of the conflict in the Middle East. Hamas has sought to paralyze normal civilian life by murdering Israelis and threatening civilian communities in Israel. Hamas has pushed its agenda as expressed in its founding Charter, namely, to destroy and inflict terror upon civilian communities in Israel, and Hamas has sought to promote its long-term agenda as stated in its charter, to exterminate the State of Israel and establish a Muslim state over all the territory of historic "Palestine." The Hamas Charter begins by declaring that "Israel will arise and continue to exist until Islam wipes it out," and rejects all "[peace] initiatives, the so-called peaceful solutions and international conferences," because they "contradict the Islamic Resistance Movement's Ideological position." It emphasizes that there is no solution to the Palestinian problem except jihad....[22]

With the termination of the lull, Israeli civilians, faced with daily attacks on their homes, schools, and work places, hurried to bomb shelters several times a day and lived in constant fear of where the next rockets or mortars might fall. Israeli authorities took a host of measures to protect its citizens, including the establishment of public shelters, fortification of public institutions, and public education for times of emergencies. Special attention was given to schools and hospitals. Schools that did not have adequate shelters and facilities were shut down for the duration of the campaign. Signs clearly marking the nearest shelter were posted in all public places, including supermarkets, shopping malls, educational facilities, government buildings, and hospitals. In many ways this was reminiscent of the conditions in Britain during the bombings in World War II.[23]

Hamas continued launching rockets and mortar rounds at Israeli cities and villages in southern Israel. The rockets had been upgraded so that 200 towns and villages in the western Negev were within range. Near the end of December 2008, Israel's patience ran out. After exhausting other alternatives and issuing warnings of an attack if the rocket and mortar fire from Gaza did not cease, Israel Defense Forces launched a military operation against Hamas and other terrorist organizations in the Gaza Strip.[24]

Operation Cast Lead Begins

On the morning of December 27, 2008, the Israeli Air Force unleashed Operation Cast Lead. Israeli fighter aircraft and attack helicopters struck Hamas terrorist infrastructure in the Gaza Strip, including headquarters, command posts, training camps, weapons stores, and armament manufacturing plants. Special priority was given to rocket and mortar launching sites. In carrying out the air strikes, the Israelis used precision-guided weapons to minimize collateral damage to civilians. In all operations, extensive precautions were taken to protect Palestinian civilians, often at the expense of military advantage and increased risk to Israeli soldiers and airmen. These efforts were frequently frustrated by the terrorist practice of deliberately basing their operations in densely populated areas. Hamas responded to the first day of Operation Cast Lead with intensive rocket and mortar fire. As many as 61 rockets and 33 mortar rounds fell on towns and villages in Israeli territory.[25]

Over the next few days, the Israeli Air Force continued pounding terrorist targets in the Gaza Strip, striking Hamas's military installations, administrative facilities, outposts, rocket and mortar launch sites, weapons production plants, and weapons storage sites. Tunnels used for smuggling weapons into the Gaza Strip from Egypt received priority targeting. On day two, 40 tunnels were hit and dozens more were struck each day of the operation. By December 31, the fifth day of the operation, Israel's air force had carried out 500 sorties, striking about 500 terrorist targets. On that same day, the air force attacked a mosque in Gaza that, according to intelligence reports, was being used as a base for terrorist operations. The strike caused a long series of secondary explosions from weapons stored in the mosque. During the campaign, it was not unusual to find mosques used for such purposes. In another operation on that day, the house of Hamas official, Nizar Ghayan, located in the Jabaliya refugee camp in northern Gaza, was struck by the Israeli Air Force causing many secondary explosions. The house was an arms storehouse with a tunnel underneath for terrorist operatives. Ghayan was killed along with his four wives and one of his sons. The son had been previously sent out on an unsuccessful suicide mission.[26]

The intensity of rocket and mortar fire dropped off on the second day of Cast Lead, probably as a result of the initial air strikes, but the fire accelerated in the next several days. A total of 312 rockets and mortars were fired in the first five days of the operation. Rockets hit Beersheba, known as the capital of the Negev region, where one damaged a kindergarten building. Many other towns in western Negev were struck, including the beach resort of Ashdod and the Village of Mefalsim where a rocket landed in a family's dining room. The effectiveness of the air strikes became evident in the first several days of 2009, with a moderate decline in the amount of rocket and mortar fire.[27]

On January 3, 2009, the eighth day of the air strikes, the ground phase of Operation Cast Lead began. This phase included a large Israeli force composed of infantry, tanks, artillery, engineer corps, intelligence units, and security forces. A sizeable contingent of Israel's Reserve Forces was also called up for participation in the ground operation. The overall goals of the ground operation were to strike at the heart of Hamas's military infrastructure, reinforce Israel's capabilities to deter attacks from the Gaza Strip, and create a better, more stable, long-term security situation around the Strip. The ground operation was supported by Israel's air force and navy. The navy joined the operation to close off the Gazan coastal waters for a distance of 20 miles from the shore, interdicted attempts to infiltrate weapons to the terrorists by sea, and attacked Hamas rocket launching positions in coastal areas. The air force continued strikes against terrorist bases and operations in the Gaza Strip. They hit more tunnels running under the Egyptian-Gaza border and destroyed a number of weapons and ammunition store houses, some of which were again located in mosques and senior Hamas operatives' homes.[28]

During the next week of the operation, January 3-10, the ground operation made steady progress, encountering various levels of resistance, including sniper fire, anti-tank rockets, explosive devices, rocket-propelled grenades, and mortar fire. The terrorists employed a battle strategy that avoided direct confrontation with Israeli forces. They gathered in population centers to draw the Israelis into the heart of densely built-up areas where fighting could be waged in house-to-house combat. In attempting to draw Israeli soldiers into urban areas and refugee camps, the terrorists deliberately exploited civilians as human shields. In a predictable example of the dangers of waging war in a populated zone, the terrorists killed about 40 Palestinian civilians when they hit the wrong target while firing a mortar at the Israelis. Suicide bombers were also a threat to Israeli troops. A paratroop force operating in the northern Gaza Strip shot a charging bomber wearing an explosive belt. The Israeli fire caused the belt to explode, wounding one soldier.

Both male and female suicide bombers were used by Hamas as part of their tactics.[29]

As Operation Cast Lead moved into the third week, the trend toward less rocket and mortar fire continued, with an average of 20 to 30 hits per day in Israeli territory. It was evident that Hamas had suffered a serious blow, but it still retained offensive and defensive capabilities at a lower level. Heavy blows were sustained by Hamas's rocket manufacturing, storage, and launching facilities, but as noted above, Hamas's rocket firing capabilities had not been completely destroyed. In the ground phase, Israeli Reserve Forces were integrated into the operation, which made it possible for the Israelis to broaden their attack and strike more deeply into the terrorist military infrastructure. The terrorists continued to avoid direct confrontation with Israeli forces and retreated into urban areas. Israeli troops encountered various obstacles and dangers as they fought in an urban warfare environment. They uncovered booby-trapped doors and windows. Sometimes entire buildings and their contents had been rigged as bombs. They also found dozens of booby-trapped houses and a large number of booby-trapped schools and mosques. The Israeli Engineering Corps had the job of clearing these traps. In carrying out this dangerous task, they blew up dozens of buildings, tunnels, weapons caches, and weapons laboratories.[30]

The Israeli Air Force continued supporting the ground forces, attacking targets of opportunity, such as rocket and mortar launchers, weapons storehouses, and armed terrorist squads. In the afternoon of January 11, 2008, Israeli aircraft struck 20 tunnels along the Egyptian-Gaza border. As of that day, the 16th day of the campaign, the air force had carried out 2,000 sorties and attacked 1,400 terrorist targets. On another front, Israeli security forces were engaged in counter-terrorism operations in Judea and Samaria in the West Bank, where dissidents demonstrated in support of Palestinians in the Gaza Strip.[31]

Meanwhile, peace proposals were being offered to end the fighting. The United Nations Security Council produced a new resolution on January 9 calling for an immediate ceasefire. French President Nicolas Sarkozy and Egypt's Hosni Mubarak presented a ceasefire proposal to Israel's Prime Minister Ehud Olmert. On January 12, U.S. President George

Bush stressed that a sustainable ceasefire must include an end to Hamas rocket attacks on Israeli towns. Hamas made certain demands before any ceasefire would be acceptable, such as ending Israel's "aggression" and lifting Israel's "siege." Hamas refused to agree to a permanent lull in fighting and would not commit to negotiations that included cessation of smuggling into the Gaza Strip. According to Iranian and Egyptian officials, Iran strongly discouraged Hamas from signing a ceasefire agreement with Israel and threatened to cut off weapons and funds for Hamas if it signed a peace agreement with Israel. A senior Hamas official was opposed to any long-term lull in fighting because such an agreement would hinder the "resistance" movement (terrorism against Israel).[32]

Ceasefire

Israeli forces continued air, naval, and ground operations through January 17, 2009 (day 22 of Operations Cast Lead). During those last few days, rocket and mortar fire from terrorists in the Gaza Strip continued at the rate of approximately 20 rockets and six mortars per day. On the night of January 17, Israel Defense Forces were instructed to cease attacks and hold fire as of 0200 hours, January 18, 2009. As of that date and time, Israel declared a unilateral ceasefire in the Gaza Strip. At first Hamas reacted with belligerent statements and launched more rockets and mortar rounds. Later in the day, the deputy head of Hamas's political bureau announced that Hamas and other terrorist organizations were declaring a ceasefire. Several contradictions in their statements raised questions about their true intentions. One statement indicated that the ceasefire was only applicable within the Gaza Strip, and it would be in effect for only a week to give the Israelis a chance to withdraw their forces from the Strip. Nevertheless, Israel signed the agreement, even though Hamas did not. Prime Minister Olmert made it clear that any future attack on Israel would be met with force.[33]

The day after the ceasefire, Hamas and Iran publicly announced a victory for Hamas and the other terrorist organizations in the Gaza Strip. They claimed Israeli forces did not weaken their military strength. Yet, Iran pledged to continue smuggling weapons into Gaza. Hamas also boasted of killing 80 Israeli soldiers, but according to Israeli casualty figures, ten of their soldiers were killed in action, four by friendly fire. Palestinian sources acknowledged 1,300 dead and over 5,400 wounded. The inference was that these were civilian casualties. The number of terrorists killed in action was not disclosed by Hamas, but based on Israel's daily battle reports, the number was probably well over 1,000 killed and several times that many wounded. As of the end of Operation Cast Lead, four Israeli people (three civilians and one soldier) were killed by rocket and mortar fire, 16 were seriously wounded, and 351 had minor injuries. During the operation, the terrorists fired 571 rockets and 205 mortar shells from the Gaza Strip into Israeli territory.[34]

The end of Operation Cast Lead on February 18, 2009, did not dissuade Iranian-backed Hamas and other terrorists in Gaza from continuing to attack Israel. Terrorist attacks such as setting explosive charges, shootings, and firing anti-tank shells at Israeli forces persisted. Rocket and mortar attacks continued sporadically, with an average of approximately 8 to 12 strikes in western Negev every month throughout 2009 and 2010.[35] Israel had no way of predicting when these attacks might occur; therefore, the Israeli people in the Negev region lived under the constant threat of death and destruction from above. Although Israel retaliated for many of these attacks, it was clear that Hamas was keeping the resistance alive, but below the threshold that would cause Israel to respond with a full-scale attack as it had done during Operation Cast Lead. It was in essence a war of attrition. Charts 1 and 2 at the end of this chapter depict the distribution of rocket and mortar fire into Israel from the Gaza Strip from 2001 to 2010, the increase leading up to Operation Cast Lead, and Hamas's efforts to avoid escalation while waging a campaign of attrition against Israel.

In 2009, Hamas also focused its attention on the political arena. Hamas challenged the legitimacy of Mahmoud Abbas as the president of the Palestinian Authority. The Justice Minister for Hamas announced that any actions and commitments made by Abbas did not obligate the Palestinian people. This raised a serious question about who could represent Palestinians in future matters, particularly peace negotiations.[36] Not long after the Gaza Operation, an international convention was held in Sharm el-Sheikh, Egypt, to enlist donations for rebuilding the Gaza Strip. Seventy representatives of Middle Eastern and other nations attended. The sum of $4.5 billion was pledged. U.S. Secretary of State Hillary Clinton pledged a donation of $900 million for the Gaza Strip and West Bank, to be coordinated with the Palestinian Authority.[37] No mention was made of compensating Israel for the damages done to its homeland by the barrages of rockets and mortars unleashed by terrorists in the Gaza Strip.

The situation in the region after the Gaza Operation was further inflamed by a belligerent, anti-Israeli speech delivered by Syria's President Bashar Assad at an Arab summit meeting on January 16, 2009. His main points, broadcast over Al-Jazeera TV to most Arab nations and around the world, were:

- Israel has based its existence on slaughter, robbery, and destruction, and the premise of its future is genocide. Israel is an enemy which understands only the language of bloodshed. The Israeli aggression in the Gaza Strip is not only a response to rocket fire but a link in a chain of steps toward the establishment of a purely Jewish state from which anyone who is not Jewish will be expelled or destroyed.

- The Arab countries must stand at the side of the residents of Gaza and the "resistance" [terrorist organizations]. The Israeli leaders should be tried so that history will record that they are "racists more dangerous than the Nazis in modern history."

- Israel will never return the land and "rights" of the Arabs unless it is forced to. Therefore, "restoring territory and rights" is the essence of the "resistance" [terrorism] and it is the way to achieve peace.

- Israel has not learned the lessons of history, because "he who has no land has no history." Thus there will be no compromise, no surrender and no withdrawal, and in the end peace will be achieved by force.

- The Arab peace initiative is dead. All the Arab countries must sever relations with Israel, close Israel's embassies and impose a boycott on it.

- Israel's "war crimes" will give birth to fiercer hatred for Israel in coming generations. For every Arab child killed in the Gaza Strip, dozens of "resistance" [fighters] will be born who will hate Israel.[38]

While surrounded by neighbors who refuse to recognize its right to exist and will not abandon the use of terrorism, what are the prospects of peace for Israel? When will their struggle for existence end? When will they be able to put down their swords? The next chapter will unmask the sponsors of terrorism against Israel and their proxies—**The Alliance of Terror.**

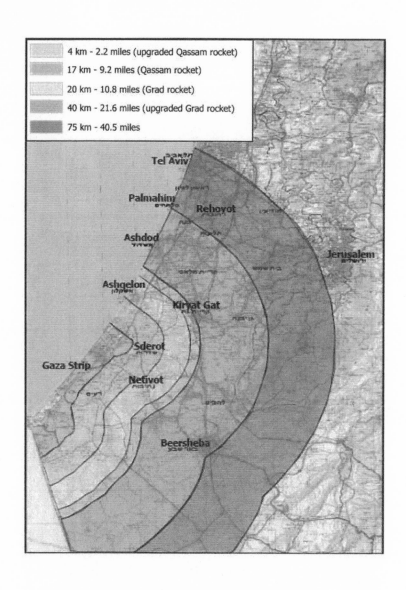

**Map 10. Rocket Threat to the Israeli Home Front from
the Gaza Strip
Source: The Meir Amit Intelligence and Terrorism
Information Center**

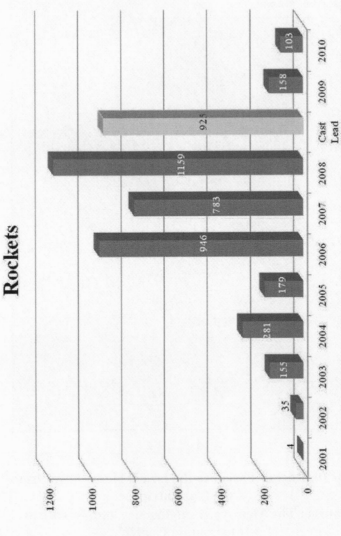

Rockets

Chart 1: Annual Distribution of Rocket Fire into Israeli Territory from the Gaza Strip
Source: The Meir Amit Intelligence and Terrorism Information Center

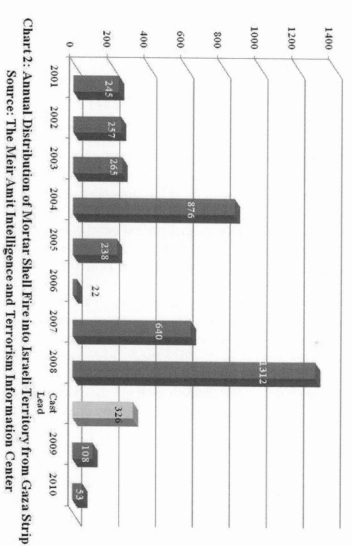

Mortars

Chart 2: Annual Distribution of Mortar Shell Fire into Israeli Territory from Gaza Strip
Source: The Meir Amit Intelligence and Terrorism Information Center

Chapter 12

Alliance of Terror

Since the State of Israel was founded 63 years ago, it has been confronted with every conceivable form of armed attack. Faced with seemingly insurmountable odds, Israel has triumphed in each of these confrontations. However, the volatile nature of today's geopolitics, alliances, ideologies, and technologies present Israel with a new array of threats and challenges. These challenges will be even more perilous than those of the past. One of the main threats to Israel today is the four pillars of evil that make up the *Alliance of Terror—Iran, Syria, Hamas, and Hezbollah*. Iran and Syria are the state sponsors of terrorism and Hamas and Hezbollah are their surrogates and partners in terror. Each of these purveyors of terror has as its primary goal the annihilation and elimination of the State of Israel. The organizational Charts 3 and 4 at the end of this chapter illustrate the relationship of these four pillars of the Alliance of Terror. The personal names in the charts might have changed, but the structure and relationships remain valid.

Iran's Quest for Dominance

Iran, the leader of this alliance, is widely known as the world's leading state sponsor of international terrorism and has been awarded this distinction by the United States for a number of years. While Iran pursues its efforts to wipe Israel off the map, its network of terror reaches into many other parts of the world where it funds, trains, and provides weapons to terrorist groups that aspire to its ideology. Iran makes extensive use of its proxies, Hamas and Hezbollah, to spread its radical Islamic revolution. Iran remains behind the curtains as it instigates and directs terrorist operations. It is important to unveil the true nature and extent of Iran's threat to Israel and other parts of the world. There is ample evidence that Iran has embarked on a quest to expand its influence around the globe and become a major power in the world. Israel is at the tip of the spear of this treacherous plot.[1]

At first glance, Iran's worldwide ambitions and defiance of world powers are reminiscent of the Third Reich, but there are stark and ominous differences. The Islamic Republic of Iran is driven by an ideology that transcends the nation-state. It is a radical revolutionary movement, tasked with fulfilling the ideological mission of jihad in God's (Allah's) way and extending the sovereignty of God's law throughout the world. Thus, the goal of the Iranian regime is not to become a part of the world community but to overpower and dominate it.[2]

Iran's revolution is based on the Islamic worldview and doctrine of its founder, Ayatollah Khomeini. This doctrine consists of an ideology that advocates internal and external revolutionary violence. Khomeini placed jihad (holy war) and shahada (self-sacrifice or martyrdom) at the forefront of his ideology.[3] The crusade to export the Islamic revolution to all Muslim societies (and the rest of the world) was an integral part of the philosophy of Ayatollah Khomeini, who led the revolution and founded the Islamic Republic of Iran in 1979. Khomeini and his followers sought to create a revolutionary Islamic force that would, under Iranian leadership, destroy the "root of evil," the superpowers led by the United States ("the great evil") and its ally, Israel ("the little evil"). For Khomeini and his successor, Ali Khamenei, exporting the revolution is a tool for advancing Iran's strategic interests to achieve regional dominance and further the campaign against Israel and the West.[4]

Iran and Syria view Hezbollah and Hamas as important strategic assets in achieving their national goals. These are summarized below:

- Weakening the State of Israel by forming rifts in its society, damaging its economy by terrorist attacks from the Palestinian Authority-administered territories and from Lebanon, and preventing sustained ceasefires in the campaign of terrorism being waged against Israel. Hezbollah's extensive military infrastructure in Lebanon, especially its significant rocket arsenal, is also meant to serve Iran and Syria's military-strategic objectives, such as reprisal in the event of an attack against Iran or in an armed conflict between Israel and Iran and Syria.

- Strengthening the radical Iranian-Syrian axis in the Middle East and on the international scene by entrenching Iranian and Syrian influence in Lebanon, in the Palestinian Authority, and throughout the entire Arab world. The terrorist organizations are also perceived as a means of strengthening Iran and Syria's status vis-à-vis the United States and Western countries.

- Weakening pro-Western Arab regimes and rulers which are fundamentally hostile to Iran and Syria, such as Fouad Siniora's government in Lebanon and Mahmoud Abbas (Abu Mazen) in the PA-administered territories. At the same time, Iran and Syria strive to strengthen radical Islamic powers in Lebanon, the PA-administered territories, and other Arab countries.

- Ideologically, Iran considers Hezbollah an effective instrument for exporting Khomeini's Islamic revolution, effectively serving Iran's desire to achieve hegemony over the Middle East. The importing of radical Islamic ideology to Lebanese Shiites is so far the only successful example. The Syrian Baath ideology is not as attractive as the Iranian Islamic radical ideology.[5]

The Revolutionary Guard

Iran uses the Quds (Jerusalem) Force, one of five branches of the Islamic Revolutionary Guard Corps, as the spearhead of its revolution. The Quds Force is an elite unit of several thousand or more operatives and is the strongest military-security organization in the country. It was formed in the early 1990s to export the revolution. The Quds Force's primary mission is to advance the Iranian Islamic regime's strategic goals:

- Implementing Iran's ideological-political doctrines, the most important of which are installing Iranian hegemony throughout the Arab-Muslim world, extending Shi'a over all Islam and continuing the campaign to destroy the State of Israel.

- Destroying American supremacy and harming American interests in the Arab-Muslim world in general and the Middle East in particular, through subversion and terrorist attacks against the West and its allies, without, insofar as possible, leaving Iranian footprints.[6]

The Quds Force conducts a wide range of operations, mostly in secret, beyond Iran's borders, including indoctrination programs in Iran's radical ideology, setting up and operating armed terrorist and guerilla cells, and acting to subvert pro-Western Arab-Muslim regimes. It also trains terrorist operatives in the use of a wide range of weapons, tactics, and guerilla operations. It serves as a conduit for funneling funds and weapons to terrorist organizations. It also assists terrorist groups in the deployment of weapons systems and in planning and executing operations. There are reports that Quds operatives hold operational positions within some terrorist organizations, such as Hezbollah.[7]

The Quds Force is not the only Iranian apparatus involved in exporting terrorism. Iran's Intelligence Ministry is well known for its participation in terror activity outside of Iran. Under the diplomatic cover of its embassies throughout the world, it provides funding, technical services, and training of agents for Iranian-supported terrorist organizations. The Iranian Foreign Ministry takes part in spreading the ideology of the Islamic revolution and assists the Intelligence Ministry and the Revolutionary Guard by providing diplomatic cover for their operations. By virtue of its diplomatic status in foreign countries, it is able to provide documentation to terrorist operatives and transfer equipment and weapons via its diplomatic pouch. The Foreign Ministry is believed to have been involved in the preparation for the attacks on the Israeli Embassy and Community Center in Argentina in the 1990s.[8]

Iran's Support of Terrorism

The roots of the Iranian support of Palestinian terrorist organizations are well defined in a paper by the Intelligence and Terrorism Information Center in Tel Aviv:

> Iran adopts a consistent strategy of encouraging and inciting Palestinian violence and terror. It achieves this by closely cooperating with its strategic ally, Syria, also defined by the U.S. State Department as a country that sponsors terror. At the base of this strategy lies the connection between radical Islamic ideology which perceives Israel as an enemy that should be annihilated (the little Satan)—and the perception of Israel as the main threat to Iran's national security and the hegemony it seeks to achieve in the region.
>
> Iranian assistance to Palestine terror is a chief component of the overall use that Iran makes of the weapon of terror as a tool for promoting its national interests. Through encouraging and assisting Palestinian terror . . . the Iranians seek to achieve a number of objectives, including reinforcement of the radical Iranian-Syrian axis in the Middle East; weakening Israel by creating rifts and cleavages in the society and inflicting damage on its economy; causing Israel to direct its resources to the Palestinian conflict, thus detracting from its capabilities against Iran; reinforcing the extremist Islamic forces in the Palestinian territories; and sabotaging any chance of reaching an Israeli-Palestinian settlement and restarting the political process....[9]

Hamas's violent takeover of the Gaza Strip in 2007 fulfilled its goal of establishing a radical Islamic entity in Gaza. This was (and is) clearly in Iran's strategic interest, for it has transformed Gaza into a base from which to export the Iranian revolution and expand its influence in the region. Iran is thus motivated to provide a variety of assistance to Palestinian terrorist organizations, mainly Hamas and the Palestinian

Islamic Jihad. The importance that Iran places on sponsoring Hamas's Islamic regime in the Gaza Strip, and potentially the West Bank, is illustrated by the fact that the Iranian leader, Ali Khamenei, is personally involved in directing the strategic support provided to Hamas by Iran.[10]

Iran's media glorifies the terrorist suicide attacks and encourages continuation of the intifada (uprising) in the Palestinian territories. In exchange for Iranian assistance, Palestinian organizations are obliged to carry out the policies as determined and dictated by Iranian operatives. Large sums of money (as much as $100 to $200 million a year) are transferred to Palestinian organizations to enable and encourage them to continue terrorist activities. Massive quantities of high quality weapons are provided to Palestinian terrorists to enable them to attack Israel, and thousands of operatives have received extensive military training at terrorist camps in Iran and Syria. The Quds Force also operates training camps inside Palestinian territories. As indicated in previous chapters, the weapons given to terrorist organizations are continuously upgraded to increase offensive and defensive capabilities against Israel. Weapons stores are replaced almost immediately after being destroyed by Israeli forces, as in the two intifadas and the recent Cast Lead Operation. In Lebanon, where Hezbollah and other terrorists groups reside, the support by Iran and Syria is quite similar.[11]

The Revolutionary Guard was behind the original establishment of Hezbollah in the early 1990s. As conceived, Hezbollah was to be the spearhead for the Islamic war against Israel. Hezbollah's radical Shiite ideology positioned it as a natural instrument for this role. From its beginning, the Quds Force of the Guard has supported Hezbollah, and in cooperation with Syria, has established a vast military infrastructure in Lebanon with the capabilities of a state instead of a terrorist organization. Iran has pumped hundreds of millions of dollars a year into this operation and has supplied Hezbollah with offensive and defensive weapons, even though UN Resolution 1701, which ended the Second Lebanon War, called for Hezbollah to disarm. Since that war, Iran has supplied Hezbollah with an arsenal of 40,000 rockets, including long-range Zelzal-2 ballistic missiles that can penetrate 124 miles into Israeli territory. Hezbollah's infrastructure was constructed, supervised, and advised by operatives of the Revolutionary Guard. The Guard gave Hezbollah massive support during the most recent war in Lebanon, including the integration of its operatives into Hezbollah's command structure. The supplies of weapons for Hezbollah are transported by air on Iranian aircraft to the international airport in Damascus, with Syrian collaboration. From there they are smuggled over land to Hezbollah in Lebanon.[12]

The Quds Force has a central role in training Hezbollah operatives at Revolutionary Guard's bases in Iran. There are as many as 20 terrorist camps and centers operated by the Revolutionary Guard in Iran. The two camps used mostly for training foreign terrorists are the Imam Ali camp in Tehran and the camp at Bahonar near Karaj, north of Tehran. There, operatives are trained to use modern weapons that Iran provides them. The operatives undergo training in integrated maneuvers, firing anti-tank and anti-aircraft weapons, and operating advanced weapons, such as ground-to-ground rockets used to strike deep into Israel. Hezbollah terrorists captured by Israeli forces during the second Lebanon war disclosed they were trained in Iran along with many others from Lebanon. Their passports were not stamped by Syria or Iran to hide their travel to Iran.[13]

Syria's Support of Terrorism

Syria, along with Iran, has consistently supported Hezbollah and the Palestinian terrorist organizations to further its strategic goals, which include:

> Strengthening the radical Iranian-Syrian axis in the Middle East; weakening Israel economically and militarily; strengthening Syria's influence in Lebanon; strengthening radical Islamic forces in the Palestinian Authority; and sabotaging agreements and arrangements in Lebanon and the PA which are not consistent with their interests.[14]

Since Hezbollah's early formation by Iran, Syria has viewed it as an important tool in its struggle against Israel. The Syrian regime has helped establish Hezbollah in Lebanon and supported it against Israel and other opponents. In compliance with the Taef Accord, which ostensibly brought the Lebanese civil war to an end, Syria was supposed to disband and disarm all militias operating in Lebanon. However, Hezbollah was allowed to continue to operate unchecked with the acquiescence and even support of Syria. Over time, Hezbollah evolved into an influential force in Lebanese internal affairs and a major terrorist organization aligned against Israel. Hezbollah evolved from a tool against Israel to a strategic partner and a major player in Syrian and Lebanese politics.[15]

When Syria was pressured by the international community to remove its forces from Lebanon in April 2005, after 30 years of occupation, Hezbollah became even more important to Syria. Without a military presence in Lebanon, Syria increased its support of Hezbollah, complementing the massive arms received from Iran. Syria's buildup of weapons for Hezbollah has included Syrian-made rockets with large warheads and long-ranges, advanced anti-tank missiles, and the latest version of the Russian-made man-portable surface-to-air missile system, the SA-18.[16] This advanced version of the man-portable missile system has improved tracking and countermeasures, which make it a greater threat to Israel's low flying planes and helicopters.

Hezbollah as a Political Force

Backed by Syria's political power over the weak Lebanese government, Hezbollah was free to seize military and political control of southern Lebanon and several areas of the Beqa'a Valley region. These areas of Lebanon essentially became a Hezbollah state-within-a-state. Hezbollah has set itself up, with Syria's acquiescence, as the main power broker in the region, unhindered by the Lebanese regime or the UN international peace force in the area. Hezbollah has infiltrated the political arena in Lebanon and has become a major political party in Lebanon's cabinet and parliament. Hezbollah, motivated by its Syrian and Iranian puppet masters, actively sought to subvert the political process in Lebanon. In 2007 Hezbollah boycotted the Lebanese parliament in an attempt to topple the pro-Western government. On numerous occasions, Hezbollah has also actively assisted Syria in preventing the election of a pro-Western president in Lebanon. In 2008, in an effort to gain more power in the Lebanese government, Hezbollah demanded and received 11 of the Lebanese cabinet's 30 seats and insisted on having veto power in the parliament's cabinet. Evidence of Hezbollah's growing influence is illustrated by the political crisis it created in January 2011 when it toppled the Western-backed Lebanese government and essentially took control of Lebanon's parliament. The invisible hand of Iran is undoubtedly behind this move. Hezbollah considers Iran and its leader Khamenei to be the highest source of authority guiding its activity and policy; accordingly, Hezbollah's actions are consistent with Iran's goal to transform Lebanon into an Iranian radical Shiite entity.[17]

Syria, which has been on the U.S. State Sponsor of Terrorism list since 1979, not only sponsors Hezbollah but continues to support Hamas and other terrorist organizations, such as the Palestinian Islamic Jihad (PIJ) and the Popular Front for the Liberation of Palestine (PFLP). When Hamas was expelled from Jordan in 1999, it was granted permission by Syrian officials to establish its headquarters in Syria. Since then, the Syrian regime has maintained close ties with the Hamas leadership and is involved in forming terrorist policies. The regime also encourages the continuation of the terrorism campaign against Israel. Syria actively provides military support to Hamas, including arms and funds that are often funneled through Hezbollah in Lebanon. Syria complements Iran's programs to train terrorist operatives. By March 2008, 650 Hamas operatives had been trained in Syria in that year alone, and another 62 were in Syrian camps undergoing training.[18]

Projecting the Arm of Terror

Although Syria and the other pillars of the "Alliance of Terror" have as their main objective the destruction of Israel, they share the same ideological vision for spreading radical Islam far beyond their borders. Iran is actively expanding its terror network on a global scale. It has been undermining U.S. and coalition forces in Iraq. Its clerics, Quds agents, and Hezbollah operatives have been involved in sabotaging U.S. and allied efforts in the region by provoking sectarian violence, gathering intelligence, providing millions of dollars, and supplying arms and training for enemy insurgents. Iranian-made explosively-formed penetrators (EFPs) especially designed to penetrate armor have been responsible for an untold number of U.S. combat casualties. Insurgents used rockets bearing Iranian markings to attack U.S. and coalition forces. Moreover, the Iranian Quds Force has been engaged in improving the operational capabilities of the elements in Iraq that oppose the Iraqi government and the remaining coalition forces. This will enable dissidents to carry out attacks directed by Iran. From behind the scenes, the Iranians are determined to strengthen their influence over Iraq and undermine the United States and coalition influence.[19]

At a hearing before the U.S. Senate Armed Services Committee on February 27, 2007, the Director of National Intelligence, Mike McConnell, made the following comments concerning the Quds Force's involvement in Iraq: "We know that Quds Forces are bringing them [Iranian manufactured weapons] into Iraq."[20] McConnell submitted that a large quantity of the weapons entering Iraq came through Syria, and attributed it to Iranian-Syrian collaboration. Most importantly, McConnell made a strong case that (as of the hearing) 170 American soldiers had been killed as a result of these weapons supplied by the Iranian Quds Force.[21] This number does not include the soldiers of the allied coalition who have been killed or injured by Iranian-made weapons. McConnell's report implicating Iranian and Syrian support for insurgents in Iraq raises a troubling question: What has the United States and its coalition partners done to stop, or at least discourage, Iran and Syria from sabotaging the war effort in Iraq?

Iran has also extended its long arm of terror into Afghanistan where it provides weapons to the Taliban for use against NATO forces. Iran has given the Taliban powerful mortars, rocket propelled grenades (RPGs), explosives, small arms, and surface-to-air missiles. The missiles present a grave danger to U.S. and NATO aircraft. Iran is also known to support certain warlords and drug traffickers in Afghanistan. Iranian operations in Afghanistan are carried out covertly, while at the same time Iran publicly supports the legitimate government in Afghanistan.[22] Here again very little has been done by U.S. and NATO to discourage Iran's efforts to undermine the fight against the Taliban.

Iran and its proxies have expanded their reach into Europe and beyond. The European Union (EU) has uncovered 800 Iranian-sponsored

Hezbollah operatives residing in Germany and sleeper cells in 20 EU nations. Hezbollah operatives in Europe's capitals conduct fundraising and intelligence gathering activities. Iran uses small groups linked to the Revolutionary Guard to recruit potential suicide bombers for operations in Israel, Europe, and the United States. Evidence suggests that Hezbollah has planned possible terrorist attacks in Rome and Paris and considered kidnapping high level officials. In the 1990s, Iran sent arms to the Muslim government in Bosnia. Between 2004 and 2007, while the conflict raged in that area, Iran is reported to have sent Iranian operatives into Bosnia-Herzegovina.[23]

In the Asian region, Iran has maintained close ties with North Korea and has established cultural and scientific agreements with that nation. North Korea has shared its nuclear technology with Iran and provided arms and training to Hezbollah. North Korea, Syria, and Iran have jointly conducted rocket experiments and tests of Scud missiles.[24] Considering Iran's ambition to acquire nuclear weapons and a missile delivery system, its close ties with nuclear North Korea are cause for alarm.

In the past few years, Iran has intensified its activities in Central and South America. A recent Rand Corporation study indicates that the tri-border area of Brazil, Argentina, and Paraguay has become the most important financing center for Islamic terrorism outside the Middle East. Hezbollah is active in the region and maintains a regional base in Venezuela, from which it recruits terrorists and indoctrinates others in radical Islamic views. Iranian-backed Hezbollah is suspected of being responsible for the attack on the Jewish Center in Buenos Aires, Argentina, in 1994 in which 85 people were killed and 300 were injured. The Iranian-backed Islamic Jihad claimed responsibility for the bombing of Israel's Embassy in Buenos Aires, Argentina, in 1992 in which 29 were killed and 242 wounded.[25]

Brazil and Iran have expanded their economic and political ties. The volume of trade between the two nations quadrupled between 2002 and 2007. In 2007 Brazil's president publicly announced support for Iran's nuclear energy program. Iran has expanded its relationship with Bolivia, giving that nation more than $1.1 billion in industrial cooperation funds in the past several years. During the Gaza Operation, which ended in January 2009, Bolivia severed ties with Israel in protest of Israel's actions. A report in the *Associated Press* last year raised suspicions that Bolivia was providing uranium to Iran for its nuclear program. According to a U.S. Justice Department report, Columbian and U.S. law enforcement agents broke up an Iranian-backed Hezbollah drug trafficking operation with ties that reach into Europe and the United States. As late as March 2009, the commander of U.S. forces in Latin America expressed concern over the level of Iranian and Hezbollah activities in the region: "We have seen in Columbia a direct connection between Hezbollah and the narco-trafficking activity."[26]

Cuba and Iran have signed an economic cooperation agreement to promote Iranian exports, along with engineering and technical services for Cuba. Ecuador and Iran have agreed to economic and military cooperation. In 2009 military instructors from Iran (probably the Revolutionary Guard) specializing in guerrilla and anti-guerrilla warfare were scheduled to begin supervising the Ecuadorian military. Iranian-backed Hezbollah has used the Mexican border to enter the United States. Arrests were made in Mexico in 2002 of traffickers who smuggled 200 Lebanese into the United States, many of whom were suspected of having ties to Iranian-backed Hezbollah. According to a *Washington Times* story in March 2009, Hezbollah is smuggling drugs and people across the U.S. border for profit and developing ties with drug cartels. In Nicaragua, President Ortega has allowed 21 Iranians into the country without visas. Iranian officials assigned to Iran's embassy in Managua have immunity to travel anywhere without restrictions. U.S. officials fear that the secluded Iranian embassy will become a hub for importing weapons.[27]

In the 2009 elections in Panama, the defeat of the left-wing candidate, Herrera, of the Democratic Revolutionary Party, probably saved that nation from joining Venezuela in a strategic alliance with China and Iran against the United States. Fortunately the winner, Ricardo Martinelli, leans to the right. Hezbollah's operation in Paraguay funnels large sums of money to militia groups in the Middle East and finances training camps, propaganda operations, and bomb attacks in South America. Iran and Venezuela have sponsored fund-raising efforts in the Muslim areas of Paraguay, helping leftist Fernando Lugo to be elected in 2008. In 2007 the Uruguayan government was discovered attempting to purchase munitions from Iran. The transaction was diverted through Venezuela to bypass UN sanctions on Iran. Iran's President Ahmadinejad met with the Uruguayan ambassador in 2008, vowing that Iran was determined to broaden relations with Uruguay.[28]

The relationship between Iran and Venezuela bodes dangers for Latin America, the United States, and the West. Iran and Venezuela have strategic alliances that join the two countries at the hip in many ways:

- Iranian officials are involved in every sector of Venezuela's economy.

- Venezuelan businesses launder money for Hezbollah. In 2008 the U.S. Treasury Department froze assets of a Venezuelan diplomat and a prominent businessman with connections to terrorist group funds.

- Since 2001, Iran and Venezuela have signed more than 180 trade agreements worth more than $20 billion in potential investment.

- In early 2007, Iran and Venezuela set up a $2 billion Liberation Fund for countries wishing to free themselves from supposed "U.S. domination." Ahmadinejad said Iran and Venezuela are *"promoting revolutionary thought in the world."*

- In November 2007, Chavez and Ahmadinejad signed four memorandums of understanding with the intention of creating a joint bank, a fund, an oil industry technical training program, and an industrial accord.

- In March 2007, IranAir began operating flights on a Tehran-Damascus-Caracas route. The following October, Venezuela's state–run airline, Conviasa, also began such a route. A Syrian official said the flights were a way to circumvent the "harassment" that Muslim travelers were undergoing after September 11, 2001.

- In December 2008, the Italian newspaper *La Stampa* reported that several Conviasa flights had transported intelligence officials, military officers and materials banned by the UN, including components for Iran's ballistic missile program.

- Iranian diplomats, as well as members of Hezbollah and Iran's Revolutionary Guard, can now fly directly to Venezuela and then to other Latin American countries. In fact, members of Hezbollah are flying back and forth. U.S. intelligence suggests that Hezbollah and the Iranian Revolutionary Guard have a task force in place to kidnap Jewish travelers in Venezuela and ship them via IranAir to Lebanon.

- The recently appointed Minister of Interior and Justice in Venezuela was accused of giving false documentation and illegally issuing passports to members of Hamas and Hezbollah.

- In September 2009, Chavez made his eighth official visit to the Islamic Republic of Iran, during which he agreed to export 20,000 barrels of gasoline a day to Iran. This will help to ease Tehran's fuel deficiency resulting from international sanctions.

- In October 2009, Chavez announced that Iran is helping Venezuela to explore and eventually mine its uranium deposits. Chavez is seeking Iran's help to develop a "nuclear village." On another note, Russia and Venezuela recently signed an agreement for Russia to build Venezuela's first nuclear power plant.[29]

From the foregoing information, it is evident that the "Alliance of Terror" has a global reach, while at the same time Iran and Syria have been arming and training their proxy terrorist organizations for attacks on Israel. The massive buildup and upgrade of weapons for Hamas and Hezbollah in recent years does not suggest that they are ready for peace talks with Israel. Not one member of the "Alliance of Terror" has participated in the recent peace process that began in Annapolis, Maryland, in September 2009. On the contrary, these purveyors of terrorism have opposed, undermined, and attempted to sabotage this latest peace process, just as they have done with each of the many attempts over the past years to negotiate a peace settlement in the Middle East. Every indication is that they will continue their efforts to destroy Israel.

With Hezbollah's recent seizure of Lebanon's parliament and Hamas's control of Gaza, Israel now has two terrorist organizations lawfully constituted on its borders. This puts Israel in an extremely vulnerable national security position. However, it could get worse. Since taking over Gaza, Hamas has been challenging the legitimacy of the Palestinian Authority (PA) and infiltrating agents into Judea and Samaria, the areas of the West Bank under the PA's control. With the backing of Iran, Hamas has set its sights on becoming the sole representative of the Palestinians and acquiring jurisdiction over all of the Palestinian territories.[30]

A related development that bodes ill for Israel recently came to light. On April 27, 2011, Hamas officials in Gaza and the Palestinian Authority's Fatah party in the West Bank announced they have reached a power-sharing agreement that calls for a single caretaker government to administer day-to-day business until new presidential and legislative elections can be held next year. This means that a terrorist organization, which has for years called for the destruction of Israel, will be part of the Palestinian Authority government. It is worth recalling that Hamas came to power by winning a landslide victory in the 2006 elections for the Palestinian Authority's Legislative Council. Hamas defeated its main rival, Fatah, by 74 to 45 council seats. If the past is any indication, Hamas will subvert the democratic process and gain control of the Palestinian Authority and all of the Palestinian territories, including the West Bank. If these events come about, Israel would be in extreme danger.[31]

Fatah came into being in the mid-1960s as a faction of the PLO. From the beginning, it was a terrorist organization that carried out numerous attacks on Israel. Its stated purpose was the liquidation of Israel. Its goals are outlined in its political program, included in Appendix D. While under Yasser Arafat's control, the Palestinian Authority and Fatah reportedly moderated their stance against Israel; however, the power sharing with Hamas seems to have changed that. During a meeting of the Arab league on May 28, 2011, Mahmoud Abbas, President of the Palestinian Authority, said that there will be no Israel at all in the future Palestine.[32] The *Jerusalem* Post reported on June 2, 2011, that Azzam al-Ahmed, a member of the Fatah Central Committee and close associate of President Abbas, commented in an interview with an Egyptian newspaper, "Fatah has never recognized Israel's right to exist and will never do so."[33]

The reconciliation agreement does not require Hamas to recognize Israel's right to exist and end the violence. During the signing ceremony for the agreement, on May 4, 2011, Hamas vowed that it will continue to use violence. This is consistent with the Hamas charter which rejects peaceful efforts to end the Israeli-Palestinian conflict and calls for the destruction of the State of Israel....[34] The clear and obvious question that stands out is, how can Israel or any other nation negotiate a peace agreement with an entity that vows to destroy it? Any agreement including Hamas would be like signing a pact with the devil. Is it any wonder why Israel refuses to bow to the pressure from the Obama Administration to accept a peace agreement with the Palestinians based on the pre-1967 borders? Israeli officials echoed these thoughts:

> Israeli Prime Minister Benjamin Netanyahu said on May 4, 2011, that the reconciliation agreement is "a tremendous blow to peace and a great victory for terrorism.... The only way we can make peace is with our neighbors who want peace. Those who want to eliminate us, those who practice terror against us, are not partners for peace."[35]

> Israeli President Shimon Peres also denounced the agreement. "The agreement between Fatah and the

terrorist organization of Hamas is a fatal mistake which
will prevent the establishment of a Palestinian state, and
destroy the chances of achieving peace and stability in
the region."[36]

In a broader arena, Israel is in the midst of a volatile Middle East. The
unrest in Egypt and Syria is of special concern since these two states
have common borders with Israel. Under Egypt's previous regime,
there was a long-standing peace treaty with Israel, and there was some
control over the infiltration of weapons across the border into the Gaza
Strip. Soon after President Mubarak was removed from office, the
military caretaker government of Egypt lifted the blockade of the Gaza
Strip and began allowing travel between Egypt and Gaza. It remains to
be seen if Egypt's soon-to-be elected government will become aligned
with Hamas and continue the open border with the Gaza. If it does, it
would seriously undermine Israel's security, for it would likely mean
the unrestricted flow of terrorists and weapons into the Gaza Strip.[37]

If the events unfold as suggested above, Israel's future could be in
grave peril. However, there are even greater dangers for Israel on the
horizon.

The Organizational structure of Hezbollah

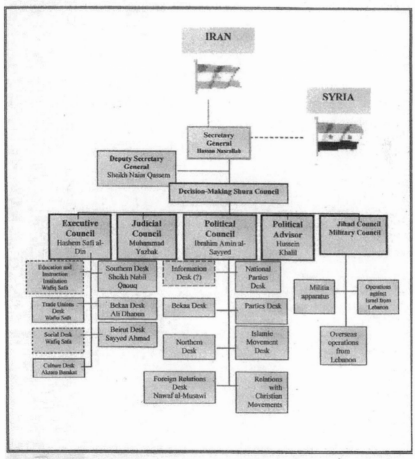

IRAN

SYRIA

Secretary General
Hassan Nasrallah

Deputy Secretary General
Sheikh Naim Qassem

Decision-Making Shura Council

| Executive Council Hashem Safi al-Din | Judicial Council Muhammad Yazbak | Political Council Ibrahim Amin al-Sayyed | Political Advisor Hussein Khalil | Jihad Council Military Council |

Education and Instruction Institution Wafiq Safa

Trade Unions Desk Wafiq Safa

Social Desk Wafiq Safa

Culture Desk Akram Barakat

Southern Desk Sheikh Nabil Qaouq

Bekaa Desk Ali Dhaoun

Beirut Desk Sayyed Ahmad

Information Desk (?)

Bekaa Desk

Northern Desk

Foreign Relations Desk Nawaf al-Musawi

National Parties Desk

Parties Desk

Islamic Movement Desk

Relations with Christian Movements

Militia apparatus

Operations against Israel from Lebanon

Overseas operations from Lebanon

Chart 3. Hezbollah's ties with Iran and Syria. Intelligence and Terrorism Center (ITIC) at the Center for Special Studies (C.S.S.). Hezbollah (Part). 6/2003.

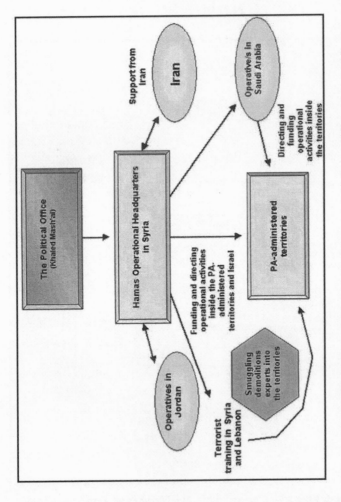

Chart 4. Hamas's Operational Structure and ties with Iran and Syria. Source: Intelligence and Terrorism Center (ITIC) at the Center for Special Studies (C.S.S.). Hamas: Portrait of a Terrorist Organization. 9/1/2004

Chapter 13

Dangers on the Horizon

Danger is nothing new to the people of Israel. Most have lived with it throughout their lives. The dangers were not always the same; for example, the threat of large armies invading Israel's homeland is not as likely today as it was in the past. However, there are dangers that Israel faces today and in the near future that pose a serious threat to its existence. Iran's quest for nuclear weapons is the greatest threat to Israel's survival.

In an interview on March 23, 2011, direct from Jerusalem on Israeli Television Channel 2 News, Israel's Prime Minister, Benjamin Netanyahu, made these comments to a question about the biggest problem facing Israel: "The greatest mission we have is to prevent a militant Islamic regime from meeting up with nuclear weapons, and nuclear weapons from meeting up with a militant Islamic regime." He added that the first comment related to Iran and the second referred to Pakistan, with its stockpile of nuclear weapons, being taken over by a militant Islamic group like the Taliban. He emphasized that we have to stop them from getting nuclear weapons, and this was the greatest mission for this and the next generation.[1]

Countdown to the Bomb

The main issue about Iran's nuclear program is not if, but when, the development of a nuclear bomb will be completed. Among major Western military and intelligence agencies, there is little doubt that Iran has been pursuing a nuclear weapons program for a number of years. Iran still denies the existence of any nuclear program other than for peaceful purposes. If this were true, why has Iran gone to such lengths to keep secret most aspects of its nuclear program? Why do the Iranians refuse to fully disclose their activities to the UN International Atomic Energy Agency (IAEA)? It is obvious that Iran has much to hide. Experts have differing opinions about when Iran will be able to build its first nuclear bomb.

In May 2010, the IAEA disclosed that Iran had accumulated over two tons of low-enriched uranium, which would be enough to build two nuclear warheads when enriched to weapons grade (90%). The IAEA inspectors stated in February 2010 that they had extensive evidence of past or current undisclosed activities by Iran's military to develop a nuclear warhead. The former Director of IAEA, General El Baradei, revealed in November 2007 that Iran had a blueprint for a nuclear warhead, which was provided by the rogue Pakistani nuclear scientist, A. Q. Khan, in the 1990s. As far back as May 2007, El Baradei stated that Iran could acquire nuclear weapons within three years.[2]

In January 2007, the London–based International Institute for Strategic Studies reported that Iran was two to three years away from having the capacity to build a nuclear weapon. In that same year, the former head of the United States National Intelligence, John Negroponte, indicated that it was more likely that it would be four years before Iran would have the necessary capacity to produce a nuclear weapon. The International Institute for Strategy Studies estimated that by 2009 Iran would have produced enough low-grade uranium, which if further enriched, could be enough material for one nuclear bomb. According to the Institute, further enrichment to produce weapons-grade uranium would take at least 12 months. The Institute also reported that Iran had stockpiled enough un-enriched uranium for 30 to 50 weapons.[3]

In 2009, *The Times* (London) reported that it had obtained confidential intelligence documents that described an Iranian test program for a neutron initiator, which is the component of a nuclear bomb that triggers an explosion. According to the report, independent experts confirmed there was no other possible use for this device except in a nuclear weapon.[4]

In an article updated September 7, 2010, the *New York Times* reported, "Top American military officials said in April 2010 that Iran could produce bomb-grade fuel for at least one nuclear weapon within a year but would most likely need two to five years to manufacture a workable atomic bomb."[5]

A report posted on *Arutz Sheva*—IsraelNationalNews.com, January 25, 2010, states:

> A secret intelligence dossier currently being reviewed by U.S., Israeli, German, and Austrian governments reveals secret Iranian tests and hierarchies of power dedicated to the successful development of a nuclear bomb, and predicts that Iran will have a primitive nuclear bomb by years end....

> According to this classified document featured in Germany's *Der Spiegel* magazine, Iran is well on its way toward obtaining its first nuclear bomb. The country's nuclear research program, it turns out, has a military wing answering to the Defense Ministry which the West was not aware of until now....[6]

There are conflicting assessments among Israeli intelligence officials about the status of Iran's nuclear program. Israeli news media reported on January 7, 2011, that retiring Mossad chief, Meir Dagan, recently said he believes Iran will be unable to acquire a nuclear weapon until 2015. Dagan suggested that this delay was the result of the Stuxnet computer worm that has damaged Iran's centrifuges along with tougher economic sanctions. Dagan added that the Iranians are moving full steam ahead, and speculating about dates was a mistake.[7] Less than a week later, Iian Mizahi, a senior Mossad official, stated that Iran's nuclear program may be further along than some Israeli Intelligence officials accept.[8]

Israel's Prime Minister, Benjamin Netanyahu, is reported to have been displeased with the retiring Mossad chief's public comments about the status of Iran's nuclear program. He made his feelings known on January 11, 2011, when he told foreign correspondents: "I think that intelligence estimates are exactly that, they are estimates. They range from best to worst case possibilities, so I think there is room for some differing assessments." He went on to say, "They [Iranians] are determined to move ahead despite every difficulty, every obstacle, every setback, to create nuclear weapons."[9]

The most credible assessment of the status of Iran's nuclear program is included in a clear and convincing report released on January 21, 2011, by the Federation of American Scientists (FAS), an independent, nonpartisan think tank that studies national and international security issues, located in Washington, D.C. Analysis by FAS experts in nuclear weapons proliferation, using IAEA data, shows that the total enrichment capacity of Iran's enrichment facility at Natanz grew during 2010 relative to previous years. The effective production capability in 2010 is estimated to be a 60 percent increase over 2009. The FAS study concludes that the quickest way Iran could achieve a breakout potential (the time required to make a bomb) would be to further enrich its stockpile of low-enriched uranium to bomb-grade uranium. This scenario would take from five months to a year to produce enough highly-enriched uranium to make a single crude bomb. The report suggests that this is not a viable option, but if Iran continues to increase its total enrichment capacity and improve performance, it could have a significant effect on the time to acquire a bomb.[10] In essence, the FAS report contradicts the claims that the Stuxnet worm has had a significant impact on Iran's enrichment program.

The delivery system is another aspect of the timetable for Iran's acquisition of nuclear weapons capability. The *Artuz* article previously cited estimates that it will take two to four years to compress the primitive bomb into a size capable of fitting into a nuclear warhead. This projection assumes that the nuclear weapon would have to be carried by a long-range missile; however, there are other ways to deliver such a weapon to Israel.

(1) It could be dropped from an aircraft,

(2) It could be smuggled into Israel in a vehicle, or

(3) It could be brought into an Israeli port via a boat or ship.

Accordingly, the anticipated timeline for a possible nuclear strike on Israel does not need to be based on the time required to design a bomb to fit into a missile. The tight lid of secrecy over Iran's nuclear program and other internal affairs make it difficult, if not impossible, for anyone outside Ahmadinejad's inner circle to know exactly when the nuclear threat will materialize. It is even more impossible to predict what the radical leaders of Iran will do with the bomb once they have it. That is why it is crucial for Israel, the United States, and the international community to know as much as they can about those in Iran who are making the decisions.

Iran's Radical Leaders

The Supreme Leader, Ayatollah Ali Hoseini Khamenei, was selected by Iran's Assembly of Experts in 1989. The Supreme Leader is viewed as Allah's divine representative on earth. The word and decision of the Supreme Leader are, therefore, the word and decision of Allah on earth. Anyone who questions the Supreme Leader is a traitor and an apostate. It has been suggested that Ayatollah Khamenei selected Ahmadinejad as president because of his fervor for spreading the Islamic revolution worldwide.[11] Iran's President Ahmadinejad dictates state policy according to the Ayatollah's guiding hand and his own radical interpretation of theology. He exercises dominance over the regime on the basis that God selected him to hasten the return of the messiah, or Mahdi, who will install a global Islamic kingdom after an apocalypse in which all non-believers are eradicated. President Ahmadinejad also believes his government must prepare Iran for the Mahdi's imminent return. The most frightening characteristic of Ahmadinejad is that he believes it is his duty to trigger a period of chaos, war, and bloodshed which will lead to the coming of the Mahdi, who will eventually rule the world.[12]

The Mahdi, also known as the Missing Imam, the Twelfth Imam, and the Hidden Imam, is said to have disappeared down a well when he was five years old in the ninth century. His return is believed to bring world peace by installing Islamic law through a global caliphate, after an

apocalypse in which all the "infidels" are killed. Ahmadinejad claims
to have a "private personal channel" to the Mahdi and called for his
re-emergence in his speech before the UN in September 2005. When
he invoked the name of God, the almighty, the merciful, during that
speech, one of the members of his group told him he saw a light around
him, and he was placed inside an aura. He claims to have felt it himself.
Ahmadinejad is reported to have said that Islam will conquer all the
mountain tops of the world. In one of his prophetic statements, he is
quoted as saying, "We must prepare ourselves to rule the world, and the
only way to do that is to put forth views on the basis of the Expectation
of Return [the return of the Mahdi or Twelfth Imam]."[13]

Juxtapose Ahmadinejad's maniacal belief in the Twelfth Imam with
the numerous public statements he has made about annihilating Israel,
and his intentions become crystal clear. Here is just a sampling of his
rantings:

- As the Imam said, Israel must be wiped off the map.

- Israel is a disgraceful stain on the Islamic world and a rotten
  tree that will be eliminated by one storm. [Possible reference to
  a nuclear detonation]

- Like it or not, the Zionist regime is heading towards
  annihilation.

- The annihilation of the Zionist regime will come...Israel must
  be wiped off the map...And God willing, with the force of God
  behind it, we shall soon experience a world without the United
  States and Zionism.

- Thanks to the grace of God and (the Iranian people) resistance,
  we are on the final stage of the path to the nuclear peak. Not
  more than one step is left to be taken. By the end of the year,
  we will organize a celebration across the country to mark the
  stabilization of our nuclear rights.[14]

It is clear that Iran will not relent on its quest to acquire nuclear weapons. The Iranian officials reject UN resolutions relating to its nuclear programs and insist that the sanctions are of no consequence. This leaves very few alternatives, if any, to prevent Iran from becoming a nuclear power, with all its ramifications for Israel, the United States, and the international community. Consequently, the road ahead is fraught with great dangers, some of which are discussed below.

Preemptive Strike

A preemptive strike against Iran's nuclear facilities could be seen by the Israelis as their only option, once it is certain that Iran has, or is close to having, a nuclear device. Israel cannot afford to disregard the numerous threats that Iran has made. It would be inviting destruction to just sit back and wait for Iran to unleash nuclear weapons upon its people. Unfortunately, this scenario carries with it many perils.

Iran has spent many years dispersing, concealing and hardening its nuclear facilities. Its nuclear assets are estimated to be spread over two dozen locations, and some are buried deep underground. Some of the critical components are duplicated at other facilities to provide redundancy. It is even possible that some parts of the nuclear program are not even known to Israeli or Western intelligence. For these reasons, Israel could not be certain of the amount of damage an air strike would cause. Moreover, it is known that some of the nuclear facilities are located near populated areas and have hundreds, even thousands, of personnel working and living inside. Consequently, Israel would be severely criticized by some in the international community for the loss of civilian lives.

Another drawback to a preemptive strike is the retaliation that would surely be launched by Iran, Hamas, Hezbollah, and other terrorist organizations. If Iran were to detect an Israeli strike with early warning radars, it could launch a counter strike against Israel, if not with nuclear missiles, with its arsenal of long-range, conventional rockets. In any event, Israel would be pummeled with missiles from Iran and possibly strikes by Iranian fighter-bombers. Hamas and Hezbollah have already promised they would attack Israel if Iran were attacked. These terrorist organizations have been equipped with thousands of rockets and mortars by Iran and Syria for just this contingency.

The next level of retaliation by Iran would most likely involve an attempt to disrupt the oil trade in the Persian Gulf. Iran is situated in a position to restrict the flow of oil in the Straits of Hormuz, through which 40 percent of the world's internationally traded oil passes. Iran has stated more than once that it would disrupt the global oil trade in the event of hostilities. The major oil fields in Iraq, Kuwait, and Saudi Arabia are in striking distance of Iran's missiles and could be attacked to further interrupt the flow of oil from the region. The impact of any disruption of oil shipments from the region would send oil prices through the roof and potentially cause severe economic damage for many nations. Rising tensions could lead to a conflagration involving major world powers.

A preemptive strike by Israel might be the only way to ensure its survival; however, the consequences for such action could be disastrous for Israel and the international community.

Nuclear Attack by Iran

This scenario has Iran launching a surprise nuclear strike against Israel. To those who say this would never happen, consider this: Israel is the only bulwark of non-Muslim culture in the midst of the surrounding Arab nations and occupies the sacred land of Palestine. It is an affront to Ahmadinejad's power as long as Israel prevents Muslims from taking complete control of the holy places in Jerusalem. On many occasions, Iran's leaders have sworn to correct this situation by driving the Israelis out of Palestine. Most importantly, a nuclear strike on Israel could ignite the apocalypse that Ahmadinejad believes is necessary to pave the way for the Twelfth Imam to return.

The consequences of a nuclear attack on Israel would undoubtedly result in a massive counter strike against Iran. Israel could be expected to attack with its nuclear assets that survive the Iranian strike. Syria could be expected to support Iran. Hamas and Hezbollah would bombard Israel with thousands of rockets and mortars. The greatest uncertainty is, what sort of involvement can be expected of the major powers? Russia, China, and North Korea lean toward Iran and Syria. If any of them entered the fray, how would the United States and the West react? The danger of a major conflagration erupting cannot be ruled out.

Preventing a Cataclysm

There is a high probability of a preemptive strike by Israel or a nuclear attack by Iran, unless there is some form of outside intervention. UN resolutions and various sanctions have not deterred Iran. Therefore, a different approach is necessary to prevent a cataclysm that could involve a clash of world powers, a massive disruption of world economies, the loss of thousands of lives, and the possible obliteration of Israel. The only plausible answer is for the United States to develop a strong backbone and take the following actions:

1. Execute a mutual defense pact with Israel that guarantees a commitment by the United States to respond, instantly, with the full force of its strategic military capability against Iran, should that nation, or its surrogate, launch a nuclear attack on Israel. The pact must be ratified by the U.S. Senate and signed by the President to be convincing to Iran. The pact must include attacks by biological or chemical WMDs, which Iran is known by U.S. intelligence agencies to be developing. Iran must be made to understand that an attack on Israel is an attack on the United States.

2. To fully cement the pact, Israel should be integrated into the United States' worldwide command control and early warning system.

3. The U.S. should assist Israel in hardening its nuclear capabilities to withstand a first strike by Iran and provide assistance for Israel to build a missile defense system or place Israel under the U.S. missile shield being planned for Europe.

4. To reduce the threat from Hamas and Hezbollah, the U.S. and other pro-Israel nations must demand that the UN enforce existing resolutions that require the disarmament of these two terrorist

organizations. The UN should also be pressed to stop Iran and Syria from supporting terrorist organizations.

The above call to action is borne out by the following statement by Israel's Prime Minister, Benjamin Netanyahu, as recently as January 18, 2011:

> Only the convincing threat of military action headed by the United States will persuade Iran to drop plans to build an atomic bomb . . . You have to ratchet up the pressure and . . . I don't think that this pressure [sanctions] will be sufficient to have this regime change course without a credible military option that is put before them by the international community led by the United States.[15]

In an address to the United States Congress on May 25, 2011, Prime Minister Netanyahu was even more emphatic. He spoke of the dire consequences of Iran developing nuclear weapons:

> Now time is running out, and the hinge of history may soon turn. For the greatest danger facing humanity could soon be upon us—A militant Islamic regime armed with nuclear weapons.
>
> A nuclear-armed Iran would ignite a nuclear arms race in the Middle East. It would give terrorists a nuclear umbrella. It would make the nightmare of nuclear terrorism a clear and present danger throughout the world....

The stakes are high. Time may be short. The United States must step up to the challenge and stand with Israel.

Chapter 14

Conclusion

The threat to Israel's survival today is just as real as it has been throughout the past 63 years of its existence as an independent Jewish state. The nature of the threat has changed over the years from clashes between large conventional armies to unconventional warfare where the enemy consists of guerrillas and terrorists. However, as the United States learned in Vietnam, an unconventional war can in many ways be harder to fight than open aggression of a conventional army. It is important to recognize that Israel is not alone in the fight against radical Islam. Iran and terrorist organizations like Al-Qaeda, Hamas, Hezbollah, and the Palestinian Islamic Jihad are just as adamant about destroying the United States and the West as they are about annihilating Israel. On Jerusalem Day 2011, Rahim Safavi, commander of the Iranian Revolutionary Guard, forewarned the West for support of Israel: "The hearts of the people of the Middle East are full of hatred and loathing for the United States and Israel.[1] On the same day Iran's Ahmadinejad warned those who support Israel's continued existence: " . . . the Western powers should not complain [that] they were not forewarned. The Muslims were saying very clearly that if the hurricane began, the West could rest assured that its dimensions would carry it beyond the geographic borders of Palestine…the Zionist regime would drag its supporters into the abyss . . ."[2]

Since World War II, the conflict over Palestine has been much broader than about Israel and the Palestinians. The interests of major world powers like the United States and the Soviet Union/Russia have been at play as part of the struggle for influence in the Middle East and access to the regions oil resources. There were times when the major powers were close to armed conflict over events in the region, often involving Israel. The Arab nations in the region also acted on their respective interests, although not reflective of their concern for Palestine. In fact, there is ample evidence that some of the Arab states used the Palestinian conflict as a means to achieve some of their own ends. Unfortunately, the Palestinian people, particularly those in the refugee camps, have been used as pawns in the Arab-Israeli conflict. The terrorist organizations and their sponsors have used the plight of the Palestinians to justify wars and terrorist attacks against Israel. As presented in previous chapters, terrorist groups like Hamas, Hezbollah, and the Palestinian Islamic Jihad have located their rocket and mortar launchers within population centers, endangering the civilian people. During the Gaza conflict, Hamas leaders and senior officials protected themselves in underground hideouts, while the civilians were left exposed to the fighting.

In reality, the Palestinian-Israeli conflict stems from the Arab states' unwillingness, with the exception of Egypt and Jordan, to accept a Jewish State in the Middle East. Paradoxically, if the Arab states and Palestinians had not gone to war with Israel in 1947-48 in opposition to the UN partitioning resolution, the two-state plan would have been implemented, and there would have been an independent Palestinian state along side of Israel for the past 63 years. Moreover, if the Arab states had not provoked six major wars and supported terrorism against Israel, the conflict might have been settled long ago. Instead of opposing and sometimes sabotaging the peace process, the Arab states could have been much more forthcoming in solving the Palestinian problem. Why haven't they supported the many peace initiatives? Why did they not come forward when the Gaza Strip and the West Bank were under Arab rule from 1948-67, a time when these lands could have been made into an independent Palestinian State? These lands did not become an issue until Israel occupied them during the 1967 War. The Arab nations in the region, some with enormous wealth, could have helped to resolve one of the major issues by resettling the Palestinian refugees in the vast Arab lands. The absence of Arab support of the refugee problem gives rise to the conclusion that most Arab states have little interest in the refugees except as a political weapon against Israel.[3]

The prospects for the settlement of the Palestinian problem and peace for Israel are not promising as long as most of the Arab states in the region and Iran with its terrorist surrogates refuse to recognize Israel's right to exist. Israel is but a tiny island in a sea of millions of Muslims, some of whom embrace radical Islamic ideology. The question is will Israel stand alone or will the United States and Western nations stand with it. The consequences if left to stand alone could be disastrous for the United States and the West as well as for Israel. The Muslim nations have four-fifths of the world's oil reserves, and as previously mentioned, Iran is in a position to cause a major disruption in the flow of oil from the Middle East. Iran and its Arab neighbors could devastate the economies and the way of life in the U.S and Western nations. Any disruption in the oil flow from the Middle East could lead to major military confrontations.

We know that Ahmadinejad has threatened many times to wipe Israel off the map, but the real danger is that he professes to be the chosen one with a divine mission to ignite a clash of civilizations, paving the way for Islam to dominate the world. Ahmadinejad's mission to create a world conflagration is at the heart of his quest for nuclear weapons. If we believe Ahmadinejad and the Ayatollah, Israel is first in line to be swept away by this movement, with the United States and the West next in line.

As if the danger of a nuclear holocaust weren't enough, yet another threat to Israel's survival has arisen. While the final words of this book were being penned, the president of the Palestinian Authority (PA), Mahmoud Abbas, presented a formal request to the United Nations for Palestinian statehood and full recognition as a member of the United Nations. His appeal for a Palestinian state called for the return to the pre-1967 borders and designation of East Jerusalem as its capital. In reality, the use of the pre-1967 borders would mean a return to the 1949 Armistice lines which were drawn at the end of Israel's War of Independence with the Arabs. When the armistice took effect, Jordan occupied the Holy City of Jerusalem and the West Bank, and Egypt controlled the Gaza Strip. Israel gained control of these territories during the Six-Day War in 1967.[4] It is worth noting that during the years when Egypt and Jordan were in control of these lands there was no demand to turn them into a Palestinian state.

Establishment of a Palestinian state based on the 1949 Armistice lines would severely impact Israel's economy, national security, and very existence as a Jewish state. Israel would have to give up important segments of the Holy City and the regions of Judea and Samaria. A half million Jews would be expelled from their homes in these areas.[5] The arbitrary, unilateral declaration of a Palestinian state by the UN, which excludes Israel's participation, would result in more conflict, strife, and destruction than ever seen before in Palestine.

President Obama has supported a Palestinian state, with the pre-1967 borders as the basis for negotiations. However, he has pledged to veto Palestinian statehood if it comes before the UN Security Council. This would deny the Palestinians official member status, but they can seek observer status in the UN General Assembly as a non-member state. Observer status could be viewed by the Palestinians as de facto recognition of a Palestinian state and embolden them to take matters into their own hands to form a state.

There is clearly a bias in the UN favoring the Palestinians and opposing Israel. This is illustrated by the UN's complete disregard for Israel in its consideration of Palestinian statehood. There seems to be a willingness by some members of the UN to accede to the Arab's demands at the expense of Israel's security and survival. This air of appeasement reminds us of a profound observation by the late Winston Churchill on the eve of Hitler's annexation of Czechoslovakia in 1938. He warned, "It is not Czechoslovakia alone which is menaced, but also the freedom and democracy of all nations. The belief that security can be obtained by throwing a small state to the wolves is a fatal delusion."[6]

It would be inconceivable for the United Nations to grant statehood to an entity like the Palestinian Authority (Fatah and Hamas) that has perpetrated thousands of terrorist attacks on Israel, has refused to accept the existence of a Jewish state, and has vowed to destroy Israel. In the days leading up to his appearance at the UN, President Abbas still insisted that the Palestinians will not recognize the Jewish state.

The UN was founded on the principle of nations living together in peace, but the Palestinians have demonstrated that they are not willing to live in peace. Furthermore, since 2000 the Israelis have made major concessions on three separate occasions to the Palestinians for an independent state, but each offer has been rejected.

The UN should not grant full membership or statehood to the Palestinians until they end all attacks on Israel, disarm all internal terrorist organizations such as Hamas (as required by previous UN resolutions), end their fanatical obsession to annihilate Israel, and once and for all, recognize Israel as a Jewish state in Palestine. Only when these conditions have been met, should the UN consider Palestinian statehood. Even then, it should be based on a peace settlement negotiated between Israel and the Palestinians.

Today, Israel is faced with some of the gravest threats to its survival in its history. Now, more than ever, is the time for Israel's friends to stand with her. The United States must make an ironclad commitment to stand with Israel. It must be crystal clear to Israel's adversaries that an attack on Israel is an attack on the United States. For this commitment to be credible and convincing, it must be a formal document ratified by the United States Congress.

Moshe Dayan was right: Israel is destined to live by the sword for the foreseeable future!

Appendix A

The Palestine National Charter (PLO Charter)

(July 17, 1968)

Stuart Hersh Comments: The Fourth Palestine National Assembly, meeting in Cairo July 10-17, 1968, was charged with forming a committee to revise the 1964 Palestinian National Charter [sometimes called the PLO Covenant] in a manner that reflected a more Palestinian-oriented organization. This included revising the objective of Palestine's liberation as being the creation of a sovereign Palestinian state. Pan-Arabism, the dominant theme of the 1964 version, became subordinate to the re-emerging Palestinian nationalism.

This Charter shall be known as "The Palestine National Charter." (Al-Mithaq Al-Watanee Al-Philisteeni)

Articles of the Charter:

Article 1. Palestine is the homeland of the Arab Palestinian people; it is an indivisible part of the greater Arab homeland, and the Palestinian people are an integral part of the Arab nation.

Article 2: Palestine, with the boundaries it had during the British Mandate, is an indivisible territorial unit.

Article 3: The Palestinian Arab people possess the legal right to their homeland and to self-determination after the completion of the liberation of their country in accordance with their wishes and entirely of their own accord and will.

Article 4: The Palestinian identity is a genuine, essential, and inherent characteristic; it is transmitted from fathers to children. The Zionist occupation and the dispersal of the Palestinian Arab people, through the disasters which befell them, do not make them lose their Palestinian identity and their membership in the Palestinian community, nor do they negate them.

Article 5: The Palestinians are those Arab nationals who, until 1947, normally resided n Palestine regardless of whether they were evicted from it or stayed there. Anyone born, after that date, of a Palestinian father—whether in Palestine or outside it—is also a Palestinian.

Article 6: The Jews who had normally resided in Palestine until the beginning of the Zionist invasion are considered Palestinians.

Article 7: There is a Palestinian community and that it has material, spiritual, and historical connection with Palestine are indisputable facts. It is a national duty to bring up individual Palestinians in an Arab revolutionary manner. All means of information and education must be adopted in order to acquaint the Palestinian with his country in the most profound manner, both spiritual and material, that is possible. He must be prepared for the armed struggle and ready to sacrifice his wealth and his life in order to win back his homeland and bring about its liberation.

Article 8: The phase in their history, through which the Palestinian people are now living, is that of national (watani) struggle for the liberation of Palestine. Thus the conflicts among the Palestinian national forces are secondary, and should be ended for the sake of the basic conflict that exists between the forces of Zionism and of colonialism on the one hand, and the Palestinian Arab people on the other. On this basis the Palestinian masses, regardless of whether they are residing in the national homeland or in Diaspora (mahajir) constitute—both their organizations and the individuals—one national front working for the retrieval of Palestine and its liberation through armed struggle.

Article 9: Armed struggle is the only way to liberate Palestine. This is the overall strategy, not merely a tactical phase. The Palestinian Arab people assert their absolute determination and firm resolution to continue their armed struggle and to work for an armed popular revolution for the liberation of their country and their return to it. They also assert their right to normal life in Palestine and to exercise their right to self-determination and sovereignty over it.

Article 10: Commando (Feday'ee) action constitutes the nucleus of the Palestinian popular liberation war. This requires its escalation, comprehensiveness, and the mobilization of all the Palestinian popular and educational efforts and their organization and involvement in the armed Palestinian revolution. It also requires the achieving of unity for the national (watani) struggle among the different grouping s of the Palestinian people, and between the Palestinian people and the Arab masses, so as to secure the continuation of the revolution, its escalation, and victory.

Article 11: Palestinians have three mottoes: national unity, national (al-qawmiyya) mobilization, and liberation.

Article 12: The Palestinian Arab people believe in Arab unity. In order to contribute their share toward the attainment of that objective, however, they must, at the present stage of their struggle, safeguard their Palestinian identity and develop their consciousness of that identity, oppose any plan that may dissolve or impair it.

Article 13: Arab unity and the liberation of Palestine are two complementary goals, the attainment of either of which facilitates the attainment of the other. Thus, Arab unity leads to the liberation of Palestine, the liberation of Palestine leads to Arab unity; and the work toward the realization of one objective proceeds side by side with work toward the realization of the other.

Article 14: The destiny of the Arab Nation, and indeed Arab existence itself, depend upon the destiny of the Palestinian cause. From this interdependence springs the Arab nation's pursuit of, and striving for, the liberation of Palestine. The people of Palestine play the role of the vanguard in the realization of this sacred (qawmi) goal.

Article 15: The liberation of Palestine, from an Arab viewpoint, is a national (qawmi) duty and it attempts to repel the Zionist and imperialist aggression against the Arab homeland, and aims at the elimination of Zionism in Palestine. Absolute responsibility for this falls upon the Arab national—peoples and governments—with the Arab people of Palestine in the vanguard. Accordingly, the Arab nation must mobilize all its military, human, moral, and spiritual capabilities to participate actively with the Palestinian people in the liberation of Palestine. It must, particularly, in the phase of the armed Palestinian revolution, offer and furnish the Palestinian people with all possible help, and material and human support, and make available to them the means and opportunities that will enable them to continue to carry out their leading role in the armed revolution, until they liberate their homeland.

Article 16: The liberation of Palestine, from a spiritual viewpoint, will provide the Holy Land with an atmosphere of safety and tranquility, which in turn will safeguard the country's religious sanctuaries and guarantee freedom of worship and of visit to all, without discrimination of race, color, language, or religion. Accordingly, the Palestinian people look to all spiritual forces in the world for support.

Article 17: The liberation of Palestine, from a human point of view, will restore to the Palestinian individual his dignity, pride, and freedom. Accordingly, the Palestinian Arab people look forward to the support of all those who believe in the dignity of man and his freedom in the world.

Article 18: The liberation of Palestine, from an international point of view, is a defensive action necessitated by the demands of self-defense. Accordingly, the Palestinian people, desirous as they are of the friendship of all people, look to freedom-loving and peace-loving states for support in order to restore their legitimate rights in Palestine, to re-establish peace and security in the country, and to enable its people to exercise national sovereignty and freedom.

Article 19: The partition of Palestine in 1947, and the establishment of the state of Israel are entirely illegal, regardless of the passage of time, because they were contrary to the will of the Palestinian people and its natural right in their homeland, and were inconsistent with the principles embodied in the Charter of the United Nations, particularly the right to self-determination.

Article 20: The Balfour Declaration, the Palestine Mandate, and everything that has been based on them, are deemed null and void. Claims of historical or religious ties of Jews with Palestine are incompatible with the facts of history and the conception of what constitutes statehood. Judaism, being a religion, is not an independent nationality. Nor do Jews constitute a single nation with an identity of their own; they are citizens of the states to which they belong.

Article 21: The Arab Palestinian people, expressing themselves by armed Palestinian revolution, reject all solutions which are substitutes for the total liberation of Palestine and reject all proposals aimed at the liquidation of the Palestinian cause, or at its internationalization.

Article 22: Zionism is a political movement organically associated with international imperialism and antagonistic to all action for liberation and to progressive movements in the world. It is racist and fanatic in its nature, aggressive, expansionist and colonial in its aims, and fascist in its methods. Israel is the instrument of the Zionist movement, and the geographical base for world imperialism placed strategically in the midst of the Arab homeland to combat the hopes of the Arab nation for liberation, unity, and progress. Israel is a constant source of threat vis-á-vis peace in the Middle East and the whole world. Since liberation of Palestine will destroy the Zionist and imperialist presence people look to the progressive and peaceful forces and urge them all, irrespective of their affiliations and beliefs, to offer the Palestinian people all aid and support in their just struggle for the liberation of their homeland.

Article 23: The demand of security and peace, as well as the demand of right and justice, require all states to consider Zionism an illegitimate movement, to outlaw its existence, and to ban its operations, in order that friendly relations among peoples may be preserved, and the loyalty of citizens to their respective homelands safeguarded.

Article 24: The Palestinian people believe in the principles of justice, freedom, sovereignty, self-determination, human dignity, and the right of peoples to exercise them.

Article 25: For the realization of the goals of this Charter and its principles, the Palestine Liberation Organization will perform its role in the liberation of Palestine.

Article 26: The Palestine Liberation Organization, the representative of the Palestinian revolutionary forces, is responsible for the Palestinian Arab peoples movement in its struggle—to achieve its homeland, liberate and return to it and exercise the right to self-determination in it—in all military, political, and financial fields and also for whatever ay be required y the Palestinian cause on the inter-Arab and international levels.

Article 27: The Palestine Liberation Organization shall cooperate with all Arab states, each according to its potentialities; and will adopt a neutral policy among them in light of the requirements of the battle of liberation; and on this basis does not interfere in the internal affairs of any Arab state.

Article 28: The Palestinian Arab people assert the genuineness and independence of their national revolution and reject all forms of intervention, trusteeship, and subordination.

Article 29: The Palestinian people possess the fundamental and genuine legal right to liberate and retrieve their homeland. The Palestinian people determine their attitude toward all states and forces on the basis of the stands they adopt vis-á-vis the Palestinian resolution to fulfill the aims of the Palestinian people.

Article 30: Fighters and carriers of arms in the war of liberation are the nucleus of the popular army which will be the protective force for the gains of the Palestinian Arab people.

Article 31: This Organization shall have a flag, an oath of allegiance, and an anthem. All this shall be decided upon in accordance with a special law.

Article 32: A law, known as the Basic Statue of the Palestine Liberation Organization, shall be annexed to this Covenant. It will lay down the manner in which the Organization, and its organs and institutions, shall be constituted; the respective competence of each; and the requirements of its obligation under the Charter.

Article 33: This Charter shall not be amended save by [vote of] a majority of two-thirds of the total membership of the National Council of the Palestine Liberation Organization [taken] at a special session convened for that purpose.

Source: Jewish Virtual Library, a Division of the American-Israeli Cooperative Enterprise.

Appendix B

The PLO's Ten Point Plan

Adopted at the 12th Session of the Palestine National Council

(June 8, 1974)

Cairo, 8 June 1974

The Palestine National Council,

On the basis of the Palestine National Charter and the Political Program drawn up at the eleventh session, held from 6-12 January 1973; and from its belief that it is impossible for a permanent and just peace to be established in the area unless our Palestinian people recover from all their national rights and, first and foremost, their rights to return and to self-determination on the whole of the soil of their homeland; and in the light of a study of the new political circumstances that have come into existence in the period between the Council's last and present sessions, resolves the following:

1. To reaffirm the Palestine Liberation Organization's previous attitude to Resolution 242, which obliterates the national right of our people and deals with the cause of our people as a problem of refugees. The Council therefore refuses to have anything to do with this resolution at any level, Arab or international, including the Geneva Conference.

2. The <u>Palestine Liberation Organization</u> will employ all means, and first and foremost armed struggle, to liberate Palestinian territory and to establish the independent combatant national authority for the people over every part of Palestinian territory that is liberated. This will require further changes being effected in the balance of power in favor of our people and their struggle.

3. The Liberation Organization will struggle against any proposal for a Palestinian entity the price of which is recognition, peace, secure frontiers, renunciation of national rights, and the deprival of our people of their right to return and their right to self-determination on the soil of their homeland.

4. Any step taken towards liberation is a step towards the realization of the Liberation Organization's strategy of establishing the democratic Palestinian State specified in the resolutions of the previous Palestinian National Councils.

5. Struggle along with the Jordanian national forces to establish a Jordanian-Palestinian national front whose aim will be to set up in <u>Jordan</u> a democratic national authority in close contact with the Palestinian entity that is established through the struggle.

6. The Liberation Organization will struggle to establish unity in struggle between the two peoples and between all the forces of the Arab liberation movement that are in agreement on this program.

7. In the light of this program, the Liberation Organization will struggle to strengthen national unity and to raise it to the level where it will be able to perform its national duties and tasks.

8. Once it is established, the Palestinian national authority will strive to achieve a union of the confrontation countries, with the aim of completing the liberation of all Palestinian territory, and as a step along the road to comprehensive Arab unity.

9. The Liberation Organization will strive to strengthen its solidarity with the socialist countries, and with the forces of liberation and

progress throughout the world, with the aim of frustrating all the schemes of Zionism, reaction and imperialism.

10. In light of this program, the leadership of the revolution will determine the tactics which will serve and make possible the realization of the objectives.

The Executive Committee of the <u>Palestine Liberation Organization</u> will make every effort to implement this program, and should a situation arise affecting the destiny and the future of the Palestinian people, the National Assembly will be convened in extraordinary session.

Source: Jewish Virtual Library, a Division of the American Israeli Cooperative Enterprise.

Appendix C

The Covenant of the Islamic Resistance Movement (HAMAS)

(August 18, 1988)

In The Name of the Most Merciful Allah

"Ye are the best nation that hath been raised up unto mankind: ye command that which is just, and ye forbid that which is unjust, and ye believe in Allah. And if they who have received the scriptures had believed, it had surely been the better for them: there are believers among them, but the greater part of them is transgressors. They shall not hurt you, unless with a slight hurt; and if they fight against you, they shall turn their backs to you, and they shall not be helped. They are smitten with vileness wheresoever they are found; unless they obtain security by entering into a treaty with Allah, and a treaty with men; and they draw on themselves indignation fro [sic] Allah, and they are afflicted with poverty. This they suffer, because they disbelieved the signs of Allah, and slew the prophets unjustly; this, because they were rebellious, and transgressed.... (Allmran-verses 109111).

Israel will exist and will continue to exist until Islam will obliterate it, just as it obliterated others before it" (The Martyr, Imam Hassan alBanna, of blessed memory).

"The Islamic world is on fire. Each of us should pour some water, no matter how little, to extinguish whatever one can without waiting for the others." (Sheikh Amjad alZahawi, of blessed memory).

In The Name of the Most Merciful Allah

Introduction

Praise be unto Allah, to whom we resort for help, and whose forgiveness, guidance and support we seek; Allah bless the Prophet and grant him salvation, his companions and supporters, and to those who carried out his message and adopted his laws everlasting prayers and salvation as long as the earth and heaven will last. Hereafter:

O People:

Out of the midst of troubles and the sea of suffering, out of the palpitations of faithful hearts and cleansed arms; out of the sense of duty and in response to Allah's command, the call has gone out rallying people together and making them follow the ways of Allah, leading them to have determined will in order to fulfill their role in life, to overcome all obstacles, and surmount the difficulties on the way. Constant preparation has continued and so has the readiness to sacrifice life and all that is precious for the sake of Allah.

Thus it was that the nucleus (of the movement) was formed and started to pave its way through the tempestuous sea of hopes and expectations, of wishes and yearnings, of troubles and obstacles, of pain and challenges, both inside and outside.

When the idea was ripe, the seed grew and the plant struck root in the soil of reality, away from passing emotions, and hateful haste. The Islamic Resistance Movement emerged to carry out its role through striving for the sake of its Creator, its arms intertwined with those of all the fighters for the liberation of Palestine. The spirits of its fighters meet with the spirits of all the fighters who have sacrificed their lives on the soil of Palestine, ever since it was conquered by the companions of the Prophet, Allah bless him and grant him salvation, and until this day.

This Covenant of the Islamic Resistance Movement (HAMAS), clarifies its picture, reveals its identity, outlines its stand, explains its aims, speaks about its hopes, and calls for its support, adoption and joining its ranks. Our struggle against the Jews is very great and very serious. It needs all sincere efforts. It is a step that inevitably should be followed by other steps. The Movement is but one squadron that should be supported by more and more squadrons from this vast Arab and Islamic world, until the enemy is vanquished and Allah's victory is realized.

Thus we see them coming on the horizon "and you shall learn about it hereafter" "Allah hath written, Verily I will prevail, and my apostles: for Allah is strong and might [sic]." (The Dispute verse 21).

> "Say to them, this is my way: I invite you to Allah, by
> an evident demonstration; both I and he who followeth
> me; and, praise be unto Allah! I am not an idolator."
> (Joseph verse 107).

Hamas (means) strength and bravery (according to) AlMua'jam alWasit: cl.

Article 7:

As a result of the fact that those Moslems who adhere to the ways of the Islamic Resistance Movement spread all over the world, rally support for it and its stands, strive towards enhancing its struggle, the Movement is a universal one. It is well equipped for that because of the clarity of its ideology, the nobility of its aim and the loftiness of its objectives....

The Islamic Resistance Movement is one of the links in the chain of the struggle against the Zionist invaders. It goes back to 1939, to the emergence of the martyr Izz alDin al Kissam and his brethren the fighters, members of Moslem Brotherhood. It goes on to reach out and become one with another chain that includes the struggle of the Palestinians and Moslem Brotherhood in the 1948 war and the Jihad operations of the Moslem Brotherhood in 1968 and after.

195

Moreover, if the links have been distant from each other and if obstacles, placed by those who are the lackeys of Zionism in the way of the fighters obstructed the continuation of the struggle, the Islamic Resistance Movement aspires to the realization [sic] of Allah's promise, no matter how long that should take. The Prophet, Allah bless him and grant him salvation, has said:

"The Day of Judgment will not come about until Moslems fight the Jews (killing the Jews), when the Jew will hide behind stones and trees. The stones and trees will say O Moslems, O Abdulla, there is a Jew behind me, come and kill him. Only the Gharkad tree, (evidently a certain kind of tree) would not do that because it is one of the trees of the Jews." (related by alBukhari and Moslem).

Article 8:

Allah is its target, the Prophet is its model, the Koran its constitution: Jihad is its path and death for the sake of Allah is the loftiest of its wishes....

Article 11:

The Islamic Resistance Movement believes that the land of Palestine is an Islamic Waqf consecrated for future Moslem generations until Judgment Day. It, or any part of it, should not be squandered: it, or any part of it, should not be given up. Neither a single Arab country nor all Arab countries, neither any king or president, nor all the kings and presidents, neither any organization nor all of them, be they Palestinian or Arab, possess the right to do that. Palestine is an Islamic Waqf land consecrated for Moslem generations until Judgment Day. This being so, who could claim to have the right to represent Moslem generations till Judgment Day?

This is the law governing the land of Palestine in the Islamic Sharia (law) and the same goes for any land the Moslems have conquered by force, because during the times of (Islamic) conquests, the Moslems consecrated these lands to Moslem generations till the Day of Judgment....

Article 12:

Nationalism, from the point of view of the Islamic Resistance Movement, is part of the religious creed. Nothing in nationalism is more significant or deeper than in the case when an enemy should tread Moslem land. Resisting and quelling the enemy become the individual duty of every Moslem, male or female. A woman can go out to fight the enemy without her husband's permission, and so does the slave: without his master's permission....

Article 13:

Initiatives, and so-called peaceful solutions and international conferences, are in contradiction to the principles of the Islamic Resistance Movement. Abusing any part of Palestine is abuse directed against part of religion. Nationalism of the Islamic Resistance Movement is part of its religion. Its members have been fed on that. For the sake of hoisting the banner of Allah over their homeland they fight. "Allah will be prominent, but most people do not know...."

There is no solution for the Palestinian question except through Jihad. Initiatives, proposals and international conferences are all a waste of time and vain endeavors. The Palestinian people know better than to consent to having their future, rights and fate toyed with....

Article 14:

The question of the liberation of Palestine is bound to three circles: the Palestinian circle, the Arab circle and the Islamic circle. Each of these circles has its role in the struggle against Zionism. Each has its duties, and it is a horrible mistake and a sign of deep ignorance to overlook ay [sic] of these circles. Palestine is an Islamic land which has the first of the two kiblahs (direction to which Moslems turn in praying), the third of the holy (Islamic) sanctuaries, and the point of departure for Mohammed's midnight journey to the seven heavens (i.e. Jerusalem)....

Since this is the case, liberation of Palestine is then an individual duty of very [sic] Moslem wherever he may be. On this basis, the problem should be viewed. This should be realized [sic] by every Moslem....

Article 15:

The day that enemies usurp part of Moslem land, Jihad becomes the individual duty of every Moslem. In face of the Jews' usurpation of Palestine, it is compulsory that the banner of Jihad be raised. To do this requires the diffusion of Islamic consciousness among the masses, both on the regional, Arab and Islamic levels. It is necessary to instill the spirit of Jihad in the heart of the nation so that they would confront the enemies and join the ranks of the fighters....

It is necessary to instill in the minds of the Moslem generations that the Palestinian problem is a religious problem, and should be dealt with on this basis. Palestine contains Islamic holy sites. In it there is al Aqsa Mosque which is bound to the great Mosque in Mecca in an inseparable bond as long as heaven and earth speak of Isra' (Mohammed's midnight journey to the seven heavens) and Mi'raj (Mohammed's ascension to the seven heavens from Jerusalem)....

Article 28:

The Zionist invasion is a vicious invasion. It does not refrain from resorting to all methods, using all evil and contemptible ways to achieve its end. It relies greatly in its infiltration and espionage operations on the secret organizations it gave rise to, such as the Freemasons, the Rotary and Lions clubs, and other sabotage groups. All these organizations, whether secret or open, work in the interest of Zionism and according to its instructions. They aim at undermining societies, destroying values, corrupting consciences, deteriorating character and annihilating Islam. It is behind the drug trade and alcoholism in all its kinds so as to facilitate its control and expansion.

Arab countries surrounding Israel are asked to open their borders before the fighters from among the Arab and Islamic nations so that they could consolidate their efforts with those of their Moslem brethren in Palestine.

As for the other Arab and Islamic countries, they are asked to facilitate the movement of the fighters from and to it, and this is the least thing they could do.

We should not forget to remind every Moslem that when the Jews conquered the Holy City in 1967, they stood on the threshold of the Aqsa Mosque and proclaimed that "Mohammed is dead, and his descendants are all women."

Israel, Judaism and Jews challenge Islam and the Moslem people. "May the cowards never sleep...."

Article 32:

World Zionism, together with imperialistic powers, try through a studied plan and an intelligent strategy to remove one Arab state after another from the circle of struggle against Zionism, in order to have it finally face the Palestinian people only. Egypt was, to a great extent, removed from the circle of the struggle, through the treacherous Camp David Agreement. They are trying to draw other Arab countries into similar agreements and to bring them outside the circle of struggle.

The Islamic Resistance Movement calls on Arab and Islamic nations to take up the line of serious and persevering action to prevent the success of this horrendous plan, to warn the people of the danger emanating from leaving the circle of struggle against Zionism. Today it is Palestine, tomorrow it will be one country or another. The Zionist plan is limitless. After Palestine, the Zionists aspire to expand from the Nile to the Euphrates. When they will have digested the region they overtook, they will aspire to further expansion, and so on. Their plan is embodied in the *"Protocols of the Elders of Zion,"* and their present conduct is the best proof of what we are saying.

Leaving the circle of struggle with Zionism is high treason, and cursed be he who does that. "for whoso shall turn his back unto them on that day, unless he turneth aside to fight, or retreateth to another party of the faithful, shall draw on himself the indignation of Allah, and his abode shall be hell; an ill journey shall it be thither." (The Spoils verse 16). There is no way out except by concentrating all powers and energies to face this Nazi, vicious Tatar invasion. The alternative is loss of one's country, the dispersion of citizens, the spread of vice on earth and the destruction of religious values. Let every person know that he is responsible before Allah for "the doer of the slightest good deed is rewarded in like, and the doer of the slightest evil deed is also rewarded in like."

The Islamic Resistance Movement considers itself to be the spearhead of the circle of struggle with world Zionism and a step on the road. The Movement adds its efforts to the efforts of all those who are active in the Palestinian arena. Arab and Islamic Peoples should augment by further steps on their part; Islamic groupings all over the Arab world should also do the same, since all of these are the best equipped for the future role in the fight with the warmongering Jews....

Article 34:

Palestine is the navel of the globe and the crossroad of the continents. Since the dawn of history, it has been the target of expansionists. The Prophet, Allah bless him and grant him salvation, had himself pointed to this fact in the noble Hadith in which he called on his honourable companion, Ma'adh benJabal, saying: O Ma'ath, Allah throw open before you, when I am gone, Syria, from AlArish to the Euphrates. Its men, women and slaves will stay firmly there till the Day of Judgment. Whoever of you should choose one of the Syrian shores, or the Holy Land, he will be in constant struggle till the Day of Judgment."

Expansionists have more than once put their eye on Palestine which they attacked with their armies to fulfill their designs on it. Thus it was that the Crusaders came with their armies, bringing with them their creed and carrying their Cross. They were able to defeat the Moslems for a while, but the Moslems were able to retrieve the land only when they stood under the wing of their religious banner, united their word, hallowed the name of Allah and surged out fighting under the leadership of Salah edDin alAyyubi. They fought for almost twenty years and at the end the Crusaders were defeated and Palestine was liberated.

"Say unto those who believe not, Ye shall be overcome, and thrown together into hell; an unhappy couch it shall be." (The Family of Imran verse 12).

This is the only way to liberate Palestine. There is no doubt about the testimony of history. It is one of the laws of the universe and one of the rules of existence. Nothing can overcome iron except iron. Their false futile creed can only be defeated by the righteous Islamic creed. A creed could not be fought except by a creed, and in the last analysis, victory is for the just, for justice is certainly victorious.

"Our word hath formerly been given unto our servants the apostles; that they should certainly be assisted against the infidels, and that our armies should surely be the conquerors." (Those Who Rank Themselves verses 171172)....

Source: The Jewish Virtual Library, a Division of the American-Israeli Cooperative Enterprise.

Appendix D

Fatah's Political Program

Palestine is a part of the Arab homeland.

The Palestinian people are an indivisible part of the Arab nations. The Palestinian people have been living in their homeland Palestine, from time immemorial.... Since the dawn of Islam and up to the present, the Palestinian people have been the heart of the Arab and Islamic nation protecting the first Qiblah and the third holiest shrine [AlAqsa Mosque]....

The Zionist conquest came at the beginning of this century to uproot the Palestinian people, end their civilizations, and implant a Zionist entity designed to carry out the imperialist schemes that seek to control the Arab homeland's resources and make this homeland a part of the colonialist's spheres of influence....

The Palestinian people have held out in the face of this Zionist colonialist barbarism.... The crime was consummated by the partition of Palestine and the establishment of the Zionist entity state in 1948.

Most of the Palestinian people were scattered outside their homeland and forced to live n [sic] exile in the diaspora.... They were builders of civilization wherever they lived....

Then came the conspiracies hatched by the Syrian regime and carried out by its agent tools, including the dissension conspiracy, the double siege and elimination against the sons of our people in the camps. The conspiracy sought to contain the Palestinian revolution and to end its effective role within the equation of the conflict.

The intifada has driven a deep crack in the barbarous Zionist entity, strongly attracted the world's attention to the justice of the cause, and imposed a new political reality that has great impact on all Palestinian, Arab, and international levels....

We convene the Fifth General Congress of our Fatah movement with more resolve and determination to continue the struggle with all possible means—political and military—to liberate our homeland and establish our state, the independent state of Palestine with holy Jerusalem as its capital . . .

The Fifth General Congress of [the] Fatah Movement specifies our future objectives as follows:

1. The Palestinian question is the core of the Arab Zionist conflict.

2. Firm adherence to Palestinian Arab national inalienable rights in their homeland Palestine, including their right to repatriation, self-determination without foreign interference, and the establishment of their independent state with holy Jerusalem as its capital....

4. The Fifth Fatah General Congress affirms the historic importance of the resolutions of the 19th PNC session, particularly the documents of independence. The Congress supports the establishment of the independent state of Palestine and extends thanks to the Arab and friendly that have recognized it. The Congress authorizes the movement's central committee to work on all levels to implement the resolutions of establishing the Palestinian people's national inalienable rights, headed by the right to repatriation, self-determination, of the establishment of the state of Palestine on Palestinian soil with holy Jerusalem as its capital.

5. Continuing to intensify and escalate armed action and all forms of struggle liquidate the Israel Zionist occupation of our occupied Palestinian land and guaranteeing our people's rights to freedom and independence.

6. Bolstering national Palestinian unity on the various political and military levels, reitering [sic] the PLO's leading role, and escalating the popular intifada aimed at ending the Zionist Israeli occupation....

9 ....rejects the Shamir plan on elections and affirms that any election in our occupied must take place n [sic] a free and democratic atmosphere under international supervision after the withdrawal of the Israel forces....

13. In light of the significant effect of the demographic factor on our conflict with the Zionist enemy, and in light of the huge efforts exerted by the Zionist movement to encourage Zionist immigration to Palestinian territory, the Congress has decided to set up an ad hoc committee within the revolutionary council to oppose the Zionist immigration to our homeland and to assume all cultural, information, and political tasks to prevent the arrival of Jewish immigrants in our occupied homeland....

The Fatah Congress calls on the Arab countries to abide by and implement all the resolutions and honor their financial commitments.

Respecting the right of the Palestinian revolution to perform its militant tasks through any Arab land....

Calling on the Arab countries, especially those on the confrontation lines, to unify their forces and mobilize their masses in order to confront the Israel aggression....

The Fifth General Congress...emphasized...the Palestinian people's national inalienable rights and the right of all oppressed peoples under occupation to use all forms of struggle for their liberation and national independence....

Source: Excerpted from the political program of the Fatah Congress, August 1989; Jewish Virtual Library, a Division of the American-Israeli Cooperative Enterprise.

Endnotes

Chapter 1. Dawn of a Jewish State.

1. Colin Shindler. *A History of Modern Israel*. (New York: Cambridge University Press, 2008), 2.

2. *Israel, Dormant War*. from Library of Congress, Country Studies, Israel, 1988, 1, http://memory.loc.gov/cgi-bin/query/D?cstdy:1:./temp/-frd_FCHT. (accessed November 4, 2010).

3. Efraim Karsh. *Arab-Israeli Conflict*. (Oxford, UK: Osprey Publishing, 2002), 14-16.

4. Ahron Bregman. *A History of Israel*. (New York: Palgrave Macmillan, 2003), 21-22.

5. Ibid., 22-23.

6. Ibid., 23-24.

7. Karsh, 17.

8. Karish, 17-18; Bregman., 32-33.

9. Bregman, 33-34.

10. Bregman, 34, 37.

11. Chaim Herzog, Updated by Shlomo Gazit, *Arab-Israeli Wars* (New York: Vintage Books, 2005), 12-13.

12. Bregman, 37-38.

13. Bregman, 38.

14. Herzog, 12-13.

15. Herzog, 13; Bergman, 39-40.

16. Bregman, 39-41.

17. Bregman, 40.

18. David Dolan. *Holy War for the Promised Land.* (Nashville, TN: Thomas Nelson, 1991), 104.

19. Karsh, 8.

20. Karsh, 8.

21. Ahron Bregman and Jihan El-Tahri. *The Fifty Years War.* (London, UK: Penguin Books, 1998), 25-26.

22. University of California, Center for Muslim-Jewish Engagement, "Composition of Muslim Texts, Sunnah and Hedith," n.p., http://www.usc.edu/schools/college/crcc/engaagement/resources/texts/muslim/hedith.

23. Ibid.

24. Ibid.

25. Ibid.

26. CIA World Fact Book. *Isreal.* (January 7, 2009), 14-15, http://www.cia/library, (accessed 12 January 2010).

27. Shindler, 2.

28. Allan Dershowitz. *The Case against Israel's Enemies.* (Hoboken, NJ: John Wiley & Sons, 2008), 7.

29. "PA Television Broadcasts Call for Killing Jews and Americans," *MEMRI, The Middle East Media Research Institute*, Dispatch No.138, October 13,2000, 1-2, http://www.memri.org/report/en/0/0/0/0/0/0/378/htm.

30. "A Friday Sermon on PA TV: We Must Educate our Children on the Love of Jihad," *MEMRI, Middle East Research Institute,* Dispatch No. 240, July 13, 2001, 1-2.

31. Ibid.

Chapter 2. War of Independence.

1. *Prelude to Statehood, Problems of the New State, 1948*-1967, 1, *from* Library of Congress, Country Studies, Israel, 1988, http://lcweb2loc.govcgi-bin/query/r?frd/cstdy:@field(DOCID+il0029. (accessed January 10, 2009).

2. David Dolan. *Holy War for the Promised Land.* (Nashville, TN: Thomas Nelson, 1991), 105.

3. Ibid; and Benny Morris. *1948, First Arab-Israeli War.* (New Haven and London: Yale University Press, 2008), 70.

4. Chaim Herzog. *Arab Israeli Wars.* (New York: Vintage Books, 2005), 19.

5. Ibid. and Efraim Karsh. *Arab-Israeli Conflict.* (Oxford, UK: Osprey, 2002), 25.

6. Morris, 90.

7. Ibid.

8. Ibid.

9. Herzog, 25-27.

10. Morris, 105-108.

11. Ibid., 110, 207.

12. Ibid., 117-119.

13. Colin Shindler. *A History of Modern Israel.* (Cambridge, UK: University Press, 2008), 46; Herzog, 47.

14. Ahron Bregman. *A History of Israel.* (New York: Palgrave Macmillan, 2003), 45.

15. Dr. Mitchell G. Bard. *Declaration of Independence of the Establishment of the State of Israel (May 14, 1948).* (Jewish Virtual Library, 1998), 1-7, http://www.jewishvirtuallibrary.org/source/Declaration.html (accessed November 5, 2010).

16. Morris, 187.

17. Herzog, 68-69.

18. Bregman, 49; Morris, 207.

19. Karsh, 60.

20. Bregman, 251.

21. Ibid., 147-148.

22. Karsh, 60.

23. Morris, 201.

24. Morris, 261-262; Bregman, 50-51.

25. Morris, 264-269; Bregman, 51.

26. Bregman, 55-56; Morris, 295-296.

27. Bregman, 59-60; Morris, 296.

28. Bregman, 60-61.

29. Bregman, 64-65; Herzog, 105.

30. Morris, 391; Bregman, 65.

31. Herzog, 106-107.

32. Ibid., 106.

Chapter 3. Sinai-Suez War.

1. *Suez Crisis*: *Events leading up to the Suez Crisis.* Answers.com, 1-2, http://www.answers.com/topic/suez-canal-crisis. (accessed October 27, 2009).

2. David Dolan, *Holy War for the Promised Land*, (Nashville, TN: Thomas Nelson, 1991), 120-122.

3. *The State of Israel, From the War of Independence Until the Sinai War (1948-1956),* 3., Ynetnews.com, December 12, 2007, http://www.ynet.co.il/english/Ext/Comp/ArticleLayout/CdaArticlePrint Preview/1,2506,L-3…(accessed January 9, 2009).

4. Dr. Mitchell G. Bard, *Road to* Suez, Jewish Virtual Library, Myths and Facts Online, 2006), n.p., http://www.jewishvirtuallibrary.org/jsource/myths/mf5.html. (accessed October 27, 2009).

5. Ibid.

6. Ahron Bregman, *A History of Israel* (New York: Palgrave Macmillan, 2003), 88-89.

7. Chaim Herzog, Updated by Shlomo Gazit, *Arab Israeli Wars* (New York: Vantage Books, 2005), 113.

8. Suez Crisis, 1.

9. Bregman, 89.

10. Herzog, 113-114.

11. Colin Shindler. *A History of Modern Israel.* (New York: Cambridge University Press, 2008) 121; *Suez Crisis. (1956-1957),* 4-5.

12. Bregman, 91.

13. Herzog, 138-139; Bergman, 92.

14. Herzog, 139.

15. Ibid, 139-140.

16. Dolan, 125.

17. Herzog, 146.

18. Bregman, 101; Dolan, 126-127.

19. Dolan, 126-127.

Chapter 4. Six-Day War.

1. Jeremy Bowen, *Six Days* (New York: Thomas Dunne Books, 2005), 70; Dennis Ross, *Peace* (New York: Farrar, Straus and Giroux, 2005), 27.

2. Walter Laqueur and Barry Rubin Editors, *Israel-Arab Reader* (New York: Penguin Books, 2008), 89-96, 98-102.

3. Ruth Bondy, Ohad Zmora, Raohael Bashan, eds., comps. *Mission Survival.* (New York: Sabra Books,1968), 15.

4. Ibid., 16.

5. Ibid.

6. Laqueur, 99.

7. David Dolan. *Holy War for the Promised Land.* (Nashville, TN: Thomas Nelson, 1991), 97-98.

8. Benny Morris. *1948.* (New York: Yale University Press, 2008), 410; Bowen, 8.

9. Bowen, 8.

10. Chaim Herzog, updated by Shlomo Gazit. *Arab Israeli-Israeli Wars.* (New York: Vintage Books, 2005), 146.

11. Donald Neff. *Warriors for Jerusalem.* (New York: Linden Press, 1984), 32-34.

12. Ibid., 35-36.

13. Ibid., 37-39.

14. Herzog, 147-148.

15. Bowen, 40.

16. Herzog, 149.

17. Bowen, 41-42, 46.

18. Herzog, 149.

19. Bondy, 16.

20. Ibid.

21. Ibid.

22. Ahron Bregman. *A History of Israel.* (New York: Palgrave Macmillan, 2003), 108; Herzog, 150.

23. Dolan, 129.

24. Neff, 165.

25. Bregman, 116; Neff, 193-194; Herzog, 130.

26. Neff, 203; Herzog, 152-153.

27. Bregman, 117.

28. Neff, 203-204; Bowen, 113; Herzog, 153.

29. Herzog, 153.

30. Neff, 223-224; Bregman, 118; Herzog, 161-163.

31. Herzog, 164-165.

32. Bondy, 170-172.

33. Herzog, 173-174, 180-181.

34. Ibid., 182-183.

35. Bregman, 108.

36. Herzog, 185.

37. Hersog, 187-188; Bregman, 122-123.

38. Neff, 279-282.

39.   Bregman, 123.

40.   Ibid., 131.

Chapter 5. War of Attrition.

1.   Chaim Herzog, updated by Shlomo Gazit. *Arab-Israeli Wars.* (New York: Vintage Books, 2005), 195-197.

2.   Ibid., 198-199.

3.   Ibid., 199-200.

4.   Ahron Bregman. *A History of Israel.* (New York: Palgrave Macmillan, 2003), 130-131.

5.   Ibid., 131-132; Herzog., 210, 212.

6.   Herzog, 217-218.

7.   Bregman, 133-134.

8.   Ibid., 134.

9.   Ibid., 135-136.

10.   Ibid., 136.

11.   Herzog, 203-205.

12.   Ibid., 222-223, 205-206.

Chapter 6. Yom Kippur War.

1.   Abraham Rabinovich. *Yom Kippur War.* (New York: Schockern Books, 2004), 10-15.

2. Ibid., 13., and Ahron Bregman and Jihan El-Tahri. *Fifty Years War.* (London, UK: Penguin Books, 1998), 12-13.

3. Aharon Bregman. *A History of Israel.* (New York: Palgrave Macmillan, 2003), 140-141.

4. Chaim Herzog, updated by Shlomo Gazit. *Arab-Israeli Wars.* (Cambridge, UK University Press, 2008), 228-239.

5. Ibid., 227-229.

6. Ibid.

7. Simon Dunstan. *Yom Kippur War, Arab-Israeli War of 1973.* (Oxford, UK: Osprey, 2007), 28-29.

8. Ibid., 52.

9. Ibid., 17-19, 35; Herzog, 228-230.

10. Bregman. *Fifty Years War.* 116-120; Rabinovich. 65-84.

11. *Yom Kippur,* Judaism 101, http://www.jewfaq.org/holiday4. htm. (accessed March 26, 2010); Bregman *A History of* Israel. 150-151.

12. Rabinovich. 56-58, 72-75.

13. Dunstan, 56-57; Bregman, *Fifty Years War*, 121; Herzog, 230.

14. Dunstan. 34-36; Herzog, 239, 285.

15. Dunstan. 37-40.

16. Bregman. *A History of Israel.* 151; Dunstan. 58; Herzog. 241.

17. Bregman. *A History of Israel.* 152; Dunstan. 67; Rabinovich.103; Herzog. 242.

18. Rabinovich. 55, 142; Bregman. *A History of Israel.* 152-153.

19. Herzog. 287-288.

20. Danstan,. 72; Herzog. 247-248.

21. Bregman. *A History of Israel.* 154-155; Dunstan. 79-80.

22. Bregman. *A History of Israel.* 155; Dunstan. 86-88.

23. Dunstan. 90-91, 95, 104; Herzog. 262-273.

24. Dunstan. 106-108; Herzog. 280.

25. Bregman. *A History of Israel.* 154; Herzog. 291; Rabinovich. 314.

26. Herzog. 294-299.

27. Ibid., 310-311.

28. Bregman. *A History of Israel,* 155-156; Herzog, 278-279.

29. Bregman, *A History of Israel.* 156; Dunstsan. 122-123, 200; Herzog. 306.

30. Bregman. *A History of Israel.* 156-157.

31. Dunstan. 200.

32. Bregman. *A History of Israel.* 158.

33. David Dolan. *Holy War for the Promised Land.* (Nashville, TN: Thomas Nelson. 1991), 135; Herzog. 323.

Chapter 7. War in Lebanon.

1. David Dolan. *Holy War for the Promised Land.* (Nashville, TN: Thomas Nelson, 1991), 135-136.

2. *PLO's Phased Plan, Cairo, June 9, 1974,* http://www.iris.org.il/plophase.htm. (accessed November 16, 2009).

3. *The October 1973 War*, 2, from Library of Congress, Country Studies, Israel, 1988, http://www.lcweb2loc.govcgi-bin/query/r?frd/cstdy"@field(DOCID+il0029. (accessed January 10, 2009).

4. *Israeli Action in Lebanon 1978-1982*, 1, from Library of Congress, Country Studies, Israel, http://www.lcweb2loc.govcgi-bin/query/r?frd/cstdy"@field(DOCID+il0029. (accessed January 10, 2009).

5. Ahron Bregman. *A History of Israel.* (New York: Palgrave Madmillan, 2003) 136-137.

6. Ibid.

7. David Dolan. *Holy War for the Promised Land.* (Nashville, TN: Thomas Nelson, 1991), 143.

8. Bregman. 186-188; Dolin. 138-139.

9. Israeli Actions in Lebanon, 1.

10. Bregman. 191-194.

11. Chaim Herzog, updated by Shlomo Gazit. Arab-Israeli Wars (New York: Vintage Books, 2005), 349-350.

12. Ibid., 351-352.

13. Bregman. 198-200.

14. Herzog. 357-359.

15. Ibid., 359-362.

16. Ibid., 362.

17. Bregman. 202-203.

18. Herzog. 364-365.

19. MarkTessler.*HistoryofIsrael—PalestinianConflict.*(Bloomington and Indianapolis, IN: Indiana University Press, 1994), 636-635; Herzog, 369-370.

20. Herzog, 372, 378.

21. Ibid., 379.

22. Dr. Reuven Erlich and Dr. Yoram Kahati. *Hezbollah as a Case Study of the Battle for Hearts and Minds.* 2-9, from Intelligence and Terrorism Information Center at the Israel Intelligence and Communication Center (IICC), http://www.terrorism-info.org. il/malam_multimedia/English/eng_n/pdf/hezbollah_be0506.pdf. (accessed July 8, 2009).

23. Ibid.

Chapter 8. First Intifada.

1. Chaim Herzog, updated by Shlomo Gazit. *Arab-Israeli Wars.* (New York: Vintage Books, 2005), 380-381.

2. Colin Shindler. *A History of Modern Israel.* (New York: Cambridge University Press, 2008), 207; David Dolan. *Holy War for the Promised Land.*(Nashville, TN: Thomas Nelson, 1991), 161-162.

3. Dolan, 161-162.

4. Ahron Bregman. *A History of Israel.* (New York: Palgrave Macmillan, 2003) 215; Dolan. 166-169.

5. Meir Livak. *Palestine Islamic Jihad—Background Information TAU Notes: No. 56.* (November 28, 2002), 1-3, (Jewish Virtual Library), http://www.jewishvirtuallibrary.org/jsource/Terrorism/tau56.html. (accessed June 8, 2010).

6. Ibid.

7. Dolan. 171.

8. *Hamas, Portrait of a Terrorist Organization,* 1, (August 2004, Updated September 1, 2004), from Intelligence and Terrorism Information Center (ITIC) at the Center for Special Studies (C.S.S.), http://www.terrorism-info.org.il/malam_multimedia//ENGLISH/AUTHORITY-HAMAS/PDF/SEP2_04.PDF, (accessed June 3, 2009).

9. *Hamas Charter (1988),* 1, (March 23, 2006), from Intelligence and Terrorism Information Center (ITIC) at the Center for Special Studies (C.S.S.), http://www.terrorism-info.org.il/malam_multimedia/English/eng_n/pdf/hamas_charter.pdf. (accessed May 12, 2009).

10. *Hamas Spokesman Ismail Radwan . . .,* 1, (November 4, 2007), from Intelligence and Terrorism Information Center (ITIC) at the Center for Special Studies (C.S.S.), http://www.terrorism-info.org.il/site/home/default.asp. (accessed March 23, 2009).

11. *The Hamas Threat . . .,* 1, (October 30, 2007), The Israel Project, http://www.the israelproject.org/site/apps/nlnet/content2.aspx?c=hsJPK0PIJpH&b==883997. (accessed November 9, 2010).

12. *Hamas Charter,* 6-16.

13. Herzog. 398-399.

14. Ahron Bregman and Jihan El-Tahri. *Fifty Years War.* ((London, UK: Penguin Books, 1998), 194.

15. Bregman. *History of Israel.* 217-221.

16. Herzog. 399-400.

17. Herzog. 400-401.

18. David Dolan. *Holy War for the Promised Land.* (Nashville, TN: Thomas Nelson, 1991). 188.

19. Herzog. 380, 382-383.

20. Dolan, 191-192.

21. Bregman, *Hisory of Israel*, 227-279.

22. Ibid., 229.

23. *Israeli History, Desert Storm*, n.p., at Israeli-Weapons LTD, http://www.israeli-weapons.com/history/desert_storm/Desert_Storm.html. (accessed August 8, 2010).

Chapter 9. al-Aqsa Intifada.

1. Ahron Bregman. *A History of Israel.* New York: Palgrave Macmillan, 2003), 232-233, 236-239.

2. Ibid., 238-241.

3. Ibid., 248-249.

4. Chaim Herzog, updated by Shlomo Gazit. *Arab Israeli Wars.* (New York: Vintage Books, 2005), 417-418.

5. Ibid., 418-419.

6. Ibid., 419-420.

7. *Timeline of Arab-Israeli Conflict*, 3, The Israel Project, http://www.theisraelproject.org/site/apps/nlnet/content2. aspx?c=hsJPK0PIJpH&b==883997 (accessed April 28, 2009).

8. Herzog, 420-421.

9. Dr. Reuven Erlich. *Agreements, arrangements and understandings concerning Lebanon* . . . (June 8, 2006), 17, from Intelligence and Terrorism Information Center (ITIC) at the Center for Special Studies (C.S.S.), http://www.terrorism-info.org.il/site/home/ default.asp. (accessed February 6, 2010).

10. Ibid., 18-19.

11. Bregman. 255; Herzog. 421-422.

12. *Timeline Arab-Israeli Conflict,* 3.

13. Bregman. 257.

14. *Timeline Arab Israeli Conflict* 3-4.

15. Ibid., 4.

16. Bregman. 266-268.

17. *Timeline Arab-Israeli Conflict*, 4.

18. Dr. Mitchell Bard. *Palestinian War (September 2000-September 2005).*1, Jewish Virtual Library, http://www.jewishvirtuallibrary. org/jsource/Peace/intifada2.html. (accessed July 14, 2010).

19. Ibid., 1.

20. Ibid., 1.

21. *Israel 1991 to Present Al-Aqsa Intifada*, 1, Palestinian Facts, http:// palestinefacts.org/pf_1991to_now_alaqsa_start.php. (accessed April 21, 2009); Bard. *Palestinian War*, 1-2.

22. Bard. *Palestinian War*, 1-2.

23. Ibid.

24. Herzog. 428.

25. Ibid.

26. Ibid.

27.vIbid., 428, 432.

28. *Leading Palestinian Terrorist Organizations (August 2004)*, 1-2, from Intelligence and Terrorism Information Center (ITIC) at the Center for Special Studies (C.S.S.), http://www.terrorism-info.org. il/site/home/default.asp. (accessed March 29, 2009).

29. Ibid., 3-4.

30. Ibid.

31. Ibid., 4-5.

32. Ibid.

33. Ibid., 5-6

34. Ibid.

35. Ibid., 6-7.

36. Ibid.

37. Ibid., 6-7.

38. Ibid.

39. Ibid., 7-8.

40. Ibid.

41. *Hezbollah (Part 1)*, (June 2003), 8, from Intelligence and Terrorism Information Center (ITIC) at the Center for Special Studies (C.S.S.), http://www.terrorism-info.org.il/site/home/default.asp. (accessed October 23, 2009).

42. Ibid.

43. *Timeline Arab-Israeli Conflict*, 4.

44. Ibid., 4.

45. Ibid., 4-5.

46. Ibid., 5.

47. Ibid., 5.

48. Ibid, 5.

49. Ibid., 5.

50. Ibid., 5.

51. *Disengagement News Update No. 8, August 24, 2005*, 2, from Intelligence and Terrorism Information Center (ITIC) at the Center for Special Studies (C.S.S.), http://www.terrorism-info.org.il/site/home/default.asp. (accessed September 25, 2009).

52. *Palestinian Terrorism in 2005, (*December 31, 2005), 8-11, from Intelligence and Terrorism Information Center (ITIC) at the Center for Special Studies (C.S.S.), http://www.terrorism-info.org.il/site/home/default.asp. (accessed May 24, 2010).

53. Ibid., 12-13.

54. Bard. *Palestinian War*, 2-4.

55. *Five Years of Violent Confrontation between Israel and Palestinians*, 1, (October 2, 2005), from *Intelligence and Terrorism Information Center (ITIC) at the Center for Special Studies (C.S.S.),* http://www.terrorism-info.org.il/site/home/default.asp. (accessed May 24, 2010).

56. *Suicide Bombing Terrorism, September 2000-December 2005*, Part A, 5-6, (January 1, 2006), 5-6, from Intelligence and Terrorism Information Center (ITIC) at the Center for Special Studies (C.S.S.), http://www.terrorism-info.org.il/site/home/default.asp. (accessed May 24, 2010).

57. *Incitement on Local Radio Stations*, (July 17, 2005), 1-2, from Intelligence and Terrorism Information Center (ITIC) at the Center for Special Studies (C.S.S.), http://www.terrorism-info.org.il/site/home/default.asp. (accessed July 26, 2009).

Chapter 10. Second Lebanon War.

1. *Rocket Threat from the Gaza Strip, 2000-2007*, (December 2007), 6-7, from Intelligence and Terrorism Information Center at the Israel Intelligence and Communication Center (IICC), http://www.terrorism-info.org.il/site/home/default.asp. (accessed December 21, 2009).

2. *Profile of the Hamas Movement*, (February 12, 2006), 2, from Intelligence and Terrorism Information Center (ITIC) at the Center for Special Studies (C.S.S.), http://www.terrorism-info.org.il/malam_multimedia/English/eng_n/pdf/hamas_e0206.pdf (accessed May 5, 2009).

3. *The Road to the Second Lebanon War*, (October 30, 2007), 11-12, from Intelligence and Terrorism Information Center (ITIC) at the Center for Special Studies (C.S.S.). http://www.terrorism-info.

org.il/malam_multimedia/English/eng_n/pdf/lebanon_0_06e.pdf. (accessed May 5, 2009).

4. Ibid., 14.

5. *Countdown to Conflict*, (August 20, 2006), 4, from Intelligence and Terrorism Information Center (ITIC) at the Center for Special Studies (C.S.S.), http://www.terrorism-info.org.il/site/home/ default.asp. (June 24, 2009).

6. *Background: Hezbollah*, (August 5, 2010), 1, The Israel Project, http://www.theisraelproject.org/site/c.hsJPK0PIJpH/b.2907307/ k.429B/Background_Hezbollah. (accessed August 5, 2010).

7. *Hezbollah, Part 1*, 8, from Intelligence and Terrorism Information Center (ITIC) at the Center for Special Studies (C.S.S.), http:// www.terrorism-info.org.il/site/home/default.asp. (accessed April 3, 2010).

8. *Hezbollah as a Strategic Arm of Iran*, (September 8, 2006), 6, from Intelligence and Terrorism Information Center (ITIC) at the Center for Special Studies (C.S.S.), http://www.terrorism-info.org. il/malam_multimedia/English/eng_n/pdf/iran_hezbollah_e1.pdf. (accessed March 23, 2009).

9. *The Road to the Second Lebanon War*18-19, 21.

10. Ibid., 22-25.

11. *Katyusha Rockets Fired Deep into the Galilee.*, (May 29, 2006), 1-5 from Intelligence and Terrorism Information Center (ITIC) at the Center for Special Studies (C.S.S.), http://www.terrorism-info. org.il/malam_multimedia/English/eng_n/pdf/hezbollah_be0506. pdf. (accessed February 23, 2010).

12. *Hezbollah's Terrorist Attack on Israel's Northern Border*, (July 13, 2006), 1-3, from Intelligence and Terrorism Information Center (ITIC) at the Center for Special Studies (C.S.S.), http://

www.terrorism-info.org.il/site/home/default.asp. (accessed March 7, 2010).

13. Ibid., 4.

14. *Hezbollah's Use of Lebanon Civilians as Human Shields*, (November 2006), 6-7, from Intelligence and Terrorism Information Center (ITIC) at the Center for Special Studies (C.S.S.), http://www.terrorism-info.org.il/malam_multimedia/English/eng_n/pdf/human_shields.pdf. (accessed Mach 8, 2010).

15. *Anti-Israeli Terrorism in 2006: Data Analysis and Trends*, (March 2007), 7, from Intelligence and Terrorism Information Center at the Israel Intelligence and Communication Center (IICC), http://www.terrorism-info.org.il/malam_multimedia/English/eng_n/pdf/terrorism_2006e.pdf. (accessed June 9, 2010).

16. *Hezbollah as a Strategic Arm*, 25; *Anti-Israeli Terrorism*, 7.

17. *Anti-Israeli Terrorism*, 10.

18. *The Hezbollah-Israel Conflict: by the Numbers*, (August 17, 2006), 1, The Israel Project, http://www.theisraelproject.org/site/apps/ninct/content2.aspx?c=hsJPK0PIJpH&b=883997& . . . (accessed August 5, 2009).

19. *Anti-Israeli Terrorism in 2006,* 117-119.

Chapter 11. Gaza Operation.

1. *Hamas's Military Buildup in the Gaza Strip (Updated April 2008)*, 3, from Intelligence and Terrorism Information Center at the Israel Intelligence and Communication Center (IICC), http://www.terrorism-info.org.il/site/home/default.asp. (accessed March 8, 2010).

2. *Profile of the Hamas Movement*, (February 12, 2006), 25-27, from Intelligence and Terrorism Information Center (ITIC) at the

Center for Special Studies (C.S.S.), http://www.terrorism-info. org.il/malam_multimedia/English/eng_n/pdf/hamas_e0206.pdf (accessed May 5, 2009).

3. *Hamas' Military Buildup*, 4.

4. Ibid., 4-5.

5. *Anti-Israeli Terrorism in 2007 and its Trends in 2008.* (May 2008), 4, 10-13, from Intelligence and Terrorism Information Center at the Israel Intelligence and Communication Center (IICC), http:// www.terrorism-info.org.il/site/home/default.asp. (accessed July 8, 2009).

6. *Hamas Rocket Attack on Sderot and Settlements . . ., May 20 Bulletin update,* (May 21, 2007), 2, from Intelligence and Terrorism Information Center at the Israel Intelligence and Communication Center (IICC), http://www.terrorism-info.org.il/site/home/default. asp. (accessed July 8, 2009).

7. *News of the Israeli-Palestinian Confrontation*, (December 1-15, 2007), 1-2, from Intelligence and Terrorism Information Center at the Israel Intelligence and Communication Center (IICC), http:// www.terrorism-info.org.il/site/home/default.asp. (accessed July 8, 2009).

8. *Protest of the Annapolis Meeting Opponents-as of November 18, 2007*, 1-6, from Intelligence and Terrorism Information Center at the Israel Intelligence and Communication Center (IICC), http://www.terrorism-info.org.il/site/home/default.asp. (accessed July 8, 2009); *November 20, 2007, Terrorist Attacks and the Propaganda Campaign to Undermine the Annapolis Meeting*, 1-3, from Intelligence and Terrorism Information Center at the Israel Intelligence and Communication Center (IICC), http:// www.terrorism-info.org.il/site/home/default.asp. (accessed July 8, 2009).

9. *Summary of Rocket Fire and Mortar Shelling in 2008/2009*, 2-3, from Intelligence and Terrorism Information Center at the Israel Intelligence and Communication Center (IICC), http://www.terrorism-info.org.il/site/home/default.asp. (accessed May 12, 2010).

10. *Two Days of Hard Fighting in the South . . .*, (January 16, 2008), 2-4, from Intelligence and Terrorism Information Center at the Israel Intelligence and Communication Center (IICC), http://www.terrorism-info.org.il/site/home/default.asp. (accessed June 14, 2009).

11. *A New Round of Escalation in Rocket Attacks by Hamas . . .*, (February 18, 2008), 2-3, from Intelligence and Terrorism Information Center at the Israel Intelligence and Communication Center (IICC), http://www.terrorism-info.org.il/site/home/default.asp. (accessed June 15, 2009).

12. *May 18, 2008, A Grad Rocket Fired from the Gaza Strip Hit a Crowded Gaza Mall in Ashqelon . . .*, 1, from Intelligence and Terrorism Information Center at the Israel Intelligence and Communication Center (IICC), http://www.terrorism-info.org.il/site/home/default.asp. (accessed June 5, 2009).

13. *Country Reports on Terrorism 2009 Middle East and North Africa Overview, Israel, West Bank, and Gaza*, U.S. Department of State, 1-2, http://www.state.gov/s/ct/rls/crt/2009/140886.htm. (accessed October 6, 2010).

14. *One Month into the Lull in Fighting: an Interim Report (as of July 23)*, (July 27, 2008), 1-2, from Intelligence and Terrorism Information Center at the Israel Intelligence and Communication Center (IICC), http://www.terrorism-info.org.il/site/home/default.asp. (accessed March 23, 2009).

15. *November 16, 2008, Significant Erosion of the Lull Arrangement in the Gaza Strip*, 1-3, from Intelligence and Terrorism Information Center at the Israel Intelligence and Communication Center (IICC),

http://www.terrorism-info.org.il/site/home/default.asp. (accessed January 5, 2009).

16. *News of Terrorism and Palestinian-Israeli Conflict, November 18-25, 2008*, 1, from Intelligence and Terrorism Information Center at the Israel Intelligence and Communication Center (IICC), http://www.terrorism-info.org.il/site/home/default.asp. (accessed July 8, 2009).

17. *Weekend Escalation in the Gaza Strip, on December 5 and 6*, (December 7, 2008), 3, from Intelligence and Terrorism Information Center at the Israel Intelligence and Communication Center (IICC), http://www.terrorism-info.org.il/site/home/default. asp. (accessed July 8, 2009); *Weekend Escalation in Gaza*, 1.

18. *News of Terrorism*, 1.

19. *Weekend Escalation*, 1-2; Escalation *in Attacks from Gaza Strip as Hamas Announces the End of the Lull Arrangement*, (December 18, 2008), 1-2, from Intelligence and Terrorism Information Center at the Israel Intelligence and Communication Center (IICC), http://www.terrorism-info.org.il/site/home/default.asp. (accessed February 6, 2009).

20. *Intensive Rocket Fire Attacks against Western Negev . . .*, (December 21, 2008), 2, from Intelligence and Terrorism Information Center at the Israel Intelligence and Communication Center (IICC), http://www.terrorism-info.org.il/site/home/default.asp. (accessed September 26, 2009).

21. *Broadcasts on Hamas's Al-Aqsa and Hezbollah's Al-Mana TV Channels*, (December 15, 2008), 1, from Intelligence and Terrorism Information Center at the Israel Intelligence and Communication Center (IICC), http://www.terrorism-info.org.il/site/home/default. asp. (accessed September 26, 2009).

22. *The Operation in Gaza, 27 December 2008-18 January 2000*, 5, 14, from Intelligence and Terrorism Information Center at the

Israel Intelligence and Communication Center (IICC), http://www.terrorism-info.org.il/site/home/default.asp. (accessed July 20, 2010).

23. Ibid., 16-17.

24. Ibid., 23,32.

25. *Operation Cast Lead, Update No. 1*, (December 28, 2008), 4, 9, from Intelligence and Terrorism Information Center at the Israel Intelligence and Communication Center (IICC), http://www.terrorism-info.org.il/site/home/default.asp. (accessed July 8, 2009).

26. *Cast Lead Updates No. 2, 3, & 5,* from Intelligence and Terrorism Information Center at the Israel Intelligence and Communication Center (IICC), http://www.terrorism-info.org.il/site/home/default.asp. (accessed June 7, 2010).

27. *Cast Lead Updates No. 4 & 5,* from Intelligence and Terrorism Information Center at the Israel Intelligence and Communication Center (IICC), http://www.terrorism-info.org.il/site/home/default.asp. (accessed June 7, 2010).

28. *Cast Lead Updates No. 4, 5, & 6,* from Intelligence and Terrorism Information Center at the Israel Intelligence and Communication Center (IICC), http://www.terrorism-info.org.il/site/home/default.asp. (accessed July 8, 2010).

29. *Cast Lead Updates No. 8, 9, & 11,* from Intelligence and Terrorism Information Center at the Israel Intelligence and Communication Center (IICC), http://www.terrorism-info.org.il/site/home/default.asp. (accessed July 8, 2010).

30. *Cast Lead Updates No. 11 & 12,* from Intelligence and Terrorism Information Center at the Israel Intelligence and Communication Center (IICC), http://www.terrorism-info.org.il/site/home/default.asp. (accessed July 8, 2010).

31. *Cast Lead Updates No. 13 & 14,* from Intelligence and Terrorism Information Center at the Israel Intelligence and Communication Center (IICC), http://www.terrorism-info.org.il/site/home/default. asp. (accessed June 7, 2010).

32. *Operation in the Gaza,* 7-8.

33. *Cast Lead Update No. 17,* (January 19, 2008), 2, from Intelligence and Terrorism Information Center at the Israel Intelligence and Communication Center (IICC), http://www.terrorism-info.org.il/ site/home/default.asp. (accessed July 28, 2009); *Operation in the Gaza,* 9.

34. *Operation in Gaza,* 9; Cast Lead Update No. 18, from Intelligence and Terrorism Information Center at the Israel Intelligence and Communication Center (IICC), http://www.terrorism-info.org.il/ site/home/default.asp. (accessed July 8, 2009).

35. *Cast Lead Updates No. 16 & 18,* from Intelligence and Terrorism Information Center at the Israel Intelligence and Communication Center (IICC), http://www.terrorism-info.org.il/site/home/default. asp. (accessed July 8, 2010); *A Surge in the Number of Rockets and Mortar Shells at Israel,* (March 1, 2009), 2-4, from Intelligence and Terrorism Information Center at the Israel Intelligence and Communication Center (IICC), http://www.terrorism-info.org.il/ site/home/default.asp. (accessed Ma 10, 2010).

36. *Cast Lead Update No. 17,* (January 19, 2009), 7, from Intelligence and Terrorism Information Center at the Israel Intelligence and Communication Center (IICC), http://www.terrorism-info.org.il/ site/home/default.asp. (accessed May 11, 2009).

37. Ibid., 8.

38. *The Gaza Strip After Operation Cast Lead,* (June 2009), 33, from Intelligence and Terrorism Information Center at the Israel Intelligence and Communication Center (IICC), http://

www.terrorism-info.org.il/site/home/default.asp. (accessed May 11, 2009).

Chapter 12. Alliance of Terror.

1. *Iran at the Forefront of Multi-Pronged War Against Israel, the West*, 1, The Israel Project, http://www.theisraelproject.org/site/c.hsJPK0PIJpH/b.672631/apps/s/content.asp?ct-5083 . . . (accessed October 1, 2010); *Iran: Leading State Sponsor of Terror*, 1, The Israel Project, mhtml:file//:\Iransponsorofterror.mht. (accessed October 3, 2010).

2. Ilan Berman, *The Iranian Nuclear Crisis: Latest Developments and Next Steps*, Testimony before the U.S. House of Representatives, (March 15, 2007), 2.

3. *Iran as a State Sponsoring and Operating Terror* (April 2003), 9, from Intelligence and Terrorism Information Center (ITIC) at the Center for Special Studies (C.S.S.), http://www.terrorism-info.org.il/site/home/default.asp. (accessed March 7, 2010).

4. *Using the Quds Force of the Revolutionary Guard as the Main Tool to Export the Revolution* (April 2, 2007), 2, from Intelligence and Terrorism Information Center at the Israel Intelligence and Communication Center (IICC), http://www.terrorism-info.org.il/site/home/default.asp. (accessed May 11, 2009).

5. *Anti-Israeli Terrorism in 2006: Data Analysis and Trends*, (March 2007), 7, from Intelligence and Terrorism Information Center at the Israel Intelligence and Communication Center (IICC), http://www.terrorism-info.org.il/malam_multimedia/English/eng_n/pdf/terrorism_2006e.pdf (accessed June 9, 2010).

6. *Using the Quds Force*, 5.

7. Ibid., 3-5.

8. *Iran as a State Sponsoring*, 29-30.

9. Ibid., 31-32.

10. Lt.Gen. (ret.) Moshe Yaalon. "Iran's Race for Regional Supremacy." *Jerusalem Center for Pubic Affairs* (2008), Jerusalem, Israel, 8.

11. *Iran as a State Sponsoring*, 33-35.

12. *Using the Quds Forces*, 7-8.

13. Ibid., 8-9.

14. Dr. Reuven Erlich. *Syria as a Strategic Prop for Hezbollah and Hamas*. (August 3, 2006), 1-2, from Intelligence and Terrorism Information Center (ITIC) at the Center for Special Studies (C.S.S.), http://www.terrorism-info.org.il/site/home/default.asp. (accessed March 7, 2010).

15. Ibid.

16. *Hezbollah (Part 1)*, (June 2003), 58-60, from Intelligence and Terrorism Information Center (ITIC) at the Center for Special Studies (C.S.S.), http://www.terrorism-info.org.il/site/home/default.asp. (accessed March 10, 2010).

17. *Hezbollah (Part 1)*, 132; *Three Years After War, Dangers to Israel Intensify* (July 5, 2009), 1, The Israel Project, http://www.the israelproject.org/site/apps/nlnet/content2.asp?c=hsJPK0PIJpH&b==689705& . . . (accessed September 4, 2009); *Hezbollah (Part 1)*, 132; *Iran's Race for Regional*, 8.

18. *Syria as Strategic Support for Hamas,* (July 5, 2006), 2-3, from Intelligence and Terrorism Information Center (ITIC) at the Center for Special Studies (C.S.S.), http://www.terrorism-info.org.il/site/home/default.asp. (accessed March 7, 2010); Syria *as a Strategic Prop*, 7;

19. Mathew A. Levitt, *Iranian Sponsorship of Terror: Threatening U.S. Security, Global Stability, and Regional Peace.* Testimony

before Joint Hearing of the Committee on International Relations, U.S. House of Representatives, (February 16, 2005), 17-18; *Iran's Sponsorship of Terrorism Across the Globe*, (November 12, 2009), 1-2, The Israel Project, http://www.theisraelproject.org/site/apps/nlnet/content2.aspx?c=hsJPK0PIJpH&b=68970...(accessed November 13, 2010).

20. *Using Quds Force*, 18.

21. Ibid.

22. *Iran's Sponsorship of Terrorism*, 1-2.

23. Ibid., 3.

24. Ibid., 3.

25. *Iran Intensifies Influence throughout Latin America*, (November 18, 2009), 1-2, The Israel Project, http://www.theisraelproject.org/site/c.hsJPK0PIJpH/b.5608661/k.E577/Iran_Intensifies_I.... (accessed November 13, 2010).

26. Ibid., 2-3.

27. Ibid., 3-4.

28. Ibid., 5.

29. Ibid., 5-6.

30. *Iranian Support of Hamas,* 2-4, (January 12, 2009), from Intelligence and Terrorism Information Center (ITIC) at the Center for Special Studies (C.S.S.), http://www.terrorism-info.org.il/site/home/default.asp. (accessed May 24, 2010); *The Gaza Strip after Operation Cast Lead,* 3-5, (June 2009), from Intelligence and Terrorism Information Center (ITIC) at the Center for Special Studies (C.S.S.), http://www.terrorism-info.org.il/site/home/default.asp. (accessed May 24, 2010); Col. (Ret.) Jonathan Fighel,

"Israel's Battle in Gaza—the Future of the Palestinian Cause," *International Institute for Counter-Terrorism,* (July 1, 2009), 1-4, http://www.ict.org.il/Articles/tabid/66/Default.aspx. (accessed November 13, 2010); *Yet Another Step in the Establishment of a Totalitarian "Islamic Emirate . . ."* (November 13, 2008), 1-2, from Intelligence and Terrorism Information Center at the Israel Intelligence and Communication Center (IICC), http://www.terrorism-info.org.il/site/home/default.asp. (accessed May 11, 2009).

31. *Fatah Reaches Alliance with Iran-backed Hamas,* 1-2, (April 27, 2011), The Israel Project, (April 27, 2011) http://www.theisraelproject.org/site/c.hsJPK0PIJpH/b.689705/k.9F22/Press_Releases/apps/nl/newsletter2.asp, (accessed April 28, 2011).

32. *Arab League Says "No" to Peace Talks; Rocket Fire Resumes,* 1-2, (May 29, 2011), The Israel Project, http://www.theisraelproject.org/site, (accessed June 1, 2011).

33. *Fatah Leaders Call for End of Israel,* 1-2, (June 2, 2011), The Israel Project, http://www.theisraelproject.org/site, (accessed June 3, 2011).

34. *Palestinian Unity Deal Undermines Peace Prospects.* 1-2, (May 5, 2011), AIPAC MEMO, www.aipac.org, (accessed June 23, 2011).

35. Ibid.

36. Ibid.

37. *Egypt to Open Border with Gaza Without Israeli Involvement,* 1-2, (April 29, 2011), The Israel Project, http://www.theisraelproject.org/site/c.hsJPK0PIJpH/b.689705/k.9F22/Press_Releases/apps/nl/newsletter2.asp, (accessed April 30, 2011).

Chapter 13. Dangers on the Horizon.

1. *A World View Interview with Benjamin Netanyahu.* You Tube World View, Israel Channel 2, Jerusalem, March 23, 2011.

2. *Fact Sheet: Iran's Burgeoning Nuclear Capacities,* 1, The Israel Project, http://www.theisraelproject.org/site/c.hsJPK0PIJpH/b.2400213/k.61B6/Irans_Number_C a...(accessed November 13, 2010).

3. Ibid; and Alfanso Serrano. "Report: Iran 2-3 Years from Nuclear Weapon." *CBS News, London,* January 31, 2007, 1, http://www.cbsnews.com/stories/2007/01/3`1/world/main24. (accessed October 29, 2010).

4. Catherine Philp. "Secret Document Exposes Iran's Nuclear Trigger." *The Times,* Washington, December 14, 2009, 1-3, http://www.timesonline.co.uk/tol/newes/world/middle_east/article6955351.ece. (accessed October 27, 2010).

5. "Iran's Nuclear Program," *The New York Times,* September 7, 2010, 1-4, http://www.nytimes.com/info/iran-nuclear-program/?pagemode=print. (accessed October 27, 2010).

6. Malkah Fleisher. "Secret Report: Iran Will Have Nuclear Bomb This Year." *Arutz Sheva, Israel National News Online,* January 25, 2010, 1-2, http://www.israelnationalnews.com/SendMail.aspx?print=print&type=0&item=135679. (accessed October 27, 2010).

7. *Former Mossad Official—No Signs of Iran Stopping Nuclear Program,* (January 12, 2011), 1-2. The Israel Project. http://www.theisraelproject.org/site/c.hsJPK0PIJpH/b.672631/apps/s/content.asp?ct=9018025. (accessed January 12, 2011).

8. Ibid.

9. "Only a threat of force will halt Iran nukes: Israel," *Reuters,* January 11, 2011, 1, http://www.reuters.com. (accessed January 17, 20011).

10. Ivanka Barzashka. *Using Enrichment Capacity to Estimate Iran's Breakout Potential.* Federation of American Scientists. (Washington, D.C.: January 21, 2011), 1-16.

11. Jerome R. Corsi. Ph.D. *Why Israel Can't Wait, The Coming War Between Israel and Iraq.* New York: Threshold Editors, 2009), 87-90.

12. *Fact Sheet: Ahmadinejad's Extremist Religious Views,* 1, The Israel Project, http://www.theisraelproject.org/site/c. hsJPK0PIJpH/b.672631/apps/s/content.asp?ct=292...(accessed October 27, 2010); *Ahmadinejad's Policies and Doctrines, Religious Dogma,* (January 11, 2007, modified February 2, 2009), 1, The Israel Project, http://www.theisraelproject.org/site/c. hsJPK0PIJpH/b.672631/apps/s/content.asp?ct=342. (accessed November 13, 2010).

13. *Ahmadinejad's Extremist Views,* 1; Ahmadinejad's *Policies and Doctrines,* 1.

14. *Fact Sheet: Ahmadinejad's Views on Israel and the Holocaust,* 1, The Israel Project, mhtml:file://F:\Fact SheetAhmadinejad'sVie wsonIsraelandtheHolocaust, (accessed October 6, 2010); Iranian *President Mahmoud Ahmadinejad: In His Own Words,* 1-4.

15. "Only the threat of force will halt Iran nukes: Israel," January 11, 2011, *Reuters.* http://www.reuters.com/assets/ print?aid=USTRE70A64F20110111. (accessed January 17, 2011).

Chapter 14. Conclusion.

1. *The Hate Industry—At the Jerusalem Day* . . .4-5, (November 8, 2006), from Intelligence and Terrorism Information Center (ITIC) at

the Center for Special Studies (C.S.S.), http://www.terrorism-info. org.il/site/home/default.asp. (accessed July 30, 2009).

2.   Ibid., 3-4.

3.   Dr. Mitchell G. Bard, *The Palestinian Question is the Core of the Arab-Israeli Conflict, Myths & Facts—The Peace Process*, 1, (The Jewish Virtual Library), http://www.jewishvirtuallibrary.org/ jsource/myths/mf22.html. (accessed June 21, 2010).

4.   Dr. Mike Evans, *Abbas to Personaly Present Case for Palestinian Statehood to UN*, July 22, 2011, www.jerusalemPrayerTeam.org.

5.   Dr. Mike Evans, *Quartet "Peace Plan" Would Force Half a Million Jews from their Homes,* July 8, 2011, www.jerusalemPrayerTeam. org.

6.   Winston S. Churchill, *The Second World War: The Gathering Storm*, (Boston: Houghton Mifflin Company, 1948) 304.

Glossary of Terms

AAA   Anti-aircraft artillery.

AHC   Arab Higher Committee.

ALA   Arab Liberation Army.

Al-Aqsa Masque   Mosque on Temple Mount in the Old City of Jerusalem where the Israelite Temple once stood.

AMAN   Israel's Military Intelligence.

Bar-Lev Line   Israel's defense fortifications on the east bank of the Suez Canal.

Battalion   Army unit. Size varies by country from 300 to 1,000 troops.

Brigade   Army unit. Size varies by country from 1,500 to 5,000 troops.

Circassians   Small community concentrated in two northern Israel villages.

Diaspora   Refers to Jewish communities living among gentiles outside of Israel.

DMZ   Demilitarized Zone.

Division   Army unit. Size varies by country from 10,000 to 15,000 troops.

East Jerusalem	Arab section of Jerusalem. Includes the Old City of Jerusalem.
EFP	Explosively formed penetration. Explosive device designed to penetrate armor and be more lethal.
Eretz	Yisrael The land of Israel.
Fatah	A Palestinian organization that carried out numerous attacks against Istael. The most important organization within the PLO under Yasser Arafat.
Fedayeen	Palestinan militant organization that attacked Israel.
Gaza Strip	The narrow, 25 mile strip along the Mediterranean Sea.
Golan Heights	Mountainous region in northeastern Israel.
Ha'aretz	Leading newspaper in Israel.
Haganah	Underground Jewish defense organization in Palestine before Israel became a state. Merged to become the Israeli Defense Force.
Hamas	Palestinian Islamic fundamentalist terrorist group and political party that seized control of the Gaza Strip.
Haram	Al-Sharif The area where the done of Rock and Al-Aqsa Mosque are located in Jerusalem.
Hezbollah	AKA Hizbullah. The Party of God. Islamic fundamentalist terrorist group in Lebanon.
IAEA UN	International Atomic Energy Agency.
IAF	Israeli Air Force.

IDF   Israeli Defense Force (Israel's armed forces).

IED   Improvised explosive device.

Imam   An Islamic leadership position, often the worship leader of the mosque and the Muslim community.

Intifada   Palestinian uprising in the Gaza and West Bank (a shaking off of Israeli control).

Irgun   Jewish underground organization established during British control of Palestine.

Islamic   Jihad Splinter group of the Muslim Brotherhood in the 1880s.

Jihad   Islamic holy war against non-Muslims.

Katusha   A Soviet/Russian rocket named after a popular wartime song about a young Russian woman named Katysha (Catherine). Used by terrorists to attack Israel.

Knesset   The parliament of the State of Israel.

Lehi   A Jewish anti-British underground organization in Palestine.

Likud   Israeli political alignment, including the Herut party and centrist Liberal party, plus several smaller parties.

Mahdi   "The Guided One." An ultimate savior of humankind and the final Imam of the Twelve Imams. Twelve Shi'a Muslims believe al-Mahdi was hidden away by God and will later emerge with isa (Jesus Christ) to bring peace and justice to the world.

Mapai	Israel's major labor party.
MIG	Soviet aircraft developed by the bureau of Mikoyan and Guervich.
Mossad	Israel's government intelligence agency (comparable to the CIA).
Negev	Southern arid region of Israel.
PA	Palestinian Authority. Originally formed as the autonomous Palestinian government of the West Bank and Gaza areas.
Palestine	An ancient designation for the area between Syria to the north and Egypt to the south, between the Mediterranean Sea and the River Jordan. The name refers to the Land of Israel during the years of the Jewish exile.
Palmach	Special strike force within the Haganah.
PIJ	Palestinian Islamic Jihad. A terrorist organization.
PLC	Palestinian Legislative Council. Legislative body of the Palestinian Authority.
PLF	Palestinian Liberation Front.
PLO	Palestinian Liberation Organization. Formed by Yasser Arafat. At one time the sole representative of the Palestinians.
PNC	PLO's highest decision-making body.
Qassam	Short range rocket manufactured by Hamas.
SA	Surface-to-air. Prefix for designating SAM systems.

SAM	Surface-to-air-missile. Air defense missile system.
Sharia	The Islamic system of law.
Torah	The "five books of Moses" in the Hebrew scriptures.
UNRWA	UN Relief and Works Agency. (Palestinian emergency assistance organization).
UNSCOP	United Nations Special Committee of Palestine.
West/Western	Term used to refer to Western Europe, United States, Britain, Canada, Australia, and New Zealand.
Waaf	Palestinian Muslim religious authority.
Yom Kippur	Jewish annual day of fasting and atonement. The most solemn and important occasion of the Jewish religious year.
Zion (Zionism)	(Mount Zion) Is a Hebrew designation for Jerusalem. In biblical times it began to symbolize the national homeland. A focus for Jewish national-religious hopes for renewal over the centuries.

Bibliography

A New Round of Escalation in Rocket Attacks by Hamas . . ., (February 18, 2008).

Ahmadinejad's Policies and Doctrines, Religious Dogma, January 11, 2007, modified February 2, 2009, The Israel Project, http://www. theisraelproject.org/site/c.hsJPK0PIJpH/b.672631/apps/scontent. asp?ct=342. (accessed November 13, 2010).

Another Step in the Establishment of a Totalitarian "Islamic Emirate . . ." (November 13, 2008), from Intelligence and Terrorism Information Center (ITIC) at the Israel Intelligence and Communication Center (IICC), http://www.terrorism-info.org.il/site/home/default.asp. (accessed May 11, 2009).

Anti-Israeli Terrorism in 2006: Data Analysis and Trends, (March 2007), from Intelligence and Terrorism Information Center at the Israel Intelligence and Communication Center (IICC), http:// www.terrorism-info.org.il/malam_multimedia/English/eng_n/pdf/ terrorsm_2006epdf. (accessed June 9, 2010).

Anti-Israeli Terrorism in 2007 and its Trends in 2008, (May 2008), from Intelligence and Terrorism Information Center (ITIC) at the Israel Intelligence and Communication Center (IICC), http://www. terrorism-info.org.il/site/home/default.asp.(accessed July 8, 2009).

Background: Hezbollah, (August 5, 2010), The Israel Project, http:// www.theisraelproject.org/site/c.hsJPK0PIJpH/b.2907307/k.429B/ Background_Hezbollah. (accessed August 5, 2010).

Balmer, Crispian. "Only a threat of force will halt Iran Nukes: Israel," *Reuters*. (January 11, 2011), http://www.reuters.com/assets/print?aid==USTRE70A64F20110111. (accessed January 17, 2011).

Bard, Dr. Mitchell G. *Declaration of Independence of the Establishment of the State of Israel (May 14, 1948)*. Jewish Virtual Library, 1998. http://www.jewishvirtuallibrary.org/source/Declaration.html. (accessed July 10, 2009).

Bard, Dr. Mitchell G. *Road to Suez*. Jewish Virtual Library, Myth and Facts, 2006. http://www.jewsihvirtuallibrary.org/jsource/myths/mfs.html. (accessed October 27, 2009).

Bard, Dr. Mitchell G. *Palestinian War (September 2000-September 2005, The "al Aksa Intifada,"* Jewish Virtual Library, http"//www.jewishvirtuallibrary.org/jsource/Peace/intifada2.html. (accessed July 14, 2010).

Barzashka, Ivanka. "Using Enrichment Capacity to Estimate Iran's Breakout Potential," *Federation of American Scientists,* Washington, D.C., http://www.fas.org. (accessed January 17, 2011).

Berman, Ilan. *Iranian Nuclear Crisis: Latest Developments and New Steps,* Testimony before the U.S. House of Representatives, (March 15, 2007).

Blum, Howard. *The Eve of Destruction*. New York: Perennial, 2003.

Bondy, Ruth, Ohad Zmora and Raphael Bashan, eds. *Mission Survival*. New York: Sabra Books, 1968.

Bowen, Jeremy. *Six Days*. New York: Thomas Dunne Books, 2005.

Bregman, Ahron and Jihan El-Tahri. *The Fifty Years War*. London, UK: Penguin Books, 1998.

Bregman, Ahron. *A History of Israel*. New York: Palgrave Macmillan, 2003.

Broadcasts on Hamas's Al-Aqsa and Hezbollah's Al Mana TV Channels, (December 15, 2008), from Intelligence and Terrorism Information Center (ITIC) at the Israel Intelligence and Communication Center (IICC), http://www.terrorism-info.org.il/site/home/default.asp. (accessed September 26, 2009).

CIA World Fact Book. *Israel.* http://www.cia/library, (accessed 12 January 2009).

Composition of Muslim Texts, Sunnah and Hedith. University of California, Center for Muslim-Jewish Engagement. http://www.use. edu/schools/college/crc/engagement/resources/texts/muslim/hedith.

Corsi, Jerome R. PhD. *Why Israel Can't Wait, The Coming War Between Israel and Iran.* New York: Threshold Editors, 2009.

Countdown to Conflict, (August 20, 2006), from Intelligence and Terrorism Information Center (ITIC) at the Center for Special Studies (C.S.S.), http://www.terrorism-info.org.il/site/home/default.asp. (accessed June 24, 2009).

Country Reports on Terrorism 2009 Middle East and North Africa Overview, Israel, West Bank, and Gaza, U.S. State Department, http:// www.stae.gov/s/ct/ris/crt/2009/140886.htm. (accessed October 6, 2010).

Country Studies, Israel 1988. *Israel Action in Lebanon 1978-1982,* from the Library of Congress, http://lcweb2loc.govegi-bin/query/r?frd/ cstdy:@field(DOCID+il0029. (accessed January 10, 2009).

Country Studies, Israel 1988. *The October War,* from the Library of Congress, http://lcweb2loc.govegi-bin/query/r?frd/cstdy:@ field(DOCID+il0029. (accessed January 10, 2009).

Country Studies, Israel, 1988. *Prelude to Statehood, Problems of the New State, 1948-1967.* from Library of Congress. http://lcweb2loc. govegi-bin/query/r?frd/cstdy:@field(DOCID+il0029.

Dershowitz, Allen. *The Case Against Israel's Enemies*. Hoboken, NJ: John Wiley & Sons, 2008.

Disengagement News Update No. 8, August 24, 2005,), from Intelligence and Terrorism Information Center (ITIC) at the Center for Special Studies (C.S.S.), http://www.terrorism-info.org.il/site/home/default. asp. (accessed September 25, 2009).

Dolan, David. *Holy War for the Promised Land*. Nashville, TN: Thomas Nelson, 1991.

Dowty, Alan. *Israel/Palestine*. (Cambridge, UK: Polity, 2008).

Dunstan, Simon. *Yom Kippur War, Arab-Israeli War of 1973*. Oxford, UK: Osprey, 2007.

Erlich, Dr. Reuven. *Agreements, Arrangements and Understandings Concerning Lebanon*. (June 8, 2006), from Intelligence and Terrorism Information Center (ITIC) at the Center for Special Studies (C.S.S.), http://www.terrorism-info.org.il/site/home/default.asp.   (accessed February 6, 2010).

Erlich, Dr. Reuven and Yoram Kahati. *Hezbollah as a Case Study of the Battle for Hearts and Minds,* from Intelligence and Terrorism Information Center at the Israel Intelligence and Communication Center (IICC). http://www.terrorism-info.org.il/malam_multimedia/ English/eng_n/pdf/hezbollah_be0506.pdf. (accessed July 8, 2009).

Erlich, Dr. Reuven. *Syria as a Strategic Prop for Hezbollah and Hamas*. (August 3, 2006), from Intelligence and Terrorism Information Center (ITIC) at the Israel Intelligence and Communication Center (IICC), http://www.terrorism-info.org.il/site/home/default.asp.   (accessed March 7, 2010).

Evans, Michael D., and Jerome R. Corsi. *Showdown with Nuclear Iran*. Nashville, TN: Nelson Current, 2006.

Fact Sheet: Ahmadinejad's Extremist Religious Views, The Israel Project, http://www.theisraelproject.org/site/c.hsJPK0PIJpH/b.672631/ apps/scontent.asp?ct=292. (accessed October 27, 2010).

Fact Sheet: Ahmadinejad's Views on Israel and the Holocaust, The Israel Project. mhtml:file://F:\Fact Sheet Ahmadinejad's Views on Israel and the Holocaust, (accessed October 6, 2010).

Fact Sheet: Iran's Burgeoning Nuclear Capacities, The Israel Project, http://www.theisraelproject.org/site/c.hsJPK0PIJpH/b,2400213/ k.61B6/Irans_Number_Ca. (accessed November 13, 2010).

Fighel, Jonathan, Col. (Ret.). "Israel's Battle in Gaza—the Future of the Palestinian Cause." *ICT International Institute for Counter-Terrorism,* (July 1, 2009), http://www.ict.org.il/Articles/tabid/66/Default.aspx. (accessed November 13, 2010).

Five Years of Violent Confrontations Between Israel and Palestinians, (October 2, 2005), from Intelligence and Terrorism Information Center (ITIC) at the Center for Special Studies (C.S.S.), http://www. terrorism-info.org.il/site/home/default.asp. (accessed May 24, 2010).

Fleisher, Malkah. "Secret Report: Iran Will Have Nuclear Bomb this Year." *Arutz Sheva, Israel National News Online,* January 25, 2010, http://www.israelnationalnews.com/SendMail.aspx?print=print&type =0&item=135679. (accessed October 27, 2010).

Former Mossad Official-No Signs of Iran Stopping Nuclear Program. (January 12, 2011), The Israel Project, http://www.theisraelproject. org/site/c.hsJPK0PIJpH/b.672631/apps/scontent.asp?ct=9018025. (accessed January 17, 2011), from Intelligence and Terrorism Information Center (ITIC) at the Israel Intelligence and Communication Center (IICC), http://www.terrorism-info.org.il/site/home/default.asp. (accessed June 15, 2009).

Gaza Strip After Operation Cast Lead, from Intelligence and Terrorism Information Center (ITIC) at the Center for Special Studies (C.S.S.), http://www.terrorism-info.org.il/site/home/default.asp. (accessed May 24, 2010).

Guyatt, Nicholas. *Absence of Peace.* New York: Zed Books, Ltd., 1998.

Hamas Charter (1988), (March 23, 2006), from Intelligence and Terrorism Information Center (ITIC) at the Center for Special Studies (C.S.S.). http://www.terrorism-info.org.il/malam_multimedia/English/eng_n/pdf/hamas_charter.pdf. (accessed May 12, 2009).

Hamas Rocket Attack on Sderot and Settlements . . ., May 20 Bulletin update, (May 21, 2007), from Intelligence and Terrorism Information Center (ITIC) at the Israel Intelligence and Communication Center (IICC), http://www.terrorism-info.org.il/site/home/default.asp. (accessed July 8, 2009).

Hamas Spokesman Ismail Radwan, (November 4, 2007), from Intelligence and Terrorism Information Center (ITIC) at the Center for Special Studies (C.S.S.). http://www.terrorism-info.org.il/malam_multimedia/English/eng_n/pdf/hamas_charter.pdf. (accessed May 12, 2009).

Hamas Threat . . ., (October 30, 2007), The Israel Project, http://www.theisraelproject.org/site/apps/nlnet/content2.aspx?c=hsJPK)PIJpH&b==883997. (accessed November 9, 2010).

Hamas, Portrait of a Terrorist Organization, from Intelligence and Terrorism Information Center (ITIC) at the Center for Special Studies (C.S.S.). http://www.terrorism-info.org.il/malam_multimedia/English/authority-hamas/pdf/sep2_04.pdf. (accessed June 3, 2009).

Hamas' Military Buildup in the Gaza Strip (Updated April 2008), from Intelligence and Terrorism Information Center (ITIC) at the Israel Intelligence and Communication Center (IICC), http://www.terrorism-info.org.il/site/home/default.asp, (accessed March 8, 2010).

Harel, Amos, and Avi Issacharoff. *34 Days: Israel, Hezbollah, and the War in Lebanon.* New York: Palgrave Macmillan, 2008.

Harms, Gregory. *Palestine-Israel Conflict: A Basic Introduction.* 2nd ed. London: Palgrave Macmillan, 2008.

Herzog, Chaim, Updated by Shlomo Gazit. *Arab-Israeli Wars.* New York: Vintage Books, 2005.

Hezbollah (Part 1), (June 2003), from Intelligence and Terrorism Information Center (ITIC) at the Center for Special Studies (C.S.S.), http://www.terrorism-info.org.il/site/home/default.asp. (accessed October 23, 2009).

Hezbollah as a Strategic Arm of Iran, (September 8, 2006), from Intelligence and Terrorism Information Center (ITIC) at the Center for Special Studies (C.S.S.), http://www.terrorism-info.org.il/site/home/default.asp. (accessed March 23, 2009).

Hezbollah, Part 1, from Intelligence and Terrorism Information Center (ITIC) at the Center for Special Studies (C.S.S.), http://www.terrorism-info.org.il/site/home/default.asp. (accessed April 3, 2010).

Hezbollah's Terrorist Attack on Israel's Northern Border, (July 13, 2006), from Intelligence and Terrorism Information Center (ITIC) at the Center for Special Studies (C.S.S.), http://www.terrorism-info.org.il/site/home/default.asp. (accessed March 7, 2010).

Hezbollah's Use of Lebanon Civilians as Human Shields, (November 2006), from Intelligence and Terrorism Information Center (ITIC) at the Center for Special Studies (C.S.S.), http://www.terrorism-info.org.il/site/home/default.asp. (accessed March 8, 2010).

Hezbollah-Israel Conflict: by the Numbers, (August 17, 2006), The Israel Project, http://www.theisraelproject.org/site/apps/ninct/content2.aspx?c=hsJPK0PIJpH&b=883997&. (accessed August 5, 2009).

Incitement on Local Radio Stations, (July 17, 2005), from Intelligence and Terrorism Information Center (ITIC) at the Center for Special Studies (C.S.S.), http://www.terrorism-info.org.il/site/home/default. asp. (accessed July 26, 2009).

Institute for National Security Studies at Tel Aviv University, http://www.inss.org.it.

Intensive Rocket Fire Attacks Against Western Negev..., from Intelligence and Terrorism Information Center (ITIC) at the Israel Intelligence and Communication Center (IICC), http://www.terrorism-info.org.il/site/home/default.asp. (accessed September 26, 2009).

Iran as a State Sponsoring and Operating Terror, (April 2003), from Intelligence and Terrorism Information Center (ITIC) at the Center for Special Studies (C.S.S.), http://www.terrorism-info.org.il/site/home/default.asp. (accessed March 7, 2010).

Iran at the Forefront of Multi-Pronged War Against Israel, the West, The Israel Project, http://www.theisraelproject.org/site/c.hsJPK0PIJpH/b.672631/apps/s/content.asp?ct-5083. (accessed October 1, 2010).

Iran Intensifies Influence Throughout Latin America, (November 18, 2009), The Israel Project, http://ww.theisraelproject.org/site/c,hsJPK0PIJpH/B.5608661/k.E577/Iran_Intensifies_I. (accessed November 13, 2010).

"Iran's Nuclear Program," *The New York Times,* September 7, 2010, http://www.nytimes.com/info/iran-nuclear-program/?gagemode=print. (accessed October 27, 2010).

Iran Will Only Be Deterred by Threat of Military Action—Netanyahu. (January 11, 2011), The Israel Project, http://www.theisraelproject.org/site/c.hsJPK0PIJpH/b.672631/apps/scontent.asp?ct=672631. (accessed January 17, 2011).

Iran: Leading State Sponsor of Terror, The Israel Project, mhtml:file//:\ Iransponsorofterror.mht. (accessed October 3, 2010).

Iran's Nuclear Program Status, Congressional Research Service, Washington, D.C., 2009.

Iran's Sponsorship of Terrorism Across the Globe, (November 12, 2009), The Israel Project, http://www.theisraelproject.org/site/apps/ ninet/content2.aspx?c=hsJPK0PIJpH&b=68970(accessed November 13, 2010).

Iranian President Mahmoud Ahmadinejad: in His Own Words, The Israel Project, http://www.theisraelproject.org/site/c.hsJPK0PIJpH/b.672631/ apps/scontent.asp?ct=369. (accessed November 13, 2010).

Iranian Support of Hamas, from Intelligence and Terrorism Information Center (ITIC) at the Center for Special Studies (C.S.S.), http://www. terrorism-info.org.il/site/home/default.asp. (accessed May 24, 2010).

Israel 1991 to Present Al-Aqsa Intifada, Palestinian Facts, http:// Palestinefacts.org/pf_1991to_now_alaqsa_start.php. (accessed April 21, 2009).

Israel, Dormant War. Library of Congress. Country Studies, Israel, 1988.

Israeli History, Desert Storm, at Israeli-Weapons LTD, http://www. israeli-weapons.com/history/desert_storm/Desert_Storm.hrml. (accessed August 8, 2010).

Jaber, Hala. Hezbollah. New York: Columbia University Press, 1997.

Judaism 101. *Yom Kippur.* Http://www.jewfaq.org/holiday4.htm. (accessed March 26, 2010).

Karish, Efraim. *Arab-Israeli Conflict.* Oxford, UK: Osprey Publishing, 2002.

Katyucha Rockets Fired Deep into the Galilee, (May 29, 2006), *from* Intelligence and Terrorism Information Center (ITIC) at the Center for Special Studies (C.S.S.), http://www.terrorism-info.org.il/site/home/default.asp. (accessed February 23, 2010).

Kissinger, Henry. *Crisis.* New York: Simon & Schuster, 1999.

Laqueuer, Walter, and Barry Rubin, eds. *The Israel-Arab Reader.* New York: Penguin Group, 2008.

Leading Palestinian Terrorist Organizations (August 2004), from Intelligence and Terrorism Information Center (ITIC) at the Center for Special Studies (C.S.S.), http://www.terrorism-info.org.il/site/home/default.asp. (accessed March 29, 2009).

Levitt, Matherw A. *Iranian Sponsorship of Terror: Threatening U.S. Security, Global Stability,* and Regional Peace. Testimony before Joint Hearing on the Committee on International Relations, U.S. House of Representatives, (February 16, 2005).

Library of Congress, Federal Research Division, *Country Studies,* http://memory.loc.gov/frd/cs/iltoc.html.

Livak, Meir. *Palestine Islamic Jihad—Background Information TAU Notes: No. 56.* (November 28, 2003). Jewish Virtual Library. http://www.jewsihvirtuallibrary.org/jsource/Terrorsm/tau.html. (accessed June 8, 2010).

May 18, 2008, A Grad Rocket Fired from the Gaza Strip Hits a Crowded Gaza Mall in Ashqelon . . .from Intelligence and Terrorism Information Center (ITIC) at the Israel Intelligence and Communication Center (IICC), http://www.terrorism-info.org.il/site/home/default.asp. (accessed June 5, 2009).

MEMRI, Middle East Research Institute, "A Friday Sermon on PA TV: We Must Educate our Children on the Love of Jihad." Dispatch No. 240, July 13, 2001.

MEMRI, Middle East Research Institute, "PA Television Broadcasts Call for Killing Jews and Americans." Dispatch No. 138, October 13, 2000.

Morris, Benny. *1948, First Arab-Israeli War*. New Haven: Yale University Press, 2008.

Moshe Dayan Center for Middle Eastern and African Affairs, Tel Aviv, Israel, http://www.dayan.org/framedoc.htm.

Neff, Donald. *Warrior for Jerusalem*. New York: Linden Press, 1984.

News of Terrorism and Palestinian-Israeli Conflict, November 18-25, 2008, from Intelligence and Terrorism Information Center (ITIC) at the Israel Intelligence and Communication Center (IICC), http://www.terrorism-info.org.il/site/home/default.asp. (accessed July 8, 2009).

News of the Israeli-Palestinian Confrontation, (December 1-15, 2007), from Intelligence and Terrorism Information Center (ITIC) at the Israel Intelligence and Communication Center (IICC), http://www.terrorism-info.org.il/site/home/default.asp. (accessed July 8, 2009).

November 16, 2008, Significant Erosion of the Lull Arrangement in the Gaza Strip, from Intelligence and Terrorism Information Center (ITIC) at the Israel Intelligence and Communication Center (IICC), http://www.terrorism-info.org.il/site/home/default.asp. (accessed January 5, 2009).

One Month into the Lull in Fighting: an Interim Report (as of July 23), from Intelligence and Terrorism Information Center (ITIC) at the Israel Intelligence and Communication Center (IICC), http://www.terrorism-info.org.il/site/home/default.asp. (accessed March 23, 2009).

Operation Cast Lead Updates 1-18, from Intelligence and Terrorism Information Center (ITIC) at the Israel Intelligence and Communication Center (IICC), http://www.terrorism-info.org.il/site/home/default.asp.

Operation in Gaza, 27 December 2008-18 January 2000, from Intelligence and Terrorism Information Center (ITIC) at the Israel Intelligence and Communication Center (IICC), http://www. terrorism-info.org.il/site/home/default.asp. (accessed July 20, 2010).

Palestinian Terrorism in 2005, December 31, 20005, from Intelligence and Terrorism Information Center (ITIC) at the Center for Special Studies (C.S.S.), http://www.terrorism-info.org.il/site/home/default. asp. (accessed May 24, 2010).

Peretz, Don. *Arab-Israeli Dispute.* New York: Facts on File, 1996.

Philp, Catherine. "Secret Document Exposes Iran's Nuclear Trigger." *The Times, Washington,* December 14, 2009, http://www.timesonline. co.uk/tol/newes/world/middle_east/article6955351.ece, (accessed October 27, 2010).

PLO's Phased Plan, Cairo, June 9, 19074, http://www.iris.org.il/ plophase.htm. (accessed November 16, 2009).

Profile of the Hamas Movement, (February 12, 2006), from Intelligence and Terrorism Information Center (ITIC) at the Center for Special Studies (C.S.S.), http://www.terrorism-info.org.il/malam_multimedia/ English/eng_n/pdf/hamas_e0206.pdf. (accessed May 5, 2009).

Protest of Annapolis Meeting Opponents-as of November 18, 2007, from Intelligence and Terrorism Information Center (ITIC) at the Israel Intelligence and Communication Center (IICC), http://www. terrorism-info.org.il/site/home/default.asp. (accessed July 8, 2009).

Rabinovich, Abraham. *Yom Kippur War.* New York: Schockern Books, 2004.

Road to the Second Lebanon War, (October 30, 2007), from Intelligence and Terrorism Information Center (ITIC) at the Center for Special Studies (C.S.S.), http://www.terrorism-info.org.il/site/home/default. asp. (accessed May 5, 2009).

Rocket Threat from the Gaza Strip, 2000-200, (December 2007), from Intelligence and Terrorism Information Center (ITIC) at the Israel Intelligence and Communication Center (IICC), http://www. terrorism-info.org.il/site/home/default.asp. (accessed December 21, 2009).

Ross, Dennis. *Peace.* New York: Farrar, Straus and Giroux, 2005.

Schiff, Ze'ev and Ehud Ya'ari. *Intifada: The Palestinian Uprising—Israel's Third Front.* New York: Simon & Schuster, 1989.

Segev, Tom. *1967.* New York: Metropolitan Books, 2005.

Serrano, Alfanso. "Report: Iran 2-3 Years from Nuclear Weapons." *CBS News, London,* January 31, 2007, http://www.cbsnews.com/ stories/2007/01/3'1/world/main24. (accessed October 29, 2010).

Shapira, Dr. Shimin, Brig. Gen. *Countdown to Conflict: Hezbollah's Military Buildup and the Need for Effective Disarmament.* (August 20, 2006), from Intelligence and Terrorism Information Center (ITIC) at the Center for Special Studies (C.S.S.), http://www.terrorism-info. org.il/malam_multimedia/English/eng_pdf/hexbollah_e_0607.pdf. (accessed May 14, 2009).

Shindler, Colin. *A History of Modern Israel.* Cambridge, UK: Cambridge University Press, 2008.

State of Israel, From the War of Independence until the Sinai War (1948-1956). Ynetnews.com. December 12, 2007. http://www.ynet. co.il/English/Ext/Comp/ArticleLayout/CdaArticlePrintPreview/1, 2506.l-3…(accessed January 9, 2009).

Suez Crisis: Events Leading up to the Suez Crisis. Answers.com. http:// answers.com/topic/suez-canal-crisis. (accessed October 27, 2009).

Suicide Bombing Terrorism, September 2000-December 2005, Part A, (January 1, 2006), from Intelligence and Terrorism Information

Center (ITIC) at the Center for Special Studies (C.S.S.), http://www. terrorism-info.org.il/site/home/default.asp. (accessed May 24, 2010).

Summary of Rocket Fire and Mortar Shelling in 2008/2009, from Intelligence and Terrorism from Intelligence and Terrorism Information Center (ITIC) at the Israel Intelligence and Communication Center (IICC), http://www.terrorism-info.org.il/site/home/default.asp. (accessed May 12, 2010).

Syria as Strategic Support for Hamas, (July 5, 2006), from Intelligence and Terrorism Information Center (ITIC) at the Center for Special Studies (C.S.S.), http://www.terrorism-info.org.il/site/home/default. asp. (accessed March 7, 2010).

Terrorist Attacks and the Propaganda Campaign to Undermine the Annapolis Meeting, from Intelligence and Terrorism Information Center (ITIC) at the Israel Intelligence and Communication Center (IICC), http://www.terrorism-info.org.il/site/home/default.asp (accessed July 8, 2009).

Timeline of Arab-Israeli Conflict, The Israel Project, http://www. theisraelproject.org/site/apps/nlnet/content2.aspx?c=hsJPK) PIJpH&b==883997. (accessed April 28, 2009).

Timmerman, Kenneth R. *Countdown to Crisis*. New York: Crown Forum, 2005.

Two Days of Hard Fighting in the South . . .,(January 16, 2008), from Intelligence and Terrorism Information Center (ITIC) at the Israel Intelligence and Communication Center (IICC), http://www. terrorism-info.org.il/site/home/default.asp. (accessed June 14, 2009).

U.S. Department of State. *Country Reports on Terrorism*. Washington, D.C., http://www.state.gov/s/ct/rls/crt/index.htm.

Using the Quds Force of the Revolutionary Guard as the Main Tool to Export the Revolution, (April 2, 2007), from Intelligence and Terrorism Information Center (ITIC) at the Israel Intelligence and Communication

Center (IICC), http://www.terrorism-info.org.il/site/home/default.asp. (accessed May 11, 2009).

Weekend Escalation, Escalation in Attacks from Gaza Strip as Hamas Announces the End of the Lull Arrangement, (December 18, 2008), from Intelligence and Terrorism Information Center (ITIC) at the Israel Intelligence and Communication Center (IICC), http://www. terrorism-info.org.il/site/home/default.asp. (accessed February 6, 2009).

Yaalon, Moshe, Lt. Gen. (ret.). "Iran's Race for Regional Supremacy." *Jerusalem Center for Public Affairs, Jerusalem*, Israel 2008.

Index

S

Sadat, Anwar 51, 52, 53, 54, 55, 56, 58, 59, 66, 67, 69, 70, 76, 88

Samaria 114, 126, 128, 131, 140, 162

San Remo Conference 1, 2

Settlements xiv, 2, 5, 7, 16, 18, 22, 23, 24, 25, 33, 41, 42, 51, 52, 74, 89, 93, 99, 100, 102, 106, 110, 127, 130, 131, 152, 162, 179

Shalit, Gilad v, 133

Sharon, Ariel 66, 103, 104, 113, 114

Shultz, George 81

Sinai Peninsula 20, 24, 30, 31, 32, 38, 42, 44, 48, 52, 54, 55, 66, 75, 76

Sinai-Suez War 28, 35, 209

Six-Day War 34, 35, 42, 45, 48, 49, 51, 52, 54, 55, 56, 61, 210

Soviet Union 29, 30, 31, 33, 39, 44, 51, 55, 56, 57, 61, 64, 68, 69, 79, 81, 177

Straits of Hormuz 174

Straits of Tiran 30, 32, 38, 41, 42

Stuxnet virus 169, 170

Suez Canal 28, 30, 31, 32, 33, 40, 41, 48, 49, 50, 51, 52, 53, 54, 55, 56, 57, 58, 60, 61, 62, 63, 65, 66, 67, 69, 70, 76, 239

Suicide bombings xiii, 83, 88, 98, 106, 107, 108, 109, 113, 116, 117, 118, 119, 126, 130, 132, 135

Surface-to-air-missile (SAM) 51, 56, 57, 58, 61, 62, 63, 64, 66, 67, 69, 78, 79, 81, 130, 155, 157, 242, 243

Syria xiii, xiv, 7, 9, 14, 16, 17, 18, 20, 25, 30, 33, 34, 36, 37, 38, 39, 43, 44, 45, 54, 56, 57, 58, 60, 61, 62, 63, 64, 66, 68, 69, 70, 71, 77, 79, 80, 81, 82, 83, 88, 93, 94, 96, 99, 101, 102, 104, 105, 108, 109, 110, 115, 116, 120, 122, 125, 127, 128, 129, 130, 143, 148, 149, 150, 152, 153, 154, 155, 156, 157, 158, 161, 164, 165, 174, 175, 176, 200, 232, 242

Syrian 16, 17, 20, 21, 22, 24, 33, 37, 38, 39, 41, 43, 44, 57, 58, 60, 61, 63, 64, 68, 69, 70, 77, 78, 79, 80, 82, 87, 109, 122, 123, 129, 150, 152, 154, 155, 156, 157, 160, 200, 202

T

Taba Conference 112

Tanks 18, 20, 25, 38, 39, 41, 43, 44, 48, 49, 53, 56, 57, 61, 62, 63, 64, 65, 66, 67, 68, 69, 70, 79, 82, 100, 110, 111, 119, 123, 124, 125, 129, 139, 142, 154, 155, 170

Tehran 131, 154, 160, 161

Tel Aviv 11, 16, 20, 23, 69, 73, 74, 75, 81, 88, 92, 95, 98, 107, 108, 109, 135, 152

Temple Mount 92, 93, 103, 104, 239

Terror xiv, 52, 105, 113, 120, 132, 136, 144, 148, 151, 152, 156, 157, 161, 162, 163, 231, 232

Terrorism 28, 73, 83, 84, 90, 93, 97, 101, 106, 113, 114, 116, 120, 122, 127, 129, 133, 135, 136, 140, 141, 143, 144, 148, 149, 151, 152, 154, 156, 158, 162, 163, 176, 178, 217, 218, 220, 221, 222, 223, 224, 225, 226, 227, 228, 229, 230, 231, 232, 233, 234, 236, 237

Terrorist organizations xiii, xiv, 7, 29, 33, 36, 83, 89, 90, 93, 104, 105, 106, 110, 111, 112, 115, 116, 118, 123, 126, 127, 129, 131, 133, 134, 135, 137, 141, 143, 150, 151, 152, 153, 154, 155, 156, 161, 162, 163, 164, 173,

267

Printed in Great Britain
by Amazon.co.uk, Ltd.,
Marston Gate.